# Bride's Wedding Planner

by the Editors of BRIDE'S Magazine

**FAWCETT COLUMBINE** ● **NEW YORK**

The Editor-in-Chief of BRIDE'S, Barbara D. Tober, wishes to extend a sincere thank you to all those who have contributed their time, talents, and energies to creating this wedding planner....

To the BRIDE'S Magazine staff and free-lance writers and artists whose understanding of brides-to-be, their grooms and families, and their wedding traumas, has inspired them to anticipate every last detail....

And especially to Helen Johnson, Managing Editor of BRIDE'S, who has coordinated the various materials into the one big, helpful guidebook you see here.

All sketches by Susan Gray and Marika Hahn.

Published by Fawcett Columbine Books, a unit of CBS Publications, the Educational and Professional Publishing Division of CBS, Inc.

ISBN 0-449-90005-3

Printed in the United States of America

First Fawcett Columbine Edition: October 1980

# The Wedding of

_____ and _____

# Date

_____

*Prepared especially for you by the Editors of BRIDE'S.*

You two have decided to marry—terrific! You've got a lot of happy, together times ahead of you. Your wedding, of course, will be one of the best. Full of fun and love for everyone now, a treasure of warm memories to last your whole lives.

How to make sure your wedding is all that you want it to be? An expression of your very special personalities? A celebration of sharing with your families? The most wonderful party ever for all of your friends? BRIDE'S Wedding Planner has the answers.

It's not easy to shop for just the right maid's dress when your attendants come in all shapes and sizes. It's not easy to draw up the guest list when your parents live in Wisconsin, his are out in California. It's *not* easy to pick a dinnerware pattern when you both work every day and some evenings too. That's why the editors of BRIDE'S magazine are here to help. On these pages, you'll find hints on every aspect of planning your wedding and new home. There are budget sheets to fill in, boxes to check, lists to go over, diagrams to follow. With this book, a couple of pencils, and a few hours together, you and your groom will save yourselves a lot of legwork, time, and worry. You'll be on your way to the beautiful ceremony you've always wanted, a smooth-running really great time for everyone. You'll be relaxed and ready to enjoy the festivities yourselves. And, especially, to enjoy each other.

BRIDE'S wishes you a happy wedding, and all good things for you and for him.

# CONTENTS

**1. PLANNING AHEAD FOR THE WEDDING YOU WANT     7**

Your Calendar, Your Groom's Calendar     8

Your Engagement: All about rings . . . Your engagement party . . . Announcing Your Engagement     11

How to Choose Your Wedding Style: Very formal to informal . . . Planning a reception . . . Marrying again     14

Easy Steps to Make It All Happen: The Members of Your Wedding . . . Your wedding budget . . . Who pays for what? . . .     19
Your families and your wedding . . . The guest list . . .     23

**2. WORKING WITH THE WEDDING PROS     35**

Creating a Personalized Ceremony: Talking to your clergymember . . . Choosing which traditions you'll keep . . . Involving family and friends . . . Writing your own vows     38

Flowers: Your wedding bouquet . . . Your ceremony and reception flowers     45

Talking to the Caterer: About food . . . Table Set-ups . . . The bar     53

Your Wedding Cake: How to buy it     58

Wedding Photography: Your portrait . . . Your candids     60

Your Wedding Music: For the ceremony . . . For the reception     66

Your Wedding Invitations: Ordering them . . . Wording them . . . Addressing them . . .     70
Proofreading . . . Special words for special weddings     73

Getting to the Wedding     74

Tips on Tipping: Whom to tip . . . How much . . . When     76

Your At-Home Wedding: Invitations . . . Pre-wedding planning . . . food     77

A Wedding Outdoors: Everything from the place to the weather     78

Long-Distance Weddings, Double Weddings     79

Guide to Wedding Clothes: The best dress for you . . . Your headpiece . . . Your attendants' dresses . . . Your man's wedding outfit . . . Good-grooming tips     82

8 Consumer Traps to Watch Out for When You Plan Your Wedding     92

Your Wedding Announcement     95

**3. PARTIES! PARTIES! PARTIES!     97**

Shower Guide: The gifts . . . The guests . . . The good time     98

The Maids' Luncheon, The Bachelor's Party     102

Warm welcomes for out-of-town guests     102

The Wedding Rehearsal, The Rehearsal Dinner     106

## 4. WEDDING GIFTS    109

Gifts for Attendants: For the bridesmaids . . . For the ushers . . . Something different    110

For You: Who sends wedding presents? . . . How to use the wedding gift registry . . .    111

Thanks! All-time favorites to hint around for    112

On The Receiving End: Displaying presents . . . Damaged gifts . . . Exchanges . . . Wedding gift list . . . Gifts for you and your groom to give each other . . .    112
Writing warm thank-yous    123

## 5. JUST FOR THE TWO OF YOU    125

Beauty Countdown    126

Your Trousseau: Figuring out what you need and budgeting for it    127

Guide to Birth Control: Choose what's right for you    134

What's Your Name: How to decide what your married name and monogram will be    136

How well do you really know each other?    138

Your Marriage License    140

## 6. YOUR WEDDING CEREMONY    141

Timetable for the Big Day    142

The Lineup: A traditional procession . . . A procession with parents . . . At the altar . . . The recessional . . . Special variations    143

## 7. THE RECEPTION    147

A Party Timetable    148

Your receiving line    149

Reception seating the easy way    150

Traditions: The first dance . . . The cake-cutting ceremony . . . Throwing the bouquet and garter    151

## 8. YOUR HONEYMOON—WHAT A TRIP!    153

Hassle-free Honeymoon Planning    154

Pack and Go: How to pack . . . For a tennis weekend . . . For a week in the sun . . . For two weeks abroad . . . Honeymoon beauty bag . . . Luggage    159

Tips: A Honeymoon budget guide    161

Honeymoon Catastrophes That Needn't Be:
Dealing with everything from lost tickets to newlywed embarrassment    161

## 9. AT HOME    165

Starting Out with Your Wedding Gifts: Your dinnerware, silverware, glassware, and linens    166

Buying a Mattress or Sofa Bed    176

Apartment-Hunting: How to find the right apartment for you    177

Furnishing your home—your way: Defining your tastes . . . Budgeting . . . Setting priorities . . . Drawing up a decorating plan    179

In the Kitchen: Your appliances and cookware . . . Your supermarket list    183

His-and-Hers Housework    186

Your Budget    187

# 1
# Planning Ahead For The Wedding You Want

You're engaged. That *is* exciting. But before you call up the nearest caterer, stop. Think. Decide how much time you want to take getting your ceremony and reception together. Figure out what you can really afford to spend. Talk to your parents—it's their wedding too. Get everyone's dreams of the perfect wedding down on paper. Gather the names of all the friends and relatives with whom you want to share the day—as attendants, as guests. Planning ahead is the surest way to make everything you'll do later easy and fun.

# YOUR CALENDAR

*You need at least six months to arrange a beautiful formal wedding, ten months to a year if you live in a big city or are planning to be married in the popular wedding months of June, August, September, and December. The charts and checklists are designed to help you organize every detail of your wedding for ready reference.*

## Six months before

☐ Select a wedding date and time. Early reservations are mandatory if your wedding will take place during a popular month or near a holiday.

☐ Discuss wedding budget with your parents; if you'll share expenses, include your fiancé and his parents. Together decide on the wedding style—everything from flowers to food.

☐ Decide how many guests may attend, then let your fiancé's family know how many they may invite, and by what date you need their guest list.

☐ Choose your location (home, garden, church, hotel).

☐ Plan your reception and make the necessary reservations. If your reception is to be at home, choose a caterer; if at a club or hotel, check their catering facilities. Decide what type of music will be appropriate, and, if necessary, book the musicians.

☐ Plan the color scheme for the wedding and reception.

☐ Make arrangements to visit the clergymember or other ceremony official with your fiancé.

☐ Choose and order your wedding dress, veil, and accessories. Remember that dresses often require fitting and adjustments.

☐ Go with your fiancé to shop for and pick out your engagement ring.

☐ Discuss ideas for your new home with your fiancé, and begin household shopping.

☐ Select your china, crystal, silver, linens, and other household needs, and register your preferences with the Wedding Gift Registry of your favorite store.

☐ Choose the friends you'd like as your bridesmaids and honor attendants.

☐ Set the date to order dresses and accessories for your attendants. A versatile style that will go to parties after the wedding is most suitable.

☐ Discuss honeymoon plans with your fiancé so reservations can be made. If you plan to travel outside the country, check on passports, visas, and inoculations.

## Three months before

☐ Complete your guest list, as well as an additional list for those who will receive announcements if you'll send them. Check these against your fiancé's list for possible duplication.

☐ Order a sufficient quantity of invitations and announcements (if you plan to send them). The envelopes should be sent to you right away so they can be addressed and ready to mail when the printed invitations are delivered to you.

☐ Order any personal stationery you may want, to use for thank-you notes now, as well as for correspondence after you're married.

☐ Plan a trousseau of any new clothes and cosmetics you need to fill out your current wardrobe, and start to shop.

☐ Let your mother and your fiancé's mother know the wedding color scheme so they may choose harmonizing dresses in identical lengths.

☐ Confirm the delivery date of your dress, and if you haven't already, make the final selection of the attendants' dresses.

☐ Schedule the appointment for your bridal portrait to coincide with the delivery date of your wedding dress.

☐ Engage a candid photographer.

☐ Notify the candid photographer of the location so he may familiarize himself with the setting.

☐ Arrange with your family doctor or gynecologist to have a physical examination and the blood test necessary for obtaining marriage licenses in most states, to choose a birth control method, to get any inoculations needed for a wedding trip abroad. Make appointments with dentist, dermatologist, eye doctor too if it's time.

☐ Discuss all details of your coming wedding ceremony, including flowers, music, photographs, canopies, carpets, etc., with the proper religious authorities.

☐ Discuss in detail all aspects of your reception with the person who will be in charge (hotel manager, caterer). If you must rent any equipment, make the necessary reservations now.

☐ Consult with florist and order flowers that match wedding color scheme, season too.

## One month before

☐ Mail your invitations to arrive preferably three—but no later than two—weeks before the wedding.

☐ Order your wedding cake if it was not included in the overall catering fee.

☐ Have the final fitting of your wedding dress, veil, and accessories, and confirm photography date for your bridal portrait.

☐ Choose and order gifts for your attendants; bridesmaids' presents are often identical, while the maid or matron of honor usually receives a slightly more special gift.

☐ Select your wedding ring. If you plan to have a double-ring ceremony, order your fiancé's ring at the same time, arrange to pick up and pay for it.

☐ Arrange lodging for out-of-town attendants. Unless they will be guests in someone's house, make reservations at a nearby hotel or motel, and pay in advance—even if they'll reimburse you later.

☐ Make necessary arrangements for the bridesmaids' luncheon or dinner.

☐ Discuss arrangements for the rehearsal dinner with whoever is giving it (your family, close friends or relatives or the groom's parents often do).

☐ Be sure to keep up with your correspondence. Write thank-you notes every day—and begin to address announcements (if any) so they will be ready to mail after the wedding.

☐ Choose a wedding present for your groom if you have both decided to exchange gifts—it's optional.

## Two weeks before

☐ Go with your fiancé to fill out necessary forms for your marriage license.

☐ Telephone the society editor of your local newspaper to find out what information is required for your wedding announcement. Compile and write the announcement in a style as close as possible to that of the society page.

☐ Arrange transportation for all members of the wedding party to and from the ceremony and reception by reserving limousines or confirming with friends who have agreed to "chauffeur."

☐ Discuss specifics of the ceremony and reception with your candid photographer, if you haven't already.

☐ Complete your trousseau shopping, making sure all purchases will be delivered on time and that clothes fit properly upon arrival. Transfer small amounts of cosmetics to plastic bottles and boxes for your honeymoon trip. Check with fiancé on any reservations.

☐ Plan with your hairdresser both a wedding hairdo and a workable routine for honeymoon hair care. A good cut and styling should be part of this visit. Be sure to take your headpiece and veil, and to book an appointment if you'll be having your hair done the day of the wedding.

☐ Arrange to change your name and address (if you will be) on bank and charge accounts, personnel records, social security, insurance or health policies, your driver's license, etc.

☐ Deliver your wedding announcement to the society editor of your local newspaper.

## One week before

☐ Begin packing for your honeymoon, layering non-crushables in the bottom of your suitcase. Leave space to add items that crease as well as cosmetics at the last minute.

☐ Be sure the wedding announcements (if any) are addressed, stamped, and ready for your parents to mail immediately after the wedding.

☐ Give or go to the bridesmaids' luncheon or dinner.

☐ Schedule your rehearsal. Make it a day or two in advance of the wedding, and notify all participants of exact time and date.

☐ Wrap, then present gifts to your attendants at the bridesmaids' party or rehearsal dinner.

☐ Give the caterer a final estimate on the number of reception guests expected.

☐ Check final details of ceremony and reception with all concerned (clergy member or ceremony official, organist, florist, photographer, etc.).

☐ Arrange for personal belongings and wedding gifts to be moved to your new home.

☐ Keep up those thank-you notes.

☐ Try to put your feet up and relax some part of each day. One whole day of pampering, including facial, massage, manicure, and pedicure, is the perfect prelude to a beautiful wedding.

# GROOM'S CALENDAR

*Your groom will have a lot of preparations to make too. Some things you'll be doing at the same time, and together. Others he'll have to take care of on his own. Why not give him this checklist to help with his planning.*

### Six months before

☐ Confirm with your fiancée's family the number of guests you may invite, then sit down with your own family to plan your guest list.

☐ Decide with your family what wedding or reception expenses, if any, they'll share with your fiancée's family. Typical: the flowers, the liquor, the rehearsal dinner. This is optional.

☐ Arrange with your fiancée to visit the clergymember or other official who'll perform the ceremony.

☐ Discuss with your fiancée the number of ushers you will need; decide which friends and relatives to ask.

☐ Purchase your fiancée's engagement ring. If she wants a matching set, order her wedding ring now. If not, it may be ordered later.

☐ Discuss and decide upon honeymoon plans with your fiancée, and start making necessary arrangements. If you plan to leave the country, make sure passports, visas, and inoculations for both of you are in order.

### Three months before

☐ Finish your guest list and give it to your fiancée, making sure that all names are spelled correctly and that addresses are complete.

☐ Order your attire, after consulting with your fiancée about the formality of the wedding.

☐ Ask your best man and ushers to participate in the wedding, then brief them on the proper attire. You might suggest they all order or rent from the same establishment to insure complementary dress.

☐ Complete your honeymoon reservations. Buy and pick up all plane, train, or ship tickets.

☐ Go with your fiancée to her doctor to discuss birth control, if she wishes. Make an appointment with your doctor for a complete physical, any needed blood tests or inoculations. Arrange for check-ups at the dentist, eye doctor, etc., if it's time.

☐ Go over your wardrobe to make sure it's in good shape—begin shopping for any new clothes you need.

### One month before

☐ Decide on bride's bouquet and going-away corsage with her; check with fiancée on boutonnières for men in the wedding party and mothers' corsages.

☐ Make arrangements for rehearsal dinner with your parents, if they will be giving it.

☐ Pick up bride's ring; check engraving.

☐ Check to see if health insurance will cover your wife; or if hers will cover you. Make any necessary changes. Change your life insurance to make her your new beneficiary; ask her to do the same for you.

☐ Buy gifts for your best man and ushers. While ushers' presents are usually identical, the best man often receives a more special gift.

☐ Make sure that all wedding attire has been ordered, and that it fits and will be ready on time.

☐ Arrange necessary accommodations for out-of-town ushers. If they won't be staying with friends, book rooms for them at nearby hotel or motel, and pay when you reserve, even if they'll reimburse you later.

☐ Make sure all legal, medical, and religious documents are in order.

☐ Select a gift for your bride if you've decided to exchange them. Anything lasting and personal is traditional—with the exception of clothes.

### Two weeks before

☐ Make a date with your fiancée to take out the marriage license. (P.S. Celebrate with a champagne lunch!)

☐ Make arrangements for the bachelor party (if you are to be host).

☐ Arrange with the best man for transportation from the reception to the airport, station, or dock, if you're not taking to the highways. If you are honeymooning by car, be sure the best man has an extra set of car keys in case you misplace yours.

☐ Double-check honeymoon reservations.

## One week before

- [ ] Wrap gifts for your best man and ushers. You may give them at the bachelor dinner, or, if you and your fiancée wish to give them all together, at the rehearsal dinner.

- [ ] Remind the best man and ushers of the rehearsal and rehearsal dinner, giving them time, date, and location.

- [ ] Brief the head usher on any special seating arrangements. The bride's relatives and friends usually sit on the left, the groom's on the right, but the front pews may be reserved for special guests.

- [ ] Put the clergymember or ceremony official's fee in a sealed envelope and give it to the best man to hand to that person just before or after the ceremony. Or buy and arrange for a gift to be sent to the judge.

- [ ] Get your honeymoon clothes in order for a quick get-away. Start to pack, layering non-crush items in the bottom, saving room to add crushables at the last minute.

- [ ] Have your hair trimmed.

- [ ] Move your things into your new home.

- [ ] Get to the church (hotel or wherever) on time.

# ALL ABOUT RINGS

## How to choose wedding rings you'll love forever

Ready to run out and choose your engagement and wedding rings? If this is your first venture into the world of fine jewelry, you're probably a bit confused too (can you spot a "flawless" diamond?). Best polish up on a few of the basics before you buy.

**Gold,** the most-used ring metal, is usually natural yellow or white in color. Since pure gold (24K) is too soft for durable jewelry, most rings are 14K or 18K alloys of gold and stronger metals.

**Platinum,** a shimmery white metal, is also popular, and it's the strongest ring metal on the market today. This is why it's often used for prongs (they hold stones) in rings of gold.

**Gemstones** (diamonds, rubies, emeralds, sapphires, etc.) are measured in *carats*. The more carats, the larger the stone. But larger does not always mean better.

**THE CUTTING, COLOR, AND CLARITY DETERMINE A STONE'S PER-CARAT PRICE.** Thus, a fine, one-half carat gem is more valuable and will cost more than an inferior one-carat gem.

Accuracy of **cutting** is essential to a gem's beauty. **Cabochons** are smoothly cut gems (like opals), but most stones are proportioned and **faceted** (carved) to return maximum brilliance through their **crowns** (tops). Gems are cut in several shapes; emerald (square or rectangular), oval, pear (teardrop), brilliant (round), and popular marquise (an oval pointed at both ends).

Another important factor is **color.** The best diamonds are colorless (although expensive canary diamonds are yellow, they're also extremely rare); rubies, pinkish red; sapphires, cornflower blue; emeralds, lush green; aquamarines, the bluest you can find.

**Clarity** is the term used to describe the presence or absence of blemishes. Good diamonds show no specks or bubbles when viewed without a magnifying glass. **"Flawless"** (or **"perfect"**) means no imperfections are visible when a stone is magnified ten times.

Ring extras include **baguettes** (small, squared or tapered stones), **brilliants** (small round stones), and **pavé groups** (tiny stones set closely together).

Stones are **channel set** (in parallel grooves) for a sculptured look or **prong set** (individually held in place by metal teeth) for fiery shine.

**WHAT TYPE OF RING IS BEST** for you? You might pick a narrow band, a single stone if your hands are tiny; or a bolder look, a freeform design if your hands are larger. And if you'll keep an engagement and wedding ring on one finger, you might want to pick a complementary or matching set. If you'll wear your rings every day, you would be wise to avoid fragile settings and stones (like opals and pearls). But beyond this, you should feel free to follow your own idea of perfection, whether that means a classic **solitaire** (single stone), a cluster of varied gems, or a single band. If you haven't seen the ring of your dreams, tell the jeweler what it is you'd like. Maybe the high, twisted mounting on one ring, and the oval rubies on another. Almost any good jeweler will alter a ring's design, stone, even metal. He can also change the setting, amount of gold or platinum, stone size, or cut if you see the ring you want, but really can't afford it. Keep in mind that you can alter a ring in the future (in some cases even trade it in for a new one) if your taste changes or your budget finally permits.

If your fiancé is like most men marrying today, he probably wants to wear a wedding ring too. What type? There are lots of different kinds: traditional plain gold and platinum bands; modern designs; even handsome jeweled creations. You two could buy matching his and her wedding bands. Or he might choose a ring of his own liking—maybe of the same metal as yours, or maybe to match the wristwatch he wears every day.

**SHOP TOGETHER** instead of risking a disappointing surprise. Rely on a jeweler you know, or a member of the *American Gem Society*. You might have your fiancé call ahead to reserve a selection of rings in the right price range. That way you're bound to pick a ring you really will love—and wear—forever.

**WHAT KIND OF PRICES CAN YOU EXPECT?** For a top quality ½ carat diamond in a simple setting, about $1,000 and up; ¼ carat, about $500 and up; one carat, $2,500 and up. As a guide, financial experts recommend that you try not to spend more than three weeks' salary or six percent of your annual income (that's about $900 if you earn $15,000).

If you can't possibly pay for your ring in cash, be sure to do some investigating before you accept a jeweler's own financing deal. Ask the jeweler about all the terms (carrying charges, legal warranties, insurance coverage). Then go to your bank or credit union and find out if you can get better terms on a loan from them.

Always find out the jeweler's own policy on guarantee and return of merchandise. And insist that important details (the material of which the jewelry is composed; whether or not any material is synthetic; the weight if it's a diamond; the quality of the gem) be listed in writing on your receipt.

**KEEP YOUR RINGS AT THEIR PRETTIEST** with regular good care. Clean them once a month with hot water and detergent, or cold water and ammonia (except pearls, opals, and turquoise, which should be polished with a dry cloth). Soak, scrub them with a toothbrush, rinse, then dry.

Be sure to check the stones often to see that they're secure. If loose, return your ring to your jeweler. In any case, take your rings to your jeweler every year or two for a professional mounting inspection and cleaning.

Remove your rings for heavy housework, swimming, gardening. Tuck them away in a cloth-lined jewelry box. Keep diamonds separate; since they're the hardest substance known to man, they're bound to scratch softer stones and metals.

**INSURE YOUR NEW RINGS IMMEDIATELY** through your regular agent or one recommended by your family, friends, or jeweler. If your parents wouldn't mind, you might have them add a floater (mini policy) to their basic homeowner's insurance policy; buy your own basic policy after you marry. Precious stones and metals increase in value, so keep your policy up to date by having all your good jewelry reappraised every three to five years.

# YOUR ENGAGEMENT

**TELL YOUR FOLKS THE GOOD NEWS** Of course you'll want your parents—and his—to be the first to know you've decided to marry. Each of you should speak to your own parents alone. With just you there, your parents will have the chance to hug and kiss you without feeling the least bit inhibited—especially if they don't know your fiancé very well.
After your fiancé has talked to his parents too, invite him over (without his parents) for dinner to meet your mom and dad. If you live in another state or part of the country, plan a short weekend with just the four of you. Together you'll have the time to chat about the kind of wedding you'd like (keep in mind a wedding takes six-ten months of planning), who you want to invite, where you two think you'll live after you marry. Sometime during the evening or weekend, do make a point of

slipping away and leaving your fiancé and your father alone. Don't worry—your fiancé doesn't have to ask for your hand. But they should have the chance to sit, talk, and find out something about each other.
Remember, an engagement is a time to get to know each other better too. You'll be around relatives and friends as a "couple." Undoubtedly you'll talk about important topics like jobs, children, religion, finances. This is definitely more than "going steady." You will be testing the strength of your relationship for the future.

**GET THE TWO FAMILIES TOGETHER** Traditionally, it's your fiancé's parents who make the first move toward getting to know your parents—either with a phone call or a letter. Your mother would then respond with an invitation for cocktails, dinner, or Sunday brunch.

However, many parents of the groom simply don't know this tradition (although you may want to slip him the word). So if your parents don't hear from his folks in a couple of weeks, it's not a crisis. Just have your parents phone them. It's important that both families are able to meet and talk about wedding plans *not* with hurt feelings, but with enthusiasm and friendship.

**SHARE YOUR HAPPINESS WITH FRIENDS** What better reason to have a party than your engagement! Since there'll just be close family and friends, your parents can host any kind of celebration they'd like. Perhaps a dessert-and-coffee party, a cocktail hour, a backyard barbecue. Your mother can invite everyone by phone or with handwritten invitations. She may want to drop a hint about the occasion, but it's more fun if you keep it secret until the party. You don't need to wear a ring to be engaged, but if you do, it'll be the first hint for your guests. Your father can pick the best moment to propose a sentimental toast to you and your fiancé. Your fiancé can return a toast to you and your family. Then *everyone* will join in wishing you well.

# ANNOUNCE YOUR ENGAGEMENT

Once you've told your parents, close relatives, and best friends in person, by telephone, or by personal notes, your engagement may be announced in the newspapers of your home towns. Since policies vary from paper to paper, it's best to check with the society editor in advance about the proper form, deadlines, photographs, etc. Some papers, for example, accept information over the telephone, while others insist that you complete a special printed form at least ten days before publication. Some papers publish wedding photographs only, while others publish either engagement or wedding pictures, but not both. Some papers will also accept photographs of the engaged couple together. If your newspaper does not supply printed forms, submit the necessary information to the society editor. Type it, double spaced, on one side of a sheet of paper 8½ X 11 inches. In the upper right-hand corner, put the name, address and telephone number of your parents or someone in the community who can be called for verification. Be sure to mention the date on which you want the announcement to appear. You might use this form:

To appear: _____     _____
(Date)                                      (Your parents' names)

_____
(Street address)

_____
(City, state, zip code)

_____
(Area code, telephone number)

Mr. and Mrs. _____ of _____ announce the engagement
(your parents' names)            (their city, if out of town)

of their daughter, _____, to _____,
(your first and middle names)            (your fiancé's first and last names)

the son of Mr. and Mrs. _____ of _____.
(your fiancé's parents' names)       (fiancé's parents' city)

No date has been set for the wedding. (Or, The wedding will take place in _____ .)
(wedding month)

If one of your parents has died, your announcement might read:

*The engagement of Miss Helen Louise Brown, daughter of Mrs. John Brown and the late Mr. Brown, to Mr. Stanley Forsythe, the son of Mr. and Mrs. Hugh S. Forsythe of Pasadena, is announced by the bride's mother.*

If your parents are divorced, the announcement is made by the parent with whom you live, but both parents are mentioned in the story:

*Mrs. Hoyt Brown (a combination of her maiden and married surnames) announces the engagement of her daughter, Helen Louise, to Mr. Stanley Forsythe, the son of Mr. and Mrs. Hugh S. Forsythe of Pasadena. Miss Brown is the daughter also of Mr. John Brown of San Francisco.*

Some newspapers also include information about schools, military service, club memberships or college associations, but there is no need to mention such facts unless they are customarily published in your paper. When in doubt, be brief and to the point. The editor can always call you if she wants more details. If you send a photograph with your announcement, it should be an 8 × 10″ glossy portrait (5 × 7″ is also acceptable). Be sure to attach a typed line of identification to the photograph and to protect it with a piece of stiff cardboard.

Marrying again? Traditionally, you wouldn't have an engagement announcement in the newspaper. But if you're having a large second wedding with all the trimmings (perhaps you didn't have it the first time), by all means do publish your wedding news.

## YOUR WEDDING STYLE

What kind of wedding do you want? It may be large or intimate, elaborate or simple, accompanied by a great deal of fanfare or none at all. A lot of things may influence its form—your religion, your lifestyle, the amount of money your family can afford to spend, your job commitments. And remember, you *can* have a traditional style of wedding, and still weave the personal touches through it that mean something special to the two of you. What matters most is that every part of your wedding be perfect, in terms of *you,* and the man you love.

THE HOUR FOR YOUR WEDDING may be a purely personal choice or based on religious or community customs, the convenience of your relatives and friends, even the plans for your wedding trip. At any hour, you may have the type of wedding you want, ranging from the most formal to the simplest, as outlined here. Before you decide which style is best for you, talk it over with your groom and both your families. You could, for instance, have a "second" reception in another part of the country so all your relatives can wish you well.

A VERY FORMAL WEDDING ceremony is held in a church, temple, or a large club or hotel ballroom. There are usually 200 guests or more. You may have any number of attendants from 4 to 12, one or two flower girls, one or two ring bearers and train bearers if you wish. Your groom will have at least one usher for every 50 guests. The church or ballroom will be beautifully decorated. You will have aisle ribbons, maybe even pew cards (sent to special guests) for reserved seats, a canopy from the curb to the door, perhaps an attendant to open car doors and others to park the cars. Your dress will be the most elegant, with a long train, and the clothes of the entire wedding party will reflect the same formality. Such a wedding is almost always followed by an elaborate, large reception.

A FORMAL WEDDING is the one most brides choose. The ceremony may take place in a church, temple, hotel, club, or at home. You will have any number from two to six attendants; there will be a best man plus at least one usher for every 50 guests. (The pageant is prettier and the parties more fun if there are the same number of ushers and bridesmaids.) You will wear a long wedding dress and veil. And afterwards . . . a reception for everyone.

A SEMI-FORMAL WEDDING may be held at home, in a church or temple chapel, club, or hotel living room. It is usually smaller than a formal wedding, and less traditional. You may wear a long or short dress, or a suit in any color but black. You may top it with a little flowered headpiece or hat — flowers are lovely, too. Your attendants will be just one or two, dressed as simply as you are. The ceremony is usually followed by a reception in the same warm, easy mood.

AN INFORMAL WEDDING is often in a judge's chambers or the office of the justice of the peace. You and one attendant will wear short dresses or suits, and you may wear flowers or carry tiny nosegays. Guests should be limited to the immediate family and one or two friends. Such a ceremony is usually followed by a small party to which a few more close friends may be invited. It might be a luncheon at home or in a restaurant—or an intimate late afternoon party at home. A large reception—and formal dress—is also fun.

Besides the wedding styles most brides and their families favor, there are a few traditional variations you might choose. They're briefly outlined below.

A MILITARY WEDDING finishing with the traditional arch of sabers (or swords in the Navy) is for commissioned officers of the armed forces only. Reserve officers may not have military weddings unless they are on active duty. And, of course, brides and grooms who are officers may marry without the military ceremony if they prefer. Attendants of the person in the service usually are fellow officers. If the groom's the officer, he and his groomsmen wear their dress uniforms (the fathers can wear the appropriate civilian outfits), the bride and her party, the traditional clothes. If the bride's the officer and the wedding is formal, she and her attendants may choose long dresses with hats and veils.

A DOUBLE WEDDING usually involves two sisters, with the older one going first down the aisle with her attendants. The older sister is escorted by her father, the younger by a brother, uncle, or male friend of the family. To keep down the size of the wedding party, the brides and grooms may serve as each other's honor attendants. The brides and two groups of attendants need not dress alike, but there should be an overall harmonizing of fabrics, colors, flowers.

A GARDEN WEDDING may be any degree of formality—from very formal to informal, with many personal touches. It's planned along the same lines as an indoor "at-home" wedding, except that the ceremony takes place at an altar under the trees, in the garden, or some other outdoor setting. In case of cold or rainy weather, alternate arrangements for both ceremony and reception must be made inside the house, at a nearby church or shelter, or under a tent. A garden wedding may open with a procession but usually there is no recessional. The bride and groom turn after the ceremony, are joined by their parents and attendants and form a receiving line in the same setting they were married. An aisle canvas may be drawn by the ushers to protect the bride's dress, or she may wear one without a train.

## PLANNING A RECEPTION

### How to make sure everyone has fun

**1** **Pick a party style to please.** Receptions mean good times, congratulations, and a grand finale to your wedding day, whether you include three people in the festivities or 300. Just start out right by choosing the party style that suits you, your family, and your friends. Like a backyard barbeque for sun-loving casuals, or an elegant dinner dance for a "dress-up" crowd. Then do allow at least six months' planning time. Cake along with champagne or punch for toasting are your only reception "musts"; you've lots of options beyond that. Feel free to mingle at a hotel, restaurant, reception hall, church, or your own home; party it up with cocktails and canapés, a brunch or a sit-down meal. Entertain with a band, chamber ensemble, folk singer, records.

**2** **Set realistic goals and limits.** Narrow down that wealth of options by making money, people, and time-of-day your prime considerations. Settle on a budget with your parents (or whoever's paying) first thing. Then draw up a basic guest list that tells you how many people you'll be entertaining and what manner of fun their ages and tastes indicate. Let your ceremony time offer a rough guide to an appropriate reception. Morning is best for an informal breakfast or more formal brunch; noon for a full lunch; early afternoon, a cocktail hour and/or dinner; evening, a buffet or sit-down supper. Now write down exactly what meets your idea of a perfect reception. Ask your parents, your fiancé to do the same. Then start compromising. Remember that some plans dictate special requirements (for dancing you need lots of space, a dance floor, bandstand; for hot foods and extensive meals, a kitchen; for guests with cars, plenty of parking). And realize that the more elaborate your party, the higher the bills. So if cash is limited but your guest list enormous, scale down visions of prime ribs and an open bar; rent a hall big enough for everyone and serve cake and punch instead. But with a generous budget and few guests, hire a caterer rather than stand over the stove for a week yourself.

**3** **Seek professional help.** A gifted florist, a good photographer, a capable caterer, and an able group of musicians can prove your best helpers on wedding day. So unless you plan the smallest, most casual kind of reception, pick up your telephone and start lining up the pros as soon as you've settled on budget and style. If you don't already have favorites, shop around before you sign any contracts or lay down deposits. Ask family, friends, fellow workers, especially recent brides, for suggestions. Make appointments with the two or three most highly recommended people to discuss prices and plans. Go prepared to give your preferred wedding date plus two optional ones (particularly in June and August, the most popular wedding months). Tell each florist how many centerpieces, bouquets, corsages, boutonnières, and standing arrangements you'll want. Look at sample wedding albums at each photographer's and check out package deals. Ask caterers (or the club manager or maitre d' if your reception site offers its own catering service) for menu suggestions, liquor arrangements, and per-head cost estimates; don't forget to add a 15 percent tip to the total. Tell caterers how many guests you'll have, whether you'll want hot or cold food, buffet or table service, an open bar or limited choice of drinks. Find out how wide each musical group's repertoire is—dance music should run the gamut from golden oldies to the latest hits—how many hours they'll play, and what they charge for overtime. Take notes as you talk to people, and work toward getting everything—from church reservation to limousine service—lined up for the wedding day. As soon as you've made your final decisions, call back to reserve your wedding date definitely and make appointments to finalize plans. Notify anyone you won't be using that you've made other arrangements, but do thank them for their time and courtesy.

**4** **Take your choice of traditions.** Even the most modern reception gains extra meaning from some traditional touches. So do share the first slice of cake with your groom and let the best man toast your happiness. If your guests number more than 50 or so, you might also want a receiving line where you and your groom, your mothers, his father, and your attendants can offer a personal greeting to each guest, and a bridal table. Start the dancing off with your new husband; make sure the bridal party waltzes with each other at some point. And give your guests something to remember you by (groom's cake, matches, etc.). When it's time to go, toss your bouquet and garter, then change, bid your parents good-bye, before dashing under that shower of rice and good wishes.

# WEDDING STYLE CHECKLIST

The ideal wedding is one where the bride, the groom, and their families are the people who have the most fun. And everyone's idea of the "perfect wedding" is a little different. So before you go ahead with your planning, find out what's on people's minds. First you fill out the list here, then get your groom, your mother, your father, and his mother and father to do the same. Taking everyone's thoughts into consideration, you'll be on your way to a wedding guaranteed to be a good time for all.

I want the wedding to take place on_____ , _____ , _____

Alternate dates
　　　　　　　　　　　Day of Week　　　Date　　　Year

Time of day: DAYTIME _____ Hour _____ EVENING _____ Hour _____

Wedding Style: VERY FORMAL _____ FORMAL _____ SEMI-FORMAL _____
　　　　　　　　INFORMAL _____

　　　　Special variations_____

_____

_____

Approximate number of guests _____ Bride's attendants _____

　　　　Groomsmen _____

I see the bride wearing _____

_____

I see the bridesmaids in _____

_____

I see the groom and his men wearing _____

_____

A lovely ceremony would

　　take place at _____
　　　　　　　　Name of Church, Temple, Home, etc.　City or Town

Alternate ceremony sites _____

_____

A fun reception would be a: Buffet meal _____ Sit-down _____

　　Cocktails and hors d'oeuvres _____ Punch and cake _____

Other_____

The ideal reception would last from _____ o'clock to _____ o'clock

Dancing? Yes _____ No _____ Alcoholic beverages? Yes _____ No _____

　　TOTAL ESTIMATED COST OF WEDDING $ _____

# MARRYING AGAIN

## *How to plan the perfect second wedding*

**Aren't you delighted you're marrying again?** Your second wedding can and should reflect all the joy and bright hopes you and your fiancé now share. Still, you may be more than a little concerned about "propriety" this time—you want everything to be "right." Furthermore, society's views on divorce and widowhood are changing, and so is second-wedding etiquette. So what kind of second marriage is right for you?

**Traditionally, a second marriage calls for** a small, informal ceremony with 50 or fewer guests. The bride wears a colored, street-length suit or dress, has one attendant but no procession. The reception can be as lavish as the bride desires. She can wear the most elegant long dress she can find, invite everyone in the phone book, and toast and dance till the wee hours.

**Today, the last word on what's proper really rests with you.** You can wear white, invite hundreds of people to your ceremony, and toss your bouquet at the reception if you like. When in doubt, just ask yourself: "Will this make me, my groom, our families, and the majority of our guests feel happy and relaxed?" If you can say "yes" with confidence, your plans are fine.

**Are there any guidelines at all?** Yes. They're a combination of old and new etiquette, and common sense.

**Announce your engagement to any children you have first**—especially if they're going to be part of your new household. Tell them without your fiancé. And be ready for any reaction. If they're not enthusiastic, find out why. Reassure them of your love. Then go ahead with your plans. Trust the children will adjust in good time.

**Plan to pay for your own wedding,** unless your parents *offer* to help. They probably did their part the first time. And you've been on your own for a while. Frequently couples share costs. The groom may even foot the entire bill.

**Be sure to check with your clergymember before you start planning** a church ceremony. Religions—even individual clergymembers—vary in their views on second marriages. Most Protestant churches allow them under certain conditions. So does the Episcopal church, if the minister involved gives his or her OK. Reformed Jewish rabbis generally permit all but mixed, second marriages. Roman Catholic clergy usually require proof of annulment as well as of divorce before they'll even consider performing a second marriage. Also be sure to ask if the clergymember approves before going ahead with a large ceremony, white dress, and veil.

**Give some thought to your age and to the circumstances of your first wedding too.** A young woman remarrying after a brief first marriage might naturally lean toward a formal wedding with white dress, lots of attendants, and a large ceremony. So might a young woman who never had "the works" before. An older bride, or a bride whose family isn't quite as open-minded as she'd like, might feel more comfortable following traditional guidelines.

**If you want to wear white,** you might choose an outfit that's a little less frilly than if you were a "first-time" bride—maybe a sleek jersey dress paired with a glamorous picture hat. Should you wear a veil—or not? Perhaps not. For remember that while white is the color of joy and celebration, the wedding veil has always been a symbol of youth and virginity.

**Try to include any children** of yours in the plans. Boys might be acolytes, ring bearers, ushers. Girls might be flower girls, maids, keepers of the reception guest book. Even at a simple, home-style reception, children can pass hors d'oeuvres, take coats. At the ceremony, be sure to seat children before parents.

**Consider the feelings** of your groom, any children you have, your parents, when you draw up your guest list and choose your attendants. Would your groom or parents feel uncomfortable if you invited an ex-husband or his relatives that you may still care a lot about? Would your first-wedding attendants understand if you preferred not to ask them again this time? Also, remember that guests are under no obligation to send gifts when you marry a second time.

**Decide whether or not you want to carry on any first-wedding customs.** Traditionally a second-time bride is not "given away" at the ceremony. She does not join her father for a "first dance" at the reception. Her wedding cake is usually pastel, not white. And she doesn't toss a bouquet or garter. Today, it's your choice. If you still want a procession at your ceremony, you can walk by yourself, with a sponsor, or with your father. Your father can give you away, or stop short, letting you go and take your place by the groom. Are you having dancing at your reception? You can start it with a traditional first dance with your father, or go it alone with your groom. Do you prefer a wedding cake iced in white or pastel? Either way, you might do without the bride-and-groom topper. Should you toss a bouquet—or not? If there's a dreamy-eyed teen-ager out there just dying to catch her first—why not go ahead and throw it?

**Send personal, handwritten invitations** when you're inviting fewer than 50 guests; printed ones (formal or informal) when you're inviting more. The invitations are issued by whoever's sponsoring the wedding (your parents, his, a friend, you and your groom). A formal invitation uses the same style and wording as for a first wedding—except for the bride's name. If you plan to go by the book, the following examples show how your name would appear, no matter what the situation.

If you're divorced, and your parents are sponsoring the wedding: *Mr. and Mrs. William Burke/request the honour of your presence/at the marriage of their daughter/Christine Burke O'Brien/etc.*

If you're divorced and sponsoring your own wedding: *The honour of your presence/is requested at the marriage of/Mrs. Burke O'Brien/etc.*

If you're a widow, and your parents are sponsoring your wedding: *Mr. and Mrs. William Burke/request the honour of your presence/at the marriage of their daughter/Christine Marie O'Brien/etc.*

If you're a widow and sponsoring your own wedding: *The honour of your presence/is requested at the marriage of/Mrs. James Peter O'Brien/etc.*

What if he's the one who's been married before? In the wedding of a second-time groom and a first-time bride, traditional first-wedding etiquette has always applied.

Whichever way your plans go, remember that your friends aren't coming to "judge" your wedding, but to share your joy. It's the fun everyone has that'll make your wedding great.

## THE MEMBERS OF YOUR WEDDING

You want *all* your favorite people with you on your wedding day, of course. And those relatives and friends who are extra-special you undoubtedly plan on making your attendants. They're the ones who'll share the planning, the parties, the small crises with you, almost from Day One. Then, when the big day finally comes, they'll turn *your* wedding into a fun-filled celebration you'll all talk about for years.

But before you and your groom run off helter-skelter with invitations to join the wedding party, ask yourself some tough questions. Who do you *really* want? Friends? Or family? Should you make it four attendants apiece? Or 12? Most readers of BRIDE'S have four bridesmaids, for instance. But if it's an ultra-formal wedding you may want more; an informal or semi-formal wedding, fewer. Don't be afraid to add an extra one or two to include everyone.

**Choose your honor attendants with special care.** You want people who'll be closest, most helpful to you. Some questions to consider: Who did you rush to call first with the news that you two were getting married? Who has the time and flexibility to handle the honor attendant's special responsibilities (running errands, planning showers and bachelor parties, making sure other attendants are properly outfitted)? Do you want a relative or a friend?

**Next figure out who'll be your maids and ushers.** Your attendants are *personal* choices. While it's customary for each of you to include a member of the other's family in your wedding party (his sister, your brother, for example), the most important thing is simply getting your best friends to share the day. Don't worry about things like seeing to it the maids' hair colors match or that the ushers are taller than the maids. And don't feel you have to include husbands, wives, fiancés, or steady dates of attendants in the wedding party too. A personal invitation to the wedding (though not even necessary) is fine. (If attendants aren't dating anyone special, it might be more fun, in fact, if they come "stag" so they can dance and mingle with other single guests.) If you've a friend or two from out of town, by all means have them in for the wedding. But also include local people if you can—they'll find it easier to attend the showers and luncheons that sprinkle pre-wedding days. Just don't let anyone get so overwhelmed with invitations, he or she feels it a drain on time, energy, and the pocketbook.

You might also want to include children in the party as flower girls, ring bearers, or pages. Or ask young teens to serve as junior ushers or bridesmaids. Children do add charm. They can also suffer stagefright, cause disruptions. If you've a niece who's very special to you, ask her. But don't go out of your way looking for children to invite.

**Keep your plans flexible.** Let all your attendants and your parents know who'll be in the wedding party as soon as you know. You may find you have to do some juggling. Your mother may feel you really should ask Cousin Jean; you grew up together, after all. Your groom might be upset because you asked one sister but not the other, and he really wants them both to be maids.

In each case, you have to choose whether to make room for another attendant or try to smooth over the rift as best you can. You don't *have* to invite anyone extra; point out that plans are already final, find extra little ways to include them. But if it's a decision between one more maid or a family fight, you may be happier in the end if you go ahead and ask Cousin Jean or your other sister-in-law.

**Find special jobs for friends who won't be in the wedding party.** Your roommate with the knack for organization might keep track of gifts. Your sister-in-law-to-be with the perfect handwriting could address invitations. His college quartet can give a mini-concert before the ceremony. On wedding day, ask his little sister to pass out pieces of groom's cake or packets of rice. Have your little brother escort your mother down the aisle.

**Adapt the rules to meet your needs.** Two best friends? Have two honor attendants: a maid- *and* matron-of-honor. Split duties down the middle, or ask one to handle special responsibilities, let the other just share the spotlight. More ushers than maids (or maids than ushers)? Pair the extras two by two and have them follow the customary maid/usher couples up the aisle for the recessional. A pregnant maid? Tradition says she should excuse herself from the wedding party. But if you really want her there, and she's sure she won't get overtired, do urge her to stay on. Then let your mother, your groom know the situation, so they can prepare any guests who'll think this a breach of etiquette, and you help your maid find a dress that fits, blends with other outfits.

**Dress your wedding party so everyone looks and feels terrific.** Consider the range of budgets and bodies when choosing formalwear and dresses, and give maids and ushers a voice in the final selection. You and your groom might choose two or three men's outfits, then let the ushers take a vote. You and your maids can look through BRIDE'S together, shop around a bit, talk over preferences in style, price, color. Maids will especially like clothes they can wear again—from hat to shoes. Consider a long skirt with a lacy white blouse. A long halter dress topped with a capelet or jacket. A skirt and blouse of the same fabric that look like a dress, can be worn separately too. Pair your choice with a classic pump or sandal. Or, if it's a small wedding, let each maid buy her favorite style in the color you specify. Match hats to dress style, hairstyles, and face shapes. Remember they're paying for everything but the flowers (you provide those); it's only polite to please them as much as you possibly can.

**Be prepared for last-minute "crises."** If one of your maids finds she absolutely can't afford even the moderately priced dress you've selected, offer to help out. Find a place to stay for out-of-town attendants and, if possible, pay for it. Keep a couple of people filed in the back of your mind who might fill in if a maid or usher comes down with pneumonia the day before.

**Say thank you with an extra-special gift,** something handsome and practical to serve as a lasting memento of your wedding. Traditional gifts include gold or silver jewelry, often cufflinks, tie-bars or -tacks for the ushers, pendants or pins for the maids, engraved with your initials and wedding date. But you might choose a single engraved pewter or silver cup, simple earrings, a handsome wallet or handbag, even unusual housewares like a small vase or set of bar tools. You can give the same gift to all your attendants. Or set an amount to spend on each gift and shop separately for something different for each attendant. In either case, your gift will help your attendants recall all the happy memories of sharing your wedding.

# BRIDE'S WEDDING BUDGET

|  | ESTIMATED COSTS | ACTUAL COSTS |
|---|---|---|
| **Stationery** | | |
| Invitations .................................. | $_____ | $_____ |
| Announcements ........................... | $_____ | $_____ |
| Notepaper for thank-yous ................ | $_____ | $_____ |
| Reception napkins......................... | $_____ | $_____ |
| Matches .................................... | $_____ | $_____ |
| Cake boxes ............................... | $_____ | $_____ |
| Other (maps, at-home cards) .............. | $_____ | $_____ |
| ........................................... | $_____ | $_____ |
| Total | $_____ | $_____ |
| | | |
| **Flowers** | | |
| | | |
| Wedding | | |
| Ceremony site (church, hotel, etc.) ......... | $_____ | $_____ |
| Church ...................................... | $_____ | $_____ |
| Bride's attendants' bouquets .............. | $_____ | $_____ |
| Corsages for mothers..................... | $_____ | $_____ |
| | | |
| Reception | | |
| Buffet decorations ........................ | $_____ | $_____ |
| Table centerpieces ....................... | $_____ | $_____ |
| Cake table ............................... | $_____ | $_____ |
| Other (bandstand, receiving line) .......... | $_____ | $_____ |
| Total | $_____ | $_____ |
| | | |
| **Photography** | | |
| Formal portraits ........................... | $_____ | $_____ |
| Engagement ........................... | $_____ | $_____ |
| Wedding .............................. | $_____ | $_____ |
| Candids .................................... | $_____ | $_____ |
| Extra prints for attendants, groom's parents ... | $_____ | $_____ |
| Total | $_____ | $_____ |

|  | ESTIMATED COSTS | ACTUAL COSTS |
|---|---|---|
| **Music** | | |
| Wedding (organist, soloist) .................. | $_____ | $_____ |
| Reception (orchestra, combo) .............. | $_____ | $_____ |
| Total | $_____ | $_____ |
| **Catering** | | |
| Bridesmaids' party ....................... | $_____ | $_____ |
| Rehearsal dinner (if sponsoring) ............ | $_____ | $_____ |
| Reception ................................ | $_____ | $_____ |
| Food ................................. | $_____ | $_____ |
| Liquor ................................ | $_____ | $_____ |
| Waiters, bartender, etc. .................. | $_____ | $_____ |
| Wedding cake ........................... | $_____ | $_____ |
| Total | $_____ | $_____ |
| **Bride's outfit** | | |
| Dress .................................... | $_____ | $_____ |
| Headpiece and veil...................... | $_____ | $_____ |
| Total | $_____ | $_____ |
| Trousseau ..................................... | $_____ | $_____ |
| **Fees** | | |
| Church, hotel or party rental, etc. ............ | $_____ | $_____ |
| Clergymembers, other ceremony official ...... | $_____ | $_____ |
| Ceremony assistants (sexton, cantor) ......... | $_____ | $_____ |
| Bridal consultant ......................... | $_____ | $_____ |
| Total | $_____ | $_____ |
| **Gifts** | | |
| Attendants' ................................ | $_____ | $_____ |
| Groom ................................... | $_____ | $_____ |
| Groom's wedding ring ..................... | $_____ | $_____ |
| Total | $_____ | $_____ |
| **Transportation** | | |
| Limousines ............................... | $_____ | $_____ |
| Parking................................... | $_____ | $_____ |
| Total | $_____ | $_____ |
| **Extras** | | |
| Table favors (almonds, rice bags) ........... | $_____ | $_____ |
| Hotel accommodations (guests, attendants) ... | $_____ | $_____ |
| Other ................................... | $_____ | $_____ |
| Total Wedding Costs ......................... | $_____ | $_____ |

# WHO PAYS FOR WHAT?

The bride's family is traditionally responsible for the wedding ceremony, the cost of the reception as well. Nowadays, however, the groom or his family may offer to share wedding costs (paying for all the liquor or flowers at the reception, for instance). Otherwise, costs are divided like this:

**The bride (or her family) usually pays for:**
Invitations, announcements, and enclosure cards
Bride's wedding dress, veil, and accessories
Bride's trousseau
Bouquets for honor attendants, bridesmaids, and flower girl
Flowers for the church and reception
Engagement and wedding photographs
Rental fee for the church (if any)
Fees for the sexton, organist, and soloist
Rental of aisle carpet, canopy, and other equipment
Transportation of the bridal party to church and reception
Complete reception, including all food, beverages, music, decorations, gratuities and professional services, unless the groom's family offers to assume some of this expense
Groom's wedding ring (if it's a double-ring ceremony)
Groom's wedding gift
Gifts for bride's attendants
Hotel accommodations (if any) for bridesmaids from out of town
Bride's personal stationery

**The groom (or his family) usually pays for:**
Bride's engagement and wedding rings
Marriage license
Clergymember's or ceremony official's fee (ranging from $10 to $100, depending on the size of the ceremony)
Bride's bouquet and going-away flowers (optional, see below)
Boutonnières for the men of the wedding party
Flowers for mothers and grandmothers (optional, see below)
Bride's wedding gift
Gifts for the best man and ushers
Hotel accommodations (if any) for ushers from out of town
Complete wedding trip

**Optional expenses usually set by local custom:**
Bride's bouquet—traditionally a gift from the groom, but may be included in the bridal outfit supplied by her family
Flowers for mothers and grandmothers—usually provided by the groom, but the bride may buy those for her own mother and grandmother
Attendants' dresses—usually bought by each woman, but the bride may provide them if she chooses
Bridesmaids' party—usually given by the bride, but may be given by her attendants or relatives
Bachelor party—given by groom's attendants and friends in most localities, but may also be given by the groom
Rehearsal dinner—given by groom's family in most communities, but may also be hosted by relatives or friends of the bride

# YOUR FAMILIES AND YOUR WEDDING

It's you and your groom's wedding, but most likely *your* family's going to handle most of the expenses, do most of the planning, and take most of the spotlight. After all, it's a big day for them. But it's just as special for your groom's family. So here are lots of ways you can count them in on your wedding day too.

**Get your parents acquainted after you announce your engagement.** Your fiancé's mother usually makes the first move with a friendly phone call or note; a dinner òr cocktail invitation if your parents live nearby. No sign of this? Have your mother do the honors. It's better to reverse etiquette than to get things off to a shaky start.

**Work out agreeable wedding plans with your fiancé and parents.** Sit down together and discuss what each of you considers to be "top priority" for a wedding (a traditional ceremony? an open bar? a low budget? hundreds of guests?). Your fiancé should speak up now if he thinks his family might object to dancing or drinking; if they'd feel awful not being able to invite all the families on their block. Be willing to compromise.

**Have your mother fill his in on the finalized wedding plans.** She should tell his mother how many guests her family may invite. Also what type of dress (long or short—the color as soon as she knows) she herself will be wearing.

**At this time, your fiancé's mother can offer her family's help with wedding expenses, if they wish.** Your mother can politely turn down her offer *or* accept it, suggesting *specific* expenses they might handle (liquor, music, flowers) rather than a percentage of the total bill. (Having the bills sent directly to them will avoid any further discussion of—or possible hassles about—money.) In either case, your fiancé's family should not ask for changes in plans (more guests, a different reception site, a fancier menu). They can always host their own kind of party, perhaps at housewarming time.

**Include your groom's parents' names on your invitation.** You could word it this way: "Mr. and Mrs. William James Bigham/ request the honour of your presence/ at the marriage of their daughter/ Elizabeth

Anne Bigham/ to/ John Robert Pingitore/ son of/ Mr. and Mrs. Francis John Pingitore/ . . .".

**Ask both sets of parents to participate in your wedding procession,** a Jewish tradition. So long as your clergymember approves, the ushers could enter first in pairs, followed by the best man, your groom on the arms of his parents, your maids, your maid or matron of honor, then you on the arms of your parents.

**Rather than having just your father give you away,** why not ask each of your parents to give his or her blessing of your marriage? After you exchange rings, you might also personally thank each family for the love and support that warms your lives.

## THE GUEST LIST

**Time to plan your invitation list? Here's how to get your groom's family and yours together—happily—to work out the details with the two of you.**

### "How do we arrive at a number?"

Ceremony planning: you've always dreamed of getting married in the little church where you went to Sunday school. But if that little church holds only 125 people and you have 230 potential guests, you'll have to do some compromising. How? Think of getting married in your groom's church.

Reception planning: *budget* plays a crucial part in determining numbers. First discuss with your parents or whoever is paying the bills what money you have to work with. Then the hard part—deciding what style reception. Sometimes you may feel as if you're choosing between people and things—but you *can* work it all out. Figure out what's really important to you—a seated dinner, open bar, and full orchestra for 50. Or cake and champagne for 200. What if his parents suggest you serve something more nourishing than cake at mid-day? They may have a point. You could schedule the reception around 2 p.m. after lunch. But what if they still talk about a "real meal" and offer to share the costs of a catered buffet? Your family can accept or politely decline. And perhaps his parents can host their kind of party to welcome the two of you back from your honeymoon.

*Space* is the other consideration when planning reception size—even when you're marrying outdoors. That pretty inn might have sweeping lawns, but limit your guests to the number that will fit comfortably inside the cozy dining room in case of rain or bad weather, or plan on renting a *big* tent.

**"Whose side can ask the most guests?"** You have two dozen aunts and uncles. He has a small family, but his mother wants to ask all those people she's played bridge with every Friday for 15 years and they're not relatives! How do you keep what should be a joyous occasion from turning into a tug-of-war? Follow tradition and divide the guest list in half. Or allocate a third to his parents, a third to yours, and a third to you

and your groom so your own friends can attend the wedding too—it's the fairest way. Once you decide on the number, have your mother call or write your groom's mother (or the parent who raised him if they're divorced). She might say, "We're limited to 200 guests, so each family is going to have the hard job of inviting 100 people. Perhaps we can help each other think of ways to cut down." If his family is from out of town, it's likely that only a small group of guests will be able to make the trip. There will probably be extra invitations for your side so ask his mother to give you a count as soon as possible. Then you can invite more friends or family without fear of overcrowding.

**"Who gets invited?"** Adult relatives, friends, your clergymember and spouse, fiancés of invited guests, the bridal party and spouses. And, if there's room, children, business associates, and parents of the attendants.

**"There are too many! How do we cut down?"** Both families are way over their guest limit. What to do? Except for brothers and sisters of the bride and groom, you could agree not to invite any children. Aunt Sylvia and Uncle George just might welcome a chance to socialize without having the kids in tow. But instead of writing "no children" on the invitations, ask a favorite aunt on both sides to spread the word that space and money prompted this decision. Still too many people? You might think of eliminating business associates on both sides of the family. After all, a wedding is a *social* occasion. And you both could try to delete people who live more than two hours away, second cousins too. Another possibility? Escorts for single guests. Who knows, maybe two of your unmarried friends might discover true love *and* each other at *your* wedding!

Use the spaces on the following pages to help your family and your groom's family decide whom to invite. Then when you're addressing your invitations, and announcements (if you send them), flip back to these pages to put a check in the appropriate blank to make sure no one's been forgotten. As soon as your invitations have been acknowledged, write yes or no in the R.S.V.P. blank to maintain an accurate headcount.

# GUEST LIST

| NAME AND ADDRESS | CEREMONY | RECEPTION | R.S.V.P. | ANNOUNCEMENT |
|---|---|---|---|---|
| 1. | | | | |
| 2. | | | | |
| 3. | | | | |
| 4. | | | | |
| 5. | | | | |
| 6. | | | | |
| 7. | | | | |
| 8. | | | | |
| 9. | | | | |
| 10. | | | | |
| 11. | | | | |
| 12. | | | | |
| 13. | | | | |
| 14. | | | | |
| 15. | | | | |
| 16. | | | | |
| 17. | | | | |
| 18. | | | | |
| 19. | | | | |
| 20. | | | | |
| 21. | | | | |
| 22. | | | | |
| 23. | | | | |
| 24. | | | | |
| 25. | | | | |

# GUEST LIST

| NAME AND ADDRESS | CEREMONY | RECEPTION | R.S.V.P. | ANNOUNCEMENT |
|---|---|---|---|---|
| 26. | | | | |
| 27. | | | | |
| 28. | | | | |
| 29. | | | | |
| 30. | | | | |
| 31. | | | | |
| 32. | | | | |
| 33. | | | | |
| 34. | | | | |
| 35. | | | | |
| 36. | | | | |
| 37. | | | | |
| 38. | | | | |
| 39. | | | | |
| 40. | | | | |
| 41. | | | | |
| 42. | | | | |
| 43. | | | | |
| 44. | | | | |
| 45. | | | | |
| 46. | | | | |
| 47. | | | | |
| 48. | | | | |
| 49. | | | | |
| 50. | | | | |

# GUEST LIST

| NAME AND ADDRESS | CEREMONY | RECEPTION | R.S.V.P. | ANNOUNCEMENT |
|---|---|---|---|---|
| 51. | | | | |
| 52. | | | | |
| 53. | | | | |
| 54. | | | | |
| 55. | | | | |
| 56. | | | | |
| 57. | | | | |
| 58. | | | | |
| 59. | | | | |
| 60. | | | | |
| 61. | | | | |
| 62. | | | | |
| 63. | | | | |
| 64. | | | | |
| 65. | | | | |
| 66. | | | | |
| 67. | | | | |
| 68. | | | | |
| 69. | | | | |
| 70. | | | | |
| 71. | | | | |
| 72. | | | | |
| 73. | | | | |
| 74. | | | | |
| 75. | | | | |

# GUEST LIST

| NAME AND ADDRESS | CEREMONY | RECEPTION | R.S.V.P. | ANNOUNCEMENT |
|---|---|---|---|---|
| 76. | | | | |
| 77. | | | | |
| 78. | | | | |
| 79. | | | | |
| 80. | | | | |
| 81. | | | | |
| 82. | | | | |
| 83. | | | | |
| 84. | | | | |
| 85. | | | | |
| 86. | | | | |
| 87. | | | | |
| 88. | | | | |
| 89. | | | | |
| 90. | | | | |
| 91. | | | | |
| 92. | | | | |
| 93. | | | | |
| 94. | | | | |
| 95. | | | | |
| 96. | | | | |
| 97. | | | | |
| 98. | | | | |
| 99. | | | | |
| 100. | | | | |

# GUEST LIST

| NAME AND ADDRESS | CEREMONY | RECEPTION | R.S.V.P. | ANNOUNCEMENT |
|---|---|---|---|---|
| 101. | | | | |
| 102. | | | | |
| 103. | | | | |
| 104. | | | | |
| 105. | | | | |
| 106. | | | | |
| 107. | | | | |
| 108. | | | | |
| 109. | | | | |
| 110. | | | | |
| 111. | | | | |
| 112. | | | | |
| 113. | | | | |
| 114. | | | | |
| 115. | | | | |
| 116. | | | | |
| 117. | | | | |
| 118. | | | | |
| 119. | | | | |
| 120. | | | | |
| 121. | | | | |
| 122. | | | | |
| 123. | | | | |
| 124. | | | | |
| 125. | | | | |

# GUEST LIST

| NAME AND ADDRESS | CEREMONY | RECEPTION | R.S.V.P. | ANNOUNCEMENT |
|---|---|---|---|---|
| 126. | | | | |
| 127. | | | | |
| 128. | | | | |
| 129. | | | | |
| 130. | | | | |
| 131. | | | | |
| 132. | | | | |
| 133. | | | | |
| 134. | | | | |
| 135. | | | | |
| 136. | | | | |
| 137. | | | | |
| 138. | | | | |
| 139. | | | | |
| 140. | | | | |
| 141. | | | | |
| 142. | | | | |
| 143. | | | | |
| 144. | | | | |
| 145. | | | | |
| 146. | | | | |
| 147. | | | | |
| 148. | | | | |
| 149. | | | | |
| 150. | | | | |

# GUEST LIST

| NAME AND ADDRESS | CEREMONY | RECEPTION | R.S.V.P. | ANNOUNCEMENT |
|---|---|---|---|---|
| 151. | | | | |
| 152. | | | | |
| 153. | | | | |
| 154. | | | | |
| 155. | | | | |
| 156. | | | | |
| 157. | | | | |
| 158. | | | | |
| 159. | | | | |
| 160. | | | | |
| 161. | | | | |
| 162. | | | | |
| 163. | | | | |
| 164. | | | | |
| 165. | | | | |
| 166. | | | | |
| 167. | | | | |
| 168. | | | | |
| 169. | | | | |
| 170. | | | | |
| 171. | | | | |
| 172. | | | | |
| 173. | | | | |
| 174. | | | | |
| 175. | | | | |

# GUEST LIST

| NAME AND ADDRESS | CEREMONY | RECEPTION | R.S.V.P. | ANNOUNCEMENT |
|---|---|---|---|---|
| 176. | | | | |
| 177. | | | | |
| 178. | | | | |
| 179. | | | | |
| 180. | | | | |
| 181. | | | | |
| 182. | | | | |
| 183. | | | | |
| 184. | | | | |
| 185. | | | | |
| 186. | | | | |
| 187. | | | | |
| 188. | | | | |
| 189. | | | | |
| 190. | | | | |
| 191. | | | | |
| 192. | | | | |
| 193. | | | | |
| 194. | | | | |
| 195. | | | | |
| 196. | | | | |
| 197. | | | | |
| 198. | | | | |
| 199. | | | | |
| 200. | | | | |

# GUEST LIST

| NAME AND ADDRESS | CEREMONY | RECEPTION | R.S.V.P. | ANNOUNCEMENT |
|---|---|---|---|---|
| 201. | | | | |
| 202. | | | | |
| 203. | | | | |
| 204. | | | | |
| 205. | | | | |
| 206. | | | | |
| 207. | | | | |
| 208. | | | | |
| 209. | | | | |
| 210. | | | | |
| 211. | | | | |
| 212. | | | | |
| 213. | | | | |
| 214. | | | | |
| 215. | | | | |
| 216. | | | | |

My maid-of-honor _____     The best man _____
Address _____              Address _____
_____                      _____
Phone _____                Phone _____

My matron-of-honor _____   The head usher _____
Address _____              Address _____
_____                      _____
Phone _____                Phone _____

1. Bridesmaid _____        1. Usher _____
   Address _____              Address _____
   _____                      _____
   Phone _____                Phone _____

2. Bridesmaid _____        2. Usher _____
   Address _____              Address _____
   _____                      _____
   Phone _____                Phone _____

3. Bridesmaid _____        3. Usher _____
   Address _____              Address _____
   _____                      _____
   Phone _____                Phone _____

4. Bridesmaid _____        4. Usher _____
   Address _____              Address _____
   _____                      _____
   Phone _____                Phone _____

5. Bridesmaid _____        5. Usher _____
   Address _____              Address _____
   _____                      _____
   Phone _____                Phone _____

6. Bridesmaid _____        6. Usher _____
   Address _____              Address _____
   _____                      _____
   Phone _____                Phone _____

7. Flower girl _____       7. Ring bearer _____
   Address _____              Address _____
   _____                      _____
   Phone _____                Phone _____

   Other helper _____         Other helper _____
   Address _____              Address _____
   _____                      _____
   Phone _____                Phone _____

   Special helper _____       Special helper _____
   Address _____              Address _____
   _____                      _____
   Phone _____                Phone _____

# 2

# Working With The Wedding Pros

There are many professionals who can help you pull together the perfect wedding—from the florist to the photographer. You'll be paying for their attention and expertise as well as for the *things* they provide (food, liquor, and so on). To get the most for your money, use your common sense. Comparison shop. Be firm about your budget (with yourself, not just them). Tell the pros exactly how many guests, family, and attendants you'll be having. Give them a clear picture of what you want from them. But do leave yourself open for suggestions too. They've had lots more experience with weddings than you, after all, and may offer you new ideas that are not only efficient and lovely but have that certain something about them that is unmistakably YOU.

**THE CLERGYMEMBER** or other official who'll perform the ceremony should head your list. Whether you'll be married in your faith or your fiancé's, you and he should make an appointment to call on the clergymember as soon as possible. He or she may talk to you informally about marriage as well as discuss the ceremony, explain your roles, and help you choose a wedding date. If there are any limits on decorations or music in the church or temple, you'll be told, and perhaps introduced to a sexton who can help you with future details.

The clergymember will preside at your wedding rehearsal, and will outline the ritual and procedure for everyone in the wedding party.

**THE CHURCH SECRETARY** (or sexton) is in charge of church property, and knows all about the aisle canvas or runner, entrance canopy, prayer benches, bell-ringing, fire laws, church capacity, and so on. If the church prefers certain florists, the sexton will tell you. He or she will also schedule your wedding rehearsal.

**A CREATIVE FLORIST** can make a church look like a garden spot or design a beautiful setting for the ceremony in any other place you wish to have it. He knows which flowers are available when, which are suitable for bouquets, which are not. The florist can use all kinds of greenery from feathery smilax to dramatic ropes of laurel, and can devise flower-trimmed supports for the ribbons that define an improvised aisle in a home or garden.

Starting with the type of wedding you'll have, the color scheme you'd like, your budget, and the flowers you love, the florist can create color harmony for your wedding party and a bridal bouquet that complements your dress. He can go on to beautify a buffet, bridal table, and additional tables for the guests. He might even supply potted plants the guests might take home as reception souvenirs.

**AN EXPERIENCED CATERER** can take care of every detail in connection with food, beverages, and service for a formal reception, including one at home. You may order your wedding cake from him. The caterer can also supply dinnerware, linens, serving dishes—even tables and chairs. He should be able to advise you on tasty menus for the time of day. His fee is usually calculated on a per person basis which varies with the menu you choose and the responsibilities you want him to assume.

For a hotel reception, make arrangements with the banquet manager. If your reception will be at a club, or church, find out what the customary procedure is. Some clubs can handle everything; others don't have the facilities. For a small home reception, you may not need the caterer's professional services, but some extra help will make everything go more easily. Trained people are hard to come by, so sign them up well ahead of time.

**THE PHOTOGRAPHER** who will take your portrait will want to discuss it with you, your groom too if he's to be included. The sitting may be in the studio, your home, or the bridal salon when you have the final fitting on your dress.

Candids will give you a complete picture record of your wedding. You may want to use the same photographer as for your portrait or another. Start thinking about any special moments you don't want to miss (remember your wedding party and maybe their parents, as well as special friends and relatives will want to see themselves in your album, or have their own prints to keep). You also might encourage guests to bring their pocket cameras.

**THE MUSICIANS** can provide a beautiful background for your day, starting with the organist. Then there's the solo singer or instrumentalist who'll perform the solos—they may be professionals or talented friends.

At your reception you may have an orchestra, a strolling musician to serenade the guests, or even records or tapes. Whomever you choose, just be sure to tell them your favorite songs and to give them plenty of time to practice.

**A GOOD STATIONER** should be able to show you dozens of samples of both the white or off-white invitations that are traditional and the newer colored papers and printing that can be combined into a design of your own. He can supply and tell you how to word announcements if you'll be sending them. You can buy your thank-you notes from the stationer—especially if you'll want them personalized.

Other things you might get from the stationer: wedding matches, napkins, coasters, or any similar items with your and your groom's names on them; little souvenirs; and tiny boxes (if the baker or caterer doesn't have them) to pack cake for the guests to take home and dream on.

**THE BRIDAL CONSULTANT** in your bridal shop or department store bridal salon can help you pick out your wedding dress. She should also be prepared to outfit the maids, mothers, and flower girl in co-ordinating looks. And not only should she have suitable headpieces on hand for everyone, but in large stores she can pull together underpinnings, shoes, gloves, and other accessories without your having to set foot in another department. She's the person who deals with the bridalwear manufacturers in case the fittings and delivery don't go quite right.

**THE WEDDING GIFT REGISTRY CONSULTANT** is the person in charge of your local store's Wedding Gift Registry. The consultant can guide you and your groom in picking out dinnerware, flatware, linens, appliances, and so on, as well as keep track of the gifts that guests purchase. You register by filling out a worksheet which lists your tastes and needs—patterns, sizes, brands, and colors you prefer, as well as the approximate number of each item you'd like to have. Then, when someone wishes to give you a gift (whether for a shower, engagement party, even a future anniversary), the consultant will ask how much they want to spend and what sort of gift they have in mind. According to what you've checked on your worksheet, she'll suggest several possibilities.

How do you let your friends know you're using the Wedding Gift Registry? Pass the word around to everyone. Guests often call the bride, her mother, or an honor attendant for gift ideas. Shower hosts might list the store on invitations, some newspapers will print it with engagement announcements (check). When people ask what you want, answer, "Jim and I are registered at Binnington's. You might find something you like as much as we do there."

**THE MENS' FORMALWEAR SPECIALIST** can either sell or rent your groom and his attendants the outfits they'll need for the wedding. Whether they choose traditional clothes or more contemporary suits, the menswear specialist can see that they fit properly. He also can supply most accessories, from studs and bow ties to appropriate shoes. Some formalwear chains will measure out-of-town groomsmen in one place, arrange for pick-up near the wedding site.

## PLANNING THE CEREMONY
## APPOINTMENTS TO KEEP

Ceremony site _____

Address _____ Seating capacity _____ Number of guests _____

Clergymember or ceremony official _____

Address _____ Phone _____ Date _____ Time _____

Organist _____

Address _____ Phone _____ Date _____ Time _____

Soloist _____

Address _____ Phone _____ Date _____ Time _____

Stationer _____

Address _____ Phone _____ Date _____ Time _____

Florist _____

Address _____ Phone _____ Date _____ Time _____

Photographer _____

Address _____ Phone _____ Date _____ Time _____

Limousine service _____

Address _____ Phone _____ Date _____ Time _____

Bridal consultant _____

Address _____ Phone _____ Date _____ Time _____

Other _____

Address _____ Phone _____ Date _____ Time _____

Other _____

Address _____ Phone _____ Date _____ Time _____

Other _____

Address _____ Phone _____ Date _____ Time _____

# PLANNING THE RECEPTION
## APPOINTMENTS TO KEEP

Reception location _____

Address _____ Seating capacity _____ Number of guests _____

Banquet manager _____

Address _____ Phone _____ Date _____ Time _____

Other caterer _____

Address _____ Phone _____ Date _____ Time _____

Baker for wedding cake _____

Address _____ Phone _____ Date _____ Time _____

Reception florist (if different from ceremony florist) _____

Address _____ Phone _____ Date _____ Time _____

Musicians _____

Address _____ Phone _____ Date _____ Time _____

Wedding Gift Registry Consultant _____

Address _____ Phone _____ Date _____ Time _____

Other _____

Address _____ Phone _____ Date _____ Time _____

Other _____

Address _____ Phone _____ Date _____ Time _____

Other _____

Address _____ Phone _____ Date _____ Time _____

# A CEREMONY THAT'S YOU

Something old, something new. Your ceremony will be both. A beautiful blending of family tradition and all that has special meaning for the two of you, the marriage you'll create. Where to begin?

**Talk to your clergymember.** Do it the same day you set the date. You'll need to know which parts of the classic ceremony are *must's* (the ring may be the only requirement if you're Jewish, a church service if you're Catholic), so you can either make sure to include them, or change to another church or ceremony official if you prefer. You'll probably want to make time too for more than the usual number of pre-wedding discussions. Most priests, ministers, and rabbis have helped lots of other couples personalize their weddings, and are just about the best source of ideas around.

First ask for a copy of the traditional ceremony. Then find out if your denomination has a newer, alternative service without phrases like "love, honor, and obey." (Many Protestant and Catholic churches do.) Also ask to borrow books, poems, hymnals. And should you two belong to different faiths, see if your clergymember will participate in an *ecumenical* service—by sharing the official's role with your groom's clergymember in your church or his, or by weaving prayers and customs from your groom's religion in with those from your own.

**Choose with your fiancé which traditions you'll keep.** Study the time-honored ceremony. Would it be fine if, for instance, you left out the idea of two becoming "one"? (a sensitive point for many individually minded couples). Would it express your genuine feelings if only it sounded more natural? Rewrite the ceremony in your own words: instead of "plight thee my troth," try "I give you my promise." You might come up with exactly the vows you were hoping to find in some book!

Take a second look at any customs you've considered dropping because they don't fit. Even if you have feminist views, do you get misty at the thought of your father giving you away? Your reasons for carrying on tradition don't have to be the same as your grandparents'.

**Look for natural points in the ceremony to add your own touches.** There'll probably be a procession, a welcome (that's "Dearly beloved . . ."), the giving-away or "parting" of the bride and her family, the vows, a blessing of the rings, the ring ceremony, one or more prayers, the pronouncement of marriage, a benediction, the kiss, and the recessional. You could change all—or just one—of these parts. With everything else traditional, you could still write vows like: "I will love you now, and will love you more. My home will be your home. I will share with you all the tears and laughter of my tomorrows, and they will become ours."

**Think about ways to involve your family and friends too.** Borrowing a Jewish custom, you might include your groom and parents in the procession (see the "lineup" ideas, Chapter 6). A sister or brother might read a prayer or the welcome (maybe a history of the two families). Instead of the giving-away, you might offer a kiss to your father, a flower to your mother (do the same for your new in-laws before the recessional). The clergymember might also ask, "Who supports the union of this couple?" The response: "We, their parents, do." To symbolize sharing between your families, you and your groom could light two tapers on either side of the church. After the ceremony, carry the candles to the center and kindle a single, taller candle. Another idea for the closing: the two of you, your parents, and your brothers and sisters might all join hands.

What about the guests? Have your printer make up souvenir programs of the ceremony. Include poems or thoughts for meditation, your vows, the names of all the people in the wedding, the words of responsive readings or hymns they can take part in. Make sure everyone can see too. At the altar, have your wedding party form a semicircle around the clergymember, facing the congregation; you two, face to face, stand in front. Afterwards, you might each go down the aisle, passing baskets of flowers or starting the kiss or handclasp of peace that closes morning worship in many faiths.

**Collect ideas.** Prowl stores and library for current books of wedding innovations. Your church may even have quite a few. Also get your librarian (or former English teachers) to suggest poems by everyone from Shakespeare and Elizabeth Barrett Browning to e.e. cummings and Judith Viorst. Other popular sources that might appeal to you: *The Prophet* by Kahlil Gibran, and the *Bible,* especially the Psalms, the Song of Solomon, and the Book of Ruth. Fiction and nonfiction books can be both lyrical and inspirational as well. *The Art of Loving* by Erich Fromm, a modern classic, is just one of many possibilities. Listen again to your favorite songs. Imagine speaking the words of Judy Collins' "Since You Asked" to each other ("What I'll give you since you asked is all my time together . . ."). The two of you could offer different readings, or maybe take turns on the lines of one you *both* love.

Get your parents and married friends to reminisce about their weddings—for a sense of communion with them, have the same song, flowers, prayers. And ask yourselves questions like: What does marriage mean to me? What do I want from it? From my partner? What can I give? Your answers—sincere and simple—will make the loveliest vows of all.

**Draw your most beautiful thoughts and feelings together for a wedding that's YOU.** Just remember a couple of things. It takes time. Give yourselves at least a month (two, if you'll be ordering programs from the printer or asking friends to write or memorize something). It's best the ceremony last 15 minutes to an hour—no longer. So don't try to crowd in too many songs, poems, prayers, readings, or get *too* political, *too* personal. You may be nervous, and the simpler the better.

As soon as it's ready, type a copy of your ceremony for the clergymember to approve. Make extras to pass out at the rehearsal; when everyone knows what comes next, things flow much more smoothly. The same goes for you and your groom. So practice together the week ahead, speaking as clearly and confidently as you will wedding day. If you memorize your vows, they'll take on special meaning. The whole time you're working, thinking, talking, of course, the two of you will be communicating your values, beliefs, and hopes to marriage to each other. And in creating your own ceremony, that can be the most meaningful part of all.

# PERSONALIZING YOUR CEREMONY
## Ideas to consider

### AS GUESTS ARRIVE
Ushers or young friends can hand each person something to make him feel a part of things—a colorful flower, a candle to be lit, a printed ceremony program.

A unique musical prelude of popular songs or classics might be played on a special instrument—flute, violin.

Excited to see everybody? You two can be the first to arrive and greet guests as they enter—it's a "receiving line" *before* the ceremony.

### THE PROCESSIONAL
Your parents and his might be part of the processional—you can each walk down the aisle on the arm of both your mother and father.

You and your groom might walk together. Enter the church from different doors, meet at the back of the aisle, go ahead arm-in-arm.

As you approach the altar, pause to give each mother a hanky embroidered with your initials, his, the date.

When you greet your groom, slip his boutonnière from your bouquet into his lapel. (Your florist can tie it into your bouquet for easy removal.)

### GIVING THE BRIDE AWAY
Instead of saying, "Who gives this woman in marriage?", your clergymember might ask, "Who blesses this marriage?" or, "Who rejoices in this union?" All parents can answer, "We do."

If you'd rather not have the traditional "giving away," part with your father as you reach his seat, kiss him on the cheek, then walk alone to meet your groom.

Why not a "unity" candle-lighting ceremony now. Have three candles on the altar—one in the center, two smaller ones on either side. You, your parents, or your whole family walk up and light the candle on the left; the groom's side lights the right candle. After exchanging your vows, you two light the center candle together.

### BEFORE THE VOWS
The two of you might alternate on reading lines of your favorite love song—or "your song"—to each other. Or recite your favorite poem.

Your clergymember might stand at a special altar with his back to the congregation while you, your groom, the wedding party face your guests.

Have special people perform readings. A brother or sister might offer a quote on the meaning of families. Attendants might talk about the importance in marriage of friends. Or, if it's an ecumenical service, an official from each faith can read a prayer, a scripture passage.

### DURING THE VOWS
The lights might be dimmed—your bridal party can each hold a candle, light them in succession, form a semicircle around the two of you.

Exchange two sets of vows—first the traditional ones, followed by words you've written yourselves.

Your parents and his might want to re-affirm their own wedding vows. Your clergymember can invite them to stand around you; after you recite your vows, he can read vows to your parents, then your groom's parents.

## AFTER THE VOWS
Your clergymember might introduce you two as "Mr. and Mrs." for the first time, as he asks the congregation to give you a joyful round of applause.
Have everyone join in and sing your favorite hymn.
After kissing each other, go over and give your parents, grandparents a special hug and kiss.

## THE RECESSIONAL
As you two walk down the aisle, stop and greet everyone with a quick hello, start the "Kiss of Peace" (your clergymember can show you how).
Walk to your reception site—if it's close by you two can lead the way while the bridal party, family, and guests follow in one huge march.
Spend a few minutes alone together—you might want to make a quick escape in a buggy or limousine, one that will take you to the reception. Or slip away to a shady spot or remote corner of the church to kiss and catch your breath and reflect on your new married life together.

## WRITING YOUR OWN VOWS
### A step-by-step guide

*Here among friends, I, Mary, wish for us both, John, a marriage of love and of laughter, of tears and then hope; where I am free to touch you when you are sad, you to hug me when I am happy; where my heart is open to yours, and yours to mine—always. I love you for the father you will become, the friend and equal you are, the man who helps me to grow and be one with myself. I will be faithful to you, I will work with you so that our marriage can mean forever. In good times and bad, with guidance from God, I am your partner . . . I am your wife . . . I love you.*

Here is a sample of vows that a bride might write. How can you compose something just as meaningful?

*Here among friends,*
1 Acknowledge all those who've come to witness your exchange of vows and to offer support for the new family you two are forming. You could do this at any point in your vows, but it is an especially easy way to begin.
*I, Mary, wish for us both, John, a marriage*
2 Cover the points basic to your "contract": your name, a phrase that tells you are about to make a pledge (like "vow to," "promise that"), your partner's name, and a word or two that indicates you're talking about marriage, or about yourself as a husband or wife.
*of love and of laughter, of tears and then hope; where I am free to touch you when you are sad, you to hug me when I am happy; where my heart is open to yours, and yours to mine—always.*
3 Go on to let your partner know which feelings you think vital for the two of you to share and what you are bringing him on an emotional level. Complicated? It doesn't have to be. "I will love you" may say it all for you.
*I love you for the father you will become,*

4 Touch on the most meaningful of the many dreams and goals that will shape your life together day to day, the special choices you've made for yourselves and your marriage. Thoughtfully spelling out your "practical" plans for children, ties with family and friends, financial responsibilities, where you'll live, and so on, can be the most revealing step you'll take in writing your own vows.
*the friend and equal you are, the man who helps me to grow and be one with myself.*
5 Include your ideas on whether a husband and wife should be equals, and on whether in marriage two people are meant to enrich each other's lives with their separate identities or to "become one." These ideas go together nicely.
*I will be faithful to you,*
6 Consider mentioning your beliefs about fidelity. (Does it refer to sex, secrets, what?)
*I will work with you so that our marriage can mean forever.*
7 Make a commitment to a marriage that lasts, if that is what you truly want. Do you prefer dedicating yourself "to a marriage filled with the energy of all my life"? Make sure your partner understands—but do be sincere.
*In good times and bad,*
8 Show you accept the fact that marriage will have its ups and downs, its joys and disappointments—as does all of life—and that you two will share whatever comes.
*with guidance from God,*
9 Find a way to bring in your faith. Lines from a Bible verse, religious tenets like those affecting family plans, a subtle deference to God—you decide what best reflects the place (if any) religion will hold in your marriage.
*I am your partner . . . I am your wife . . . I love you.*
10 Reaffirm your desire to be married, your love for the person who has promised himself to you.

# YOUR CEREMONY CHECKLIST

Site reserved _____ Cost, if any $ _____

Date _____ Ceremony time _____ to _____

| Part of Ceremony | Person(s) Participating | Special Idea, Reading, Poem, etc. |
|---|---|---|
| Procession | Wedding party, bride, bride's father _____ | _____ |
| | | _____ |
| | Wedding party, groom and parents, bride and parents _____ | _____ |
| | | _____ |
| | Clergy, wedding party, all grandparents, groom and parents, bride and parents _____ | _____ |
| | | _____ |
| | | _____ |
| | | _____ |
| | Other _____ | _____ |
| | _____ | _____ |
| Welcome | _____ | _____ |
| | _____ | _____ |
| | | _____ |
| Giving-Away or Other Family Gesture | _____ | _____ |
| | _____ | _____ |
| | _____ | _____ |
| Prayer or Other Meditation | _____ | _____ |
| | | _____ |
| | | _____ |
| Groom's Vows | _____ | _____ |
| | | _____ |
| | | _____ |
| | | _____ |
| Bride's Vows | _____ | _____ |
| | | _____ |
| | | _____ |
| | | _____ |

Prayer or
Other Meditation          _____          _____

                                                     _____

                                                     _____

Blessing of the Rings      _____          _____

                                                     _____

                                                     _____

Groom's Giving of the Ring _____          _____

                                                     _____

                                                     _____

Bride's Giving of the Ring _____          _____

                                                     _____

                                                     _____

Prayer or
Other Meditation          _____          _____

                                                     _____

                                                     _____

Pronouncement of Marriage  _____          _____

                                                     _____

                                                     _____

Kiss or
Other Closing             _____          _____

                          _____          _____

                          _____          _____

Recessional               Same as Procession          _____
                          without parents,
                          grandparents, clergy         _____

                                                     _____

Other_____          _____

_____          _____

_____          _____

                          Ceremony official's fee, if any $ _____

                    44    Total cost of ceremony $ _____

# YOUR WEDDING BOUQUET

WHAT FLOWERS CAN MEAN TO YOU
ROSE      *Love*
ORCHID      *Beauty*
CARNATION      *Distinction*
WHITE DAISY      *Innocence*
ORANGE BLOSSOM      *Purity, loveliness*
BLUE VIOLET      *Faithfulness*
BLUE BELL      *Constancy*
FORGET-ME-NOT      *True love*
LILY OF THE VALLEY      *Happiness*
WHITE LILAC      *Youthful innocence*
RED CHRYSANTHEMUM      *Sharing*
GARDENIA      *Joy*

Left: Crescent-shaped bouquet.
Center: Cascade of flowers and
ivy, trimmed with ribbons.
Right: Prayer book with single flowers.

Flowers have been part of weddings since ancient Roman times when brides carried bunches of herbs under their veils. Later, brides held orange blossoms as symbols of fertility. Today, wedding flowers give fresh, finishing touches to every bridal look. So consult your florist at least one month before the wedding to find just the right flowers for you. Decide on how much money you want to spend, then list the flowers you like best. Traditional favorites are white roses, gardenias, orchids, stephanotis, and carnations. When you visit the florist, find out which flowers stay fresh the longest and which ones will be in season during your wedding (they'll cost less than those that aren't). Give the florist a sketch and description of your dress and your maids' dresses. Include sleeve length, neckline, silhouette, trimmings, and formality so he can advise you on appropriately shaped and styled bouquets. Also take along fabric swatches to help him work out a color scheme. If you'd like, suggest using the Victorian custom of spelling out your fiancé's name in flowers. For example, start a nosegay with baby's breath, ivy, and lilies of the valley for Bill. Remember to order flowers for your mothers, boutonnières for the men, and reception and altar flowers. Finally, listen to the florist's suggestions, ask for a cost estimate in writing, then trust him to carry out his plans. Weeks later when you're headed down the aisle, stand tall and hold your bouquet in your right hand at waist level. At the altar, pass it to the maid on your left and take it back before the recessional. Your maids hold their bouquets with both hands, elbows resting on top of their hips. After the reception, don't forget to toss your bouquet to the lucky one who will be next to wed.

## RECEPTION HAIR FLOWERS
The newest fashion idea for brides? Special wedding blossoms to pin in your hair at reception time. Once you take off your veil, you can move about more freely. What flowers are best to wear? Anything from your bouquet of course. Just be sure the colors blend with your makeup and complexion. Quiet whites and pastels like pink and lavender are more flattering than bright orange and yellow. And don't worry—some of the prettiest blossoms will last throughout your wedding reception: roses, daisies, gardenias, baby's breath, orchids, lilies, carnations.

## YOUR WEDDING KEEPSAKE
Here's how to dry flowers from your bouquet (take a few out before you throw it): tie the flowers together tightly with a pipe cleaner, then hang them upside down in a dry, dark place (closet or attic) until they feel parched (about two weeks). Reassemble the flowers (tie ribbon around them if you like), then seal them in a see-through box or bell jar. Or press some flowers between the pages of a thick book for at least six weeks, arrange them on velvet, and encase them in a picture frame. Still another way to have a nice keepsake is to have your florist use silk flowers as well as real flowers in your wedding bouquet.

# YOUR CEREMONY AND RECEPTION FLOWERS

Left: "Presentation" or arm bouquet of long-stemmed flowers. Center: Basket of flowers for maids or flower girl. It can later go on reception tables. Right: Nosegay with streamers. These and many other floral designs are available at your local florist.

There are infinite arrangements your florist can make for your church or temple. However, you should first talk to your clergymember or the congregational group responsible for the general upkeep of the church and its relics. Many churches have definite dos and don'ts about decorating. But you can probably find a "unique" flower arrangement you love and still meet church requirements. Here are some ideas you might mention to your clergymember. Hang garlands or beribboned flowers on the aisle-side of the pews or around the choir loft. Fill vases with delicate flowers—daisies, lilacs, forsythia—or small potted plants and put them on the window sill. Bunch greenery in baskets and set them around the sides of the altar. For a beautiful effect, vary colors and textures—perhaps fluffy spring green fern with trailing ivy and magnolia branches. Your florist can tell you what's in season and what will look best together. Or you can have your florist make a medallion of greenery with one dramatic flower—a large chrysanthemum or a gladiola—in the center. The medallions can be made to stand on their own frame. Or border a graduated grouping of candles on the altar with lots of bright flowers like tulips, daffodils, and azaleas all around.

When you talk to the florist, also agree on a color scheme for your reception. Do tell him or her your preferences for flowers. But allow the florist to suggest substitutions which may be more readily available. You might ask that everything match, or plan striking contrast in your decorations by choosing colors and kinds of flowers that differ from those you and your maids will carry. After you've made these basic decisions, take your florist to the reception site. Consider trimming the staircase, fireplace, bandstand or any area people will see. Remember that all arrangements will draw the most attention placed at eye level and above and that centerpieces should stand low enough to allow diners to see each other easily. Also ask the florist to recommend colors for tablecloths and any non-floral decorations that will also accent the room. Although many hotels and clubs may refer you to a florist who best knows the surroundings, you may prefer to hire the same florist for both your reception and your wedding. The florist should willingly itemize all bills in advance and promise to assume all delivery and set-up duties anywhere you need flowers.

# FLOWER CHECKLIST

## Decorations for the ceremony site (church, hotel, etc.)

| Where | Kinds of flowers | Color | Number of arrangements | Cost |
|---|---|---|---|---|
| Altar or canopy | _____ | _____ | _____ | $_____ |
|  | _____ | _____ | _____ | $_____ |
|  | _____ | _____ | _____ | $_____ |
| Pews | _____ | _____ | _____ | $_____ |
| Aisles | _____ | _____ | _____ | $_____ |
| Windows | _____ | _____ | _____ | $_____ |
| Other | _____ | _____ | _____ | $_____ |
| _____ | _____ | _____ | _____ | $_____ |
| _____ | _____ | _____ | _____ | $_____ |
|  |  |  | TOTAL | $_____ |

## Other decorations provided

| What | Where | How Many | Flowers, if any | Cost |
|---|---|---|---|---|
| Candles | _____ | _____ | _____ | $_____ |
| Candleholders | _____ | _____ | _____ | $_____ |
| Aisle runner | _____ | _____ | _____ | $_____ |
| Other | _____ | _____ | _____ | $_____ |
| _____ | _____ | _____ | _____ | $_____ |
| _____ | _____ | _____ | _____ | $_____ |
|  |  |  | TOTAL | $_____ |

**Delivery**

Ceremony site _____

Address _____ Phone _____

Person to see _____

Date _____ Time _____

**Flowers for the wedding party**

**Bride**

Style of bouquet _____

Kinds and colors of flowers _____

_____

_____

Ribbon color _____

Cost $ _____

**Maid or matron of honor**

Style _____

Kinds and colors of flowers _____

_____

Ribbon color _____

Cost $ _____

**Bridesmaids** _____ How many _____

Style _____

Kinds and colors of flowers _____

_____

Ribbon color _____

Cost of all $ _____

**Flower girl**

Style _____

Kinds and colors of flowers _____

Ribbon color _____

Cost $ _____

**Mother of the bride**

Style of corsage _____

Kinds and colors of flowers _____

_____

Ribbon color _____

Cost $ _____

**Delivery of flowers for the bridal party**

Place (home of bride, church, etc.) _____

Address _____ Phone _____

Person to see _____

Date _____ Time _____

Cost $ _____

**Groomsmen, fathers, ring bearer** _____ How many _____

Kind and color of boutonnières _____

Cost $ _____

**Delivery of flowers for the groom's party**

Place (church, hotel, etc.) _____

Address _____ Phone _____

Person to see _____

Date _____ Time _____

**Mother of the groom**

Style of corsage _____

Kinds and colors of flowers _____

_____

Ribbon color _____

Cost $ _____

**Delivery**

Place (home of groom's parents, church, etc.) _____

Address _____ Phone _____

Person to see _____

Date _____ Time _____

**Other person (bride's grandmother, groom's grandmother, aunts, etc.)** _____

Style _____

Kinds and colors _____

Cost $ _____

Delivery address _____ Phone _____

Date _____ Time _____

**Other** _____

Style _____

Kinds and colors _____

Cost $ _____

Delivery address _____

Date _____ Time _____

TOTAL COST OF FLOWERS FOR THE WEDDING PARTY $ _____

**Party flowers (for the bridesmaids' luncheon, rehearsal dinner, etc.)**

| Where | Kinds of flowers | Color | Number of arrangements | Cost |
|---|---|---|---|---|
| Buffet table | _____ | _____ | _____ | $ _____ |
| Bridal table | _____ | _____ | _____ | $ _____ |
| Guest tables | _____ | _____ | _____ | $ _____ |
| Other _____ | _____ | _____ | _____ | $ _____ |
| _____ | _____ | _____ | _____ | $ _____ |
| _____ | _____ | _____ | _____ | $ _____ |
| | | | TOTAL | $ _____ |

**Delivery**

Party site (Bride's home, restaurant, etc.) _____

Address _____ Phone _____

Person to see _____

Date _____ Time _____

**Flowers for special guests** _____

Style, kinds, colors _____

Cost $ _____

Delivery address _____

Date _____ Time _____

**Special guest** _____

Style, kinds, colors _____

Cost $ _____

Delivery address _____

Date _____ Time _____

TOTAL COST OF PARTY FLOWERS $ _____

## Decorations for the reception

| Where | Kinds of flowers | Color | Number of arrangements | Cost |
|---|---|---|---|---|
| Receiving line area | _____ | _____ | _____ | $_____ |
| | _____ | _____ | _____ | $_____ |
| Buffet table | _____ | _____ | _____ | $_____ |
| | _____ | _____ | _____ | $_____ |
| Bridal table | _____ | _____ | _____ | $_____ |
| Parents' table | _____ | _____ | _____ | $_____ |
| Guest tables | _____ | _____ | _____ | $_____ |
| | _____ | _____ | _____ | $_____ |
| Cake table | _____ | _____ | _____ | $_____ |
| Cake knife, top of cake, etc. | _____ | _____ | _____ | $_____ |
| Punch table | _____ | _____ | _____ | $_____ |
| Bandstand | _____ | _____ | _____ | $_____ |
| Other_____ | _____ | _____ | _____ | $_____ |
| _____ | _____ | _____ | _____ | $_____ |
| _____ | _____ | _____ | _____ | $_____ |
| | | | TOTAL | $_____ |

## Delivery

Reception site _____

Address _____ Phone _____

Person to see _____

Date _____ Time _____

# TALKING TO THE CATERER

## *Partying at a club, hotel, or restaurant*

You might celebrate your marriage with a bountiful reception in a private club or community club, church parlor, hotel, or elegant restaurant. If you hope to invite more than 50 guests, you may entertain them at one of these sites much more efficiently than in a small home, for you then tap the experience of the establishment's banquet manager. He can see that all runs smoothly and free you and the reception hosts to be with your guests and enjoy the happy occasion. But do be sure to start shopping for your reception site as soon as possible. Some are booked a year in advance.

**Before you meet with the manager,** decide on the day and time you wish the reception to take place, the length of your guest list, the type of reception you want—whether a cocktail party, buffet, or dinner—and the limits of your budget. He'll be able to show you rooms which can best accommodate the number of people who will attend the reception. Be sure to get an exact cost estimate before you leave. And find out if gratuities are included in the price. If not, ask about the concern's general tipping policy (usually about 15 percent for the waiters, five percent of the total bill for the wine steward).

**Once you've negotiated the number of guests** with the manager, stick to it, as last minute additions may hamper his staff's ability to provide the best ser-vice. Also, to guarantee your guests the most appetizing food, choose a menu from the varied selection he can offer and one that he is the most familiar with. Accept too his hints for efficient room set-ups and ask for his advice on setting up the receiving line. You may, however, request your favorite brands of liquor or wine, asking that only a certain amount be served, or that the bar be closed at a certain time after you and your groom leave for your honeymoon, thereby controlling costs to some degree. Another way you can save money is by contracting for one of the special reception packages many establishments offer. These packages include such necessities as flowers and music with the price per person of the food and drinks. Find out exactly what a package includes and costs before you sign any contract. And don't worry that your "package" wedding reception will lose its individuality, for the banquet manager may recommend economical additions to personalize the party, such as offering a groom's cake packed in small, individual boxes for guests to take home.

**After the reception is over,** when the bill arrives, remember that you pay not only for the well-served food a manager's concern can provide, but also for the comfortable, welcoming surroundings everyone will enjoy.

# CHECKLIST FOR THE BANQUET MANAGER

Room reserved _____ Cost, if any $ _____

Date _____ Reception hours _____ to _____

Number of guests _____

Party style: Buffet meal _____ Sit-down _____ Cocktails/hors d'oeuvres _____

Punch and cake _____ Other_____

## MENU

_____

_____

_____

_____

_____

_____

_____

_____

Wedding cake included?     Yes _____ No _____

Cost of food $_____

## TABLE SET-UPS

| Whose | Location | How Many | Number at each | Linen color | Special Appointments |
|---|---|---|---|---|---|
| Wedding party | _____ | _____ | _____ | _____ | _____ |
| Parents' | _____ | _____ | _____ | _____ | _____ |
| Guests | _____ | _____ | _____ | _____ | _____ |
| Orchestra (if served) | _____ | _____ | _____ | _____ | _____ |
| Cake | _____ | _____ | _____ | _____ | _____ |
| Punch | _____ | _____ | _____ | _____ | _____ |
| Other_____ | _____ | _____ | _____ | _____ | _____ |

## SERVICE

Number of waiters _____ Bartenders _____ Other _____

Rate _____ Gratuities, if not included _____ Overtime rate _____

Total service cost $ _____

## WHERE WILL THEY BE?

Receiving line _____

Dance floor and bandstand _____

Women's rest room _____ Men's rest room _____

Dressing room for bride _____

Dressing room for groom _____

Parking facilities _____

Other_____

## EXTRAS REQUESTED (groom's cake, pastry cart, etc.)

Item _____ Cost $ _____

Item _____ Cost $ _____

Item _____ Cost $ _____

Item _____ Cost $ _____

Item _____ Cost $ _____

Item _____ Cost $ _____

TOTAL RECEPTION COST WITHOUT LIQUOR    $ _____

# BAR CHECKLIST

Number of guests _____ When served _____ Cocktail hours _____ to _____

Champagne toast_____ Wine with dinner _____ Punch bowls_____

## LIQUOR

| Item | Quantity | Brand | Cost |
|---|---|---|---|
| Champagne | _____ | _____ | $ _____ |
| Bourbon | _____ | _____ | $ _____ |
| Gin | _____ | _____ | $ _____ |
| Rum | _____ | _____ | $ _____ |
| Scotch | _____ | _____ | $ _____ |
| Vermouth | _____ | _____ | $ _____ |
| Vodka | _____ | _____ | $ _____ |
| Red wine | _____ | _____ | $ _____ |
| Rosé wine | _____ | _____ | $ _____ |
| White wine | _____ | _____ | $ _____ |
| Punch | _____ | _____ | $ _____ |
| Other | _____ | _____ | $ _____ |
| _____ | _____ | _____ | $ _____ |
| _____ | _____ | _____ | $ _____ |
| | | Total liquor cost | $ _____ |

## MIXERS

| Collins mix | _____ | _____ | $ _____ |
|---|---|---|---|
| Cola | _____ | _____ | $ _____ |
| Ginger ale | _____ | _____ | $ _____ |
| Soda | _____ | _____ | $ _____ |
| Tonic | _____ | _____ | $ _____ |
| Orange juice | _____ | _____ | $ _____ |
| Tomato juice | _____ | _____ | $ _____ |
| Other | _____ | _____ | $ _____ |
| _____ | _____ | _____ | $ _____ |
| _____ | _____ | _____ | $ _____ |
| | | Total mixer cost | $ _____ |

## DRINK INGREDIENTS

| Item | Quantity | Brand | Cost |
|------|----------|-------|------|
| Angostura bitters | _____ | _____ | $ _____ |
| Cocktail olives | _____ | _____ | $ _____ |
| Cocktail onions | _____ | _____ | $ _____ |
| Ice | _____ | _____ | $ _____ |
| Lemons and lemon peel | _____ | _____ | $ _____ |
| Limes | _____ | _____ | $ _____ |
| Maraschino cherries | _____ | _____ | $ _____ |
| Superfine sugar | _____ | _____ | $ _____ |
| Other | _____ | _____ | $ _____ |
| _____ | _____ | _____ | $ _____ |
| _____ | _____ | _____ | $ _____ |
| | | Total drink ingredients cost | $ _____ |

## BAR EQUIPMENT

| Item | Number | Item | Number |
|------|--------|------|--------|
| Bottle openers | _____ | Water pitchers | _____ |
| Can openers | _____ | Drink recipe book | _____ |
| Cocktail shakers | _____ | Cocktail napkins | _____ |
| Corkscrews | _____ | Stir sticks | _____ |
| Ice buckets | _____ | 8-oz. glasses | _____ |
| Ice tubs | _____ | 4-oz. glasses | _____ |
| Knives | _____ | Champagne glasses | _____ |
| Spoons | _____ | Wine glasses | _____ |
| Strainers | _____ | Serving trays | _____ |
| | | Other | _____ |
| | | _____ | _____ |
| | | _____ | _____ |
| | | Equipment costs, if any | $ _____ |
| | | Total bar costs | $ _____ |

# YOUR WEDDING CAKE

Cake is the one ingredient no wedding reception, no matter how small, can do without. It doesn't have to be the white sponge or light fruitcake that's traditional. Chocolate, spice, or yellow is fine too. And although you might prefer the more "bridal" look of white frosting swirled in baroque curlicues, you can also pick a topping that's as colorful as your wedding portrait. Whatever tastes best to you (and is in the best taste).

## How to buy it for the wedding

Start shopping the bakeries right *now.*

Discuss prices of the cakes available, ask to see *and* taste them. Take notes ("yum," "yuk," "pretty!") on your impressions.

Order the cake three months before the wedding. Specify how many it must serve, then trust the baker's judgment on size. Don't demand a spoil-prone cream filling if the weather's likely to be warm. Do ask that a fruitcake be prepared right away, that white, spice, etc. be baked no more than a day ahead to be sure it's fresh and moist.

Expect to put down a deposit. Get in writing on the receipt: cake size; flavors of cake, filling, icing; topping design; delivery date and address (make sure they *do* deliver, in some states they won't); balance to be paid. Ask for a knife and how to cut. Call and confirm *everything* two days ahead.

Find out if it's cheaper (it *is* easier) to take the cake offered in your caterer's reception package than to shop for it on your own. And figure ingredient costs carefully before baking; it *could* be more expensive.

Consider ordering a groom's cake too—packed in individual boxes, left near the door for guests to take home and dream on.

# WEDDING CAKE CHECKLIST

Number to serve_____

Size of cake_____

Shape: Two-tier _____ Three-tier _____ Four-tier _____ Flat _____ Other _____

Cake flavor: White _____ Yellow _____ Chocolate _____ Other _____

Filling flavor _____

Icing flavor and color_____

Decoration description _____

_____

Topping: Bride and groom _____ Wedding bells _____ Lovebirds _____

        Fresh flowers _____ Other _____

Cake knife included?     Yes _____ No _____

Cutting instructions _____

_____

_____

_____

                                                        Cost $ _____

Delivery _____

Reception site_____

Address _____ Phone_____

Person to see _____

Date _____ Time _____

Groom's cake?     Yes _____ No _____

Description _____

How many packages_____

                                                        Cost $ _____

                                        Total cake cost $ _____

# YOUR WEDDING PHOTOGRAPHY

Your marriage ceremony will be over in a few minutes, and the reception will be over in a few hours, but the photographs of your wedding will last a lifetime. So the person who photographs your wedding should be someone you trust—someone with the talent and experience to take the kind of pictures you'll display with pride. Most brides prefer to rely on a professional photographer who specializes in weddings. He may be a member of the Professional Photographers Association of America which has its own Code of Ethics for Wedding Photography. He knows how to conduct himself at the sacred ceremony, how to compensate for church lighting, and isn't so moved by it all he forgets to snap the ring ceremony. Though his intentions are sincere, an amateur doesn't share this expertise. But do ask friends and relatives to bring their pocket cameras to the reception; even the best professional photographer can only be in one place at a time. And you'll want to capture all the excitement you can.

There are two types of wedding photographs—formal portraits taken several weeks before the wedding and the informal candids taken during the actual ceremony and reception. You may have both types taken by the same photographer, or you may choose one to do your portraits and another to take your candids. It doesn't matter how you arrange it, as long as you study sample photographs before you make a choice, and are sure that the person you hire is the one whose samples you liked—not another photographer on the same staff. It's also wise to talk to other brides about their experiences with wedding photographers. Choose your photographer as early as possible, for the one you want may be fully booked as far as three months ahead of a popular wedding season like June, August, September, or December.

The cost of wedding photographs varies according to locality, photographer, and the amount of time necessary to complete the job. The number of pictures and whether they're color or black and white also affect the cost. In general, however, the minimum price for a portrait ranges from $90 for black and white to $100 for color. A few glossies are usually included for use by newspapers. The fee for "covering" a wedding as a candid photographer usually begins at $300 for color, including a wedding album and a set number of pictures (25 5x7s is a popular package) with an extra charge for each additional print. The majority of all wedding photographs are taken in color. It's usually more economical to have the same studio handle all your wedding photography, but it's important to know

what you're getting. The lowest price may not be the best value.

Most newspapers require that wedding photographs be submitted one or two weeks before the scheduled publication date, so it may be necessary to have your portrait taken more than a month before your wedding. This is actually to your advantage, as portrait sitting helps a bride get used to her wedding outfit. It also forces her to see how everything looks together while there's still time to make changes.

Wedding portraits are usually taken in the photographer's studio, but if the proper facilities are available, you may arrange to have yours taken in the store bridal salon during the final fitting of your dress. The latter is preferable if there's any chance that your dress and veil will be crushed on the trip to the studio. Your home and other locations are not recommended because few are able to offer the proper air conditioning, lighting, background, and peaceful surroundings necessary.

Be sure you have all your accessories—lingerie, shoes, gloves, jewelry, prayer book—with you at the studio. A detailed description of your flowers is also necessary so the photographer can provide an appropriate dummy bouquet for the pictures. And the one thing you won't need is an audience—you might get nervous.

The sensitive film now being used by most photographers eliminates the need for any special camera makeup, but it's wise to take a supply of cosmetics along to the studio with you. If you use foundation, choose a liquid or cream; a matte finish will kill natural highlights. Be light with blusher; on a black and white photo it will show black, not the sunny peach you intended. A medium shade of lipstick is best with lots of gloss. For eyes, mascara is a must—even if you never wear makeup; eyes tend to vanish in a photograph, especially in black and white. But no amount of makeup will substitute for plenty of rest and a good meal before your sitting.

The average portrait sitting takes about an hour, and includes from 10–20 different poses.

Along with your wedding candids, it's nice to include a few posed photographs—of you and your groom and of the entire bridal party, perhaps—but these should be kept to a minimum. Try to plan for photos when time permits, between the time you've finished dressing and before the ceremony begins and after the receiving line.

# PORTRAIT PHOTOGRAPHY CHECKLIST

Portrait photographer _____

Sitting location _____

Date of sitting_____ Time_____

## THINGS TO TAKE TO THE SITTING

_____ Wedding dress—all pressed and neatly boxed or hung, then covered with a dress bag

_____ Headpiece in its carrying box

_____ Veil or mantilla, pressed with a *cool, cool* iron, hung and protected with plastic

_____ Wedding shoes

_____ Gloves, if any

_____ Ultra-sheer white or flesh-toned pantyhose

_____ White or "nude color" bra, specially chosen for comfort, smoothest dress line, the barest look if dress has a low or sheer bodice

_____ Matching white or nude panties

_____ White slip or long petticoat

_____ Girdle, if needed

_____ Wedding jewelry, if any

_____ Lacy hanky and bridal garter, if desired

_____ Prayer book, if carrying one

_____ Description of bridal bouquet so photographer may substitute an appropriate dummy

_____ Wedding makeup, unless photographer's assistant will supply and apply it—ask

_____ Comb and brush

_____ Light snack

Date portrait proofs will be ready _____

Portrait package includes_____

_____

Package cost $_____

Number of black and white prints for newspapers       _____       Cost $ _____

Number of extra portrait prints       _____       Cost $ _____

Total portrait photography cost $ _____

**WEDDING CANDID PHOTOGRAPHY CHECKLIST**

**Before The Ceremony**

_____ Bride in dress

_____ Bride with mother

_____ Bride with father

_____ Bride with both parents

_____ Bride with honor attendant

_____ Bride with maids

_____ Bride touching up makeup, hair

_____ Bride at gift table

_____ Everyone getting flowers

_____ Bride leaving house

_____ Bride, father getting in car

_____ Groom alone

_____ Groom with best man

_____ Groomsmen getting boutonnières

_____ Other moments dressing

_____

_____

_____

**At The Ceremony**

_____ Guests outside church (other site)

_____ Bride, father getting out of car

_____ Bride, father going into church

_____ Ushers escorting guests

_____ Giving-away ceremony

_____ Altar or canopy during ceremony

_____ Bride and groom exchanging vows

_____ Ring ceremony

_____ Bridesmaids coming down aisle

_____ Maid or matron of honor

_____ Flower girl and ring bearer

_____ Bride and father

_____ Groom meeting bride

_____ Groom's parents being seated (or in procession)

_____ Bride's mother being seated (or in procession)

_____ Soloist and organist

_____ Groom and groomsmen at altar (or in procession)

_____ The kiss

_____ Bride and groom coming up aisle

_____ Bride and groom on church steps

_____ Bride alone in the chapel

_____ Bride and groom among guests, wedding party

_____ Bride and groom getting in car

_____ Bride and groom in back seat of car

_____ Other ceremony moments

_____

_____

## Posed Shots Before the Reception

_____ Bridesmaids looking at bride's ring

_____ Bride's and groom's hands

_____ Bride and groom together

_____ Bride with parents

_____ Groom with parents

_____ Bride and groom with honor attendants

_____ Bride and groom with children

_____ Bride with her attendants

_____ Groom with his attendants

_____ Bride, groom, all the wedding party

_____ Bride, groom, all the parents

_____ Other people with bride, groom

_____

_____

## At The Reception

_____ Bride and groom arriving

_____ Bride and groom getting out of car

_____ Bride and groom going into reception

_____ The receiving line (posed)

_____ Receiving line (candid)

_____ Bride and groom in receiving line

_____ Bride, groom dancing

_____ Bride, her father dancing

_____ Groom, his mother dancing

_____ The musicians

_____ Bride, groom talking to guests

_____ Passing the guest book

_____ The cake table

_____ Bride, groom cutting the cake

_____ Bride, groom feeding each other cake

_____ Bride's mother in receiving line

_____ Groom's parents in receiving line

_____ Buffet table

_____ Friends serving punch

_____ Bride, groom at bride's table

_____ Parents' table

_____ Bride changing into going-away clothes

_____ Groom changing

_____ Bride and groom saying good-bye to parents

_____ Bride and groom ready to leave

_____ Guests throwing rice

_____ Bride and groom getting in car

_____ Guests waving good-bye

_____ Rear of car speeding off

_____ Other reception fun

_____ Bride, groom toasting

_____ Throwing and catching bouquet

_____ Groom taking off bride's garter

_____ Throwing, catching garter

_____ Wedding party decorating car

_____ _____

_____ _____

_____ _____

_____ _____

_____ _____

_____ _____

**NAMES OF GUESTS PHOTOGRAPHER SHOULDN'T MISS**

1. _____

2. _____

3. _____

4. _____

5. _____

6. _____

7. _____

8. _____

9. _____

10. _____

11. _____

12. _____

Wedding album package includes: _____

Date candid proofs will be ready _____

_____

Package Cost $ _____

Extra prints

| Photo Description | Number | Cost |
|---|---|---|
| _____ | _____ | _____ |
| _____ | _____ | _____ |
| _____ | _____ | _____ |
| _____ | _____ | _____ |
| _____ | _____ | _____ |
| _____ | _____ | _____ |

Cost of extra prints $_____

Total candid photography cost $_____

# YOUR WEDDING MUSIC

Music is one of the easiest, most natural ways you can personalize your wedding, whether you're planning a lavish cathedral ceremony and ballroom reception, or vows and toasts by the fireplace at home. How to make sure you get the wedding music *you* love best?

**Consult with your clergymember** (if you're marrying in a church or temple) to find out if there are any rules that would keep you from having *secular* (non-religious) selections played or sung during your ceremony. Do it at the same time you and your fiancé go to reserve the church and date. Traditionally, some denominations have asked that brides and grooms stay with hymns and centuries-old religious pieces (Bach's "Sheep May Safely Graze" while guests are being seated, the familiar "Lord's Prayer" as a solo). Now, almost anything goes—from "We've Only Just Begun" beforehand to "You Light Up My Life" as guests file out afterwards. But ask. The clergymember might also suggest the organist, cantor, soloist, or ensemble accustomed to doing weddings in your church or temple. And if you're marrying in a hotel or banquet room, the manager will recommend people. In either case check whether the local musicians' union limits who may perform there. If not, feel free to bring in other musicians.

**Sit down with your fiancé next and discuss the mood of the ceremony.** There might be a soft prelude to last half an hour as the guests filter in, perhaps broken midway by the first solo; a reflective solo, choir, or ensemble work performed just after your mother has been seated; a majestic processional to herald you and your wedding party down the aisle (even if it's the staircase of your parents' house); maybe another meditative solo after your vows; for sure, a joyous recessional to march you out as husband and wife; then a quick postlude for the parade of guests.

If your ceremony will be the traditional one most couples favor, trust the organist and church soloist to offer suitable selections. But there are many more classics besides "Oh, Promise Me," so do get the musicians to play or sing several for you, then *you* pick your favorites.

If your wedding will be an expression of deep faith, consider replacing the bridal march with your church choir and the whole congregation joining in on a few hymns. Are you planning a formal candlelight ceremony? How about a woodwind or string quintet for the prelude, a trumpeter or brass choir for the processional? (Try outstanding music students from the local high school on something from an opera or symphony.) Do you want to include all the people you love in your wedding? Let Aunt Martha play preludes on the piano, have your roommate the folk guitarist strum out "your song." A word of advice: if you're concerned that every detail be perfect, better stick with the pros. As for the

two of you performing yourselves (singing vows to one another?), think hard. What with wedding-day nerves, even the most seasoned professional will fumble.

Whoever the musicians, give them plenty of time to practice. And ask if you can attend a rehearsal two weeks before wedding day. After the wedding, have your parents pay them promptly—or thank them with gifts if they're very close relatives or friends.

**Decide with both families the kind of reception music you want.** Just one piano player, an accordionist, a trio of violins, or any combo that does "dinner music" would be ideal for a small party or casual cake-and-punch buffet. (A church parlor reception, of course, means you should get an OK from the clergymember.) What about a big reception with dancing? Figure out whether you want folk tunes—Polish polkas, Italian tarantellas, for example; what age groups will be dancing most (the fox-trotting aunts and uncles, or your friends who *need* a solid hard-rock beat?); if there'll be a number of guests who object to dancing—in which case, you might be better off without it.

**Then start shopping around for the right band or orchestra.** Get names of groups from friends, check the Yellow Pages under "Orchestras and Bands," call the musicians' union in your area, contact school band or orchestra directors, look on the bulletin boards at local colleges. Now begin phoning the leaders. Ask each if the group is available the day and time of your reception, and if they routinely play the mix of music you need. Tell how long the reception will last, and get a cost estimate. Find out if they play *continuous music* (no breaks); or take time out (usually this is far less expensive, and a strolling instrumentalist can always be hired to fill in). See if the leader comes too, or if you might end up with any number of bands with the leader's name. Find out the size of the group (four to eight pieces are usually enough). Ask when you might hear the group live—preferably at a club or another wedding.

Once you've picked your band, spell out your kinds of music: "mostly old standards, a quarter pop rock, about three country ballads." Name any special requests. Specify the song for the "first dance." Indicate the role of the leader—an entertainer who can joke about Uncle Harry's tango? or a straight man? Plan any musical signals or fanfares: when the two of you arrive; as you sit down to eat; before the cake-cutting, tossing of the bouquet, garter-throwing; as you depart; when the bar closes; when the party's over. Offer your banquet manager's name and phone number so the group can arrange for any special equipment. And do ask what they'll wear; tight, red jumpsuits might look terrifically sexy to your maids, downright risqué to your grandmother. Finally, get in writing the name of the leader who'll appear, the number of musicians, their total hourly rate, the overtime rate, whether you'll be billed for partial hours as whole hours, whether you're getting continuous music, when the leader's to be paid and how.

Before you hire any group, check with your banquet manager to find out if there are any union rules governing how many musicians must play in your reception room. And don't forget to order food and drinks for all.

**Don't rule out the possibility of records or tapes** for a small, budget-wise wedding at home. Poking around a record shop or library, you may find just the music you need for a ceremony processional and recessional, as well as for dancing. Get a friend to man the controls, and tape any wires out of the way so no one trips over them. Remember that you can rent wedding tapes from many music stores, also a piano or organ that a talented friend or relative might play instead. After it's arrived, make certain the instrument's tuned—the same goes if you're using your own. Recorded or live, the music you choose can provide a beautiful background and a happy highlight to your wedding day.

# CEREMONY MUSIC CHECKLIST

| Ceremony Moment | Performance Time | Selections |
|---|---|---|
| *Ceremony Moment* | *Performance Time* | *Selections* |
| Prelude | _____ | _____ |
| | | _____ |
| | | _____ |
| | | _____ |
| | | _____ |
| | | _____ |
| First solo | _____ | _____ |
| Second solo | _____ | _____ |
| Processional | _____ | _____ |
| Other | _____ | _____ |
| Recessional | _____ | _____ |
| Postlude | _____ | _____ |
| | | _____ |
| | | _____ |
| | | _____ |
| | | _____ |
| | | _____ |

Organist (or main instrumentalist) _____ Cost $_____

Soloist_____ Cost $_____

Ensemble or choir leader _____

Ensemble members_____

_____

_____

_____

_____

Ensemble cost $_____

Total ceremony music cost $_____

# RECEPTION MUSIC CHECKLIST

| Reception Activity | Times | General Kind of Music or Specific Selections |
|---|---|---|
| Receiving Line | _____ | _____ |
| | _____ | _____ |
| | _____ | _____ |
| Arrival of Bride and Groom | _____ | _____ |
| First Dance Seating at Bride's Table | _____ | _____ |
| | _____ | _____ |
| Cake-cutting | _____ | _____ |
| Dancing or Background | _____ | _____ |
| | _____ | _____ |
| | _____ | _____ |
| Special Requests | _____ | _____ |
| | _____ | _____ |
| | _____ | _____ |
| | _____ | _____ |
| | _____ | _____ |
| Tossing of Bouquet | _____ | _____ |
| Throwing of Garter Departure of Bride and Groom | _____ | _____ |
| Last Dance | _____ | _____ |
| Other_____ | _____ | _____ |
| _____ | _____ | _____ |
| _____ | _____ | _____ |

Orchestra or band leader _____

Number of musicians _____

Hours of music _____ to _____ Continuous music? Yes _____ No _____

Regular hourly rate _____ Overtime rate _____

Total reception music cost $_____

# YOUR WEDDING INVITATIONS

## How to choose the right style for your wedding

**Invite your favorite people** to celebrate your marriage with you. It's a big part of the wedding-planning fun! If you're having the kind of wedding most brides and their families love (100 or more guests, you in a classic bride's dress, a big reception), then you'll want to send formal wedding invitations.

**Word formal invitations** the traditional way. And do write out what you want before you order. Or ask your printer to show you personalized versions. If all your guests are being invited to *both* ceremony and reception, consider the "combination" invitation, below:

*Mr. and Mrs. Raymond James Fuller*
*request the honour of your presence*
*at the marriage of their daughter*
*Susan Elizabeth*
*to*
*Mr. John North Fleming*
*on Saturday, the third of December*
*at half after four o'clock*
*St. James Church*
*Hill Oaks, Illinois*
*and afterwards*
*at Greenbriar Country Club*

Your printer should be able to show you variations if, for example, you're having a small ceremony and large reception or vice versa.

**Request replies** with an *R.S.V.P., Kindly Respond,* or *Please Respond* in the lower left corner, and below the address to mail them. Traditionally reserved for business functions only, printed response cards for the reception do make things easy for guests. It is up to you to decide if you'll send them. These small cards are engraved in the same style as the invitations. Stamped, self-addressed envelopes are included. Here is the form for the card:

*M* _____

_____ *accepts*

_____ *regrets*

*Saturday, December third*

*Greenbriar Country Club*

**Spell out everything** on formal invitations—the wedding date, time, all numerals, and names. No abbreviations, initials or nicknames are used—except *Mr., Ms., Mrs.,* and *Jr.* Traditionally, only the bride's first and middle names are printed. But if you're a doctor or military officer, you can add your title and full name below the phrase, *their daughter.* You may or may not want to add *Mr.* before your fiancé's name.

**Begin your invitations** with the name of the person(s) *sponsoring* the wedding. The name at the top of an invitation is *not* supposed to tell your guests who's paying the bills. So whether you live at home or not, your parents' names should head the invitations. You might also include the groom's parents' names below his on the invitation . . . *John North Fleming/son of/Mr. and Mrs. Robert Fleming* . . . If your parents are deceased, your guardian, a relative, or a friend can host the wedding. Or you two can be your own sponsors. If your parents are divorced, the parent who raised you usually does the inviting. If that's your mother, and she's remarried, she uses your step-father's name, inserts the phrase *at the marriage of her daughter . . . ,* then adds your full name. Divorced but friendly parents *can* issue a joint invitation.

**Have your formal invitations printed** in black script on the top page of a double sheet of paper in pale ivory or white. It can be paneled—with a raised border surrounding the print—or plain. The most popular size, 4½″ × 5¾″ fits into an envelope without folding. A larger size, 5½″ × 7½″ is folded once before mailing. It's for *very* formal weddings.

**Add more "personality"** to your invitations by choosing a translucent (parchment perhaps) or shiny paper in a pretty pastel or an earthy tone. Use colorful ink, maybe different type faces, border designs, or even a photograph of the two of you.

**Order invitations three months before** your wedding day to allow time for printing, addressing, and mailing. Visit your jeweler, department store, stationer or bridal salon to order them. Do ask to check a sample for mistakes before your order is printed up.

**Count on one invitation** for every married couple (including the clergymember and spouse), *each* single adult guest—even if they're "living together" or with their parents, each attendant and *their* parents (if you can), and everyone in the groom's family. If you're inviting dates for your single guests, avoid the phrase "and Escort" on the invitation—better to send each a separate invitation. Request extra invitations for your families as keepsakes. Order spare envelopes in case you make a mistake. Once the return address was embossed colorlessly on the back flap of the outer envelope. Now the Post Office asks it appear on the face of the envelope in the upper left-hand corner.

**Get a headstart addressing envelopes** by having your stationer send them to you early. Handwrite the addresses in blue or black ink. Use full names, no initials. Avoid abbreviations—write out states' names, avenue, street, etc. Address inner envelopes, *Mr. and Mrs. Gibbs*. Add any childrens' names below on the inner envelope *only*.

**Insert invitations** into the inner envelope with enclosure cards and printed side *facing* the back flap, as pictured above. For the large formals, fold the invitation in half across the printing, then put it *fold* down in its envelope. Tissues used to prevent ink smudges at the printers aren't needed. Place the inner envelope with its front facing the back of the outer envelope. Stamp and mail your invitations four to six weeks before your wedding to allow time for replies.

*Above:* Slide invitation, enclosures in inner envelope. *Below:* Slip inner envelope into outer one.

**Do send announcements** if you have many friends and relatives you couldn't invite to the wedding. People who receive them aren't obliged to send gifts and will be happy to get the news. Have them all addressed, so that a friend or family member can drop them in the mail as soon as you two are showered with rice.

# SPECIAL WORDS FOR SPECIAL WEDDINGS

## INVITATION TO RECEPTION ONLY

*Mr. and Mrs. Charles Miller*
*request the pleasure of your company*
*at the wedding reception of their daughter*
*Susan Ann*
*and*
*Mr. John David Smith*
*Saturday, the eighth of March*
*at half after four o'clock*
*The Edwardian Towne House*
*113 East Sixty-seventh Street*
*New York, New York*

## HIS PARENTS HOST

*Mr. and Mrs. William Smith*
*request the honour of your presence*
*at the marriage of*
*Susan Ann Miller*
*to their son*
*John David Smith*
*Saturday, the eighth of March*
*at three o'clock*
*All Saints' Church*
*New York, New York*

## TWO REMARRIED PARENTS HOST

*Mrs. Donald Jones*
*and*
*Mr. Charles Miller*
*request the honour of your presence*
*at the marriage of their daughter*
*Susan Ann Miller*
*to*
*John David Smith*
*Saturday, the eighth of March*
*at three o'clock*
*All Saints' Church*
*New York, New York*

## YOU'RE THE HOST

*The honour of your presence*
*is requested at the marriage of*
*Susan Ann Miller*
*to*
*John David Smith*
*Saturday, the eighth of March*
*at three o'clock*
*All Saints' Church*
*New York, New York*

## ONE REMARRIED
## PARENT HOSTS

*Mr. and Mrs. Donald Jones*
*request the honour of your presence*
*at the marriage of her daughter*
*Susan Ann Miller*
*to*
*John David Smith*
*Saturday, the eighth of March*
*at three o'clock*
*All Saints' Church*
*New York, New York*

## YOUR PARENTS
## SHARE PLANNING

*Mr. and Mrs. Charles Miller*
*request the honour of your presence*
*at the marriage of their daughter*
*Susan Ann Miller*
*to*
*John David Smith*
*son of Mr. and Mrs. Leo Smith*
*Saturday, the eighth of March*
*at three o'clock*
*All Saints' Church*
*New York, New York*

## PARENTS HOST YOUR
## SECOND WEDDING

*Mr. and Mrs. Charles Miller*
*request the honour of your presence*
*at the marriage of their daughter*
*Susan Miller Smith*
*to*
*Lawrence Edward White*
*Saturday, the eighth of March*
*at three o'clock*
*All Saints' Church*
*New York, New York*

## YOU HOST YOUR
## SECOND WEDDING

*The honour of your presence*
*is requested at the marriage of*
*Susan Miller Smith*
*to*
*Lawrence Edward White*
*Saturday, the eighth of March*
*at three o'clock*
*All Saints' Church*
*New York, New York*

## YOUR PARENTS ISSUE TRADITIONAL
## WEDDING ANNOUNCEMENTS

*Mr. and Mrs. Charles Miller*
*have the honour of announcing*
*the marriage of their daughter*
*Susan Ann*
*to*
*Mr. John David Smith*
*Saturday, the eighth of March*
*One thousand, nine hundred and eighty-one*
*New York, New York*

## YOU REAFFIRM YOUR
## WEDDING VOWS

*The honour of your presence*
*is requested at the reaffirmation*
*of the wedding vows of*
*Mr. and Mrs. John David Smith*
*Saturday, the eighth of March*
*at three o'clock*
*All Saints' Church*
*New York, New York*

My invitation will read:

_____

*request the honour of your presence*
*at the marriage of their daughter*

_____

to

_____

_____

_____

_____

_____

and afterwards at

_____

*Please respond*

_____

_____

# INVITATION PROOFREADING CHECKLIST

Proofreading date _____

When the printer or stationer asks you to look over a simple invitation before making up the rest, read it carefully, compare it to the one you wrote out on the preceding page, and answer the following questions:

_____ Is the invitation worded the way *you* want it?

_____ Do the lines fall in the proper places (*to* on one line, the entire date on another)?

_____ Is everyone's name spelled correctly—your parents', yours, your groom's, his parents', if listed?

_____ Is there a *u* in the word *honour*?

_____ Do the day of the week and the date correspond? (Check a calendar.) Is the time written in words, not numbers? Is it correct?

_____ Are the names of the ceremony and reception sites spelled right? Are any addresses complete and correct?

_____ Are any commas in the right places? Apostrophes? Are there periods after all abbreviations?

_____ Is the paper the color you chose? The lettering style? What about any borders or designs?

Corrections if any _____

_____

_____

Pick-up or delivery date _____    Cost per hundred $_____

Number of invitations to order _____    Total invitation cost $_____

# GETTING TO THE WEDDING

A very important step in planning your wedding is arranging transportation. After all, you want to make sure that you, the members of your wedding party, and guests all get to the church and reception on time!

## YOUR WEDDING PARTY

As the bride, you're traditionally responsible for making the transportation arrangements to the church for you and your parents, your maids, and very often the groom's parents too. The classic way to travel on wedding day is by a gleaming, sleek limousine. Call a few limousine rental places for their rates (get names from the Yellow Pages). Even if you decide against renting limos for the entire wedding party, consider securing at least *one* for you and your father to drive to church, you and your groom to make your grand getaway! Otherwise, ask among friends and relatives if their cars would be free on wedding day, and if they'd volunteer as chauffeurs (your ushers will be too busy). Offer to pay for gas and a car wash, and thank each driver with a small gift. On wedding day, have all the wedding cars arrive at your door in time to reach the church at least five to ten minutes before the ceremony (if you'll be dressing at the church, you'll want them to arrive earlier). Plan all your at-home candids well in advance of your leaving for church (don't forget to have the photographer snap one of you and your father getting into the car). In the first car goes your mother with your honor attendant, perhaps another maid or two; second, the rest of your maids; third, you and your father. A separate car can go around to pick up your groom's parents. Then it's on to the church! Your groom and his best man should take care of their own transportation to the church; they should get there 20 minutes before the ceremony begins—time enough for the best man to slip the clergymember the fee, also for your groom to straighten his tie and calm any pre-wedding jitters!

## YOUR GUESTS

If you've many out-of-town guests on hand for your wedding, try to arrange their transportation to and from the church and reception. Ask guests living near hotels where out-of-towners are staying if they'd mind taking on a passenger or two. Or rent a bus or van to pick them all up! For guests who'll be driving in from out-of-town for the day, help them reach your wedding easily. Ask your local Automobile Association or Chamber of Commerce for maps of your area, or draw your own. Include just those roads the driver will need to navigate, and identify all major landmarks. Make sure directions are clear—after all, imagine getting married without your college roommate Maureen there. Slip your directions in with the invitations. Also, ask your reception hall manager for written directions; most have cards to include with invitations. Or have ushers hand cards to guests following the ceremony. Make sure there's plenty of parking space for all cars on wedding day. Reserve parking in front of your church or synagogue for the car you drive in, space behind your place of worship for wedding party and guests' cars. Having a reception at home? Call your police department to find out if you need permission to park on the street. Otherwise, check with your reception manager for parking arrangements there.

## THE TWO OF YOU

Leaving the church, you and your new husband ride in one car together—the one that brought you and your father to church. Your parents travel to the reception in one car, bridesmaids and ushers in the remaining cars. During your reception, chances are your attendants will slip away and decorate your getaway car. Have your groom drop hints to his best man about decorations that'll be easy to clean. For instance, if "Just Married!" is going on the back of the car, it should be written in big letters with a scouring powder and water paste, not shaving cream. Other ideas: big felt hearts, dimestore bells, pinwheels, old shoes, and masking tape to attach car trimmings (it won't take off the paint). And decorating should be safe—no long streamers to obstruct the driver's vision; no rocks in the hubcaps to reduce his hearing. Honking should also be kept down to one "Here Comes the Bride" at most. Taking your getaway car to your honeymoon destination? Bring along a spare tire, a jack, flares, a flashlight, and a first aid kit—and drive safely!

## DRIVER'S CHECKLIST

(Give a copy to each driver.)

Driver's name _____

Address _____ Phone _____

*Passengers*

*1. Name* _____

    Address _____ Phone _____

2. Name _____

    Address _____ Phone _____

3. Name _____

    Address _____ Phone _____

4. Name _____

    Address _____ Phone _____

5. Name _____

    Address _____ Phone _____

Address of gathering place _____

Arrival time _____

Ceremony site_____

Ceremony address _____

Arrival time _____

Directions_____

_____

_____

Reception site_____

Reception address_____

Arrival time _____

Directions_____

_____

_____

_____

# TIPS ON TIPPING

*Decisions about tipping (or not tipping) can be embarrassing and confusing. How to handle all those people who help make your wedding run smoothly? Whom to tip and how much to tip them? Below, a chart designed to clear up the confusion. You, your fiancé, and family can refer to it in the busy wedding planning days ahead.*

| Whom to (or not to) tip | How much | When, and by whom |
|---|---|---|
| Caterer, club manager, hotel banquet manager, bridal consultant. | 1-15% for extra-special services only. The fee usually covers everything. | Reception hosts pay bill on receipt. Add any special tip to payment. |
| Waiters, waitresses, bartenders, table captains. | 15% for servers; 1-2% for captains (often included in catering or club bill). | If included, reception hosts pay tips with bill. If not, right after reception. |
| Powder room attendants, coat room attendants in hotels or clubs. | 50¢ per guest, or arrange a flat fee with the hotel or club management. | If a flat fee, reception hosts pay it with bill. If not, right after reception. |
| Florist, photographer, baker, musicians you hire, limousine driver. | 15% for driver; others tipped only for extra-special service, 1-15%. | Ceremony hosts tip driver at reception site. Add other tips to bill payments. |
| Civil-ceremony officials (Judge, Justice of the Peace, city clerk). | Usually a flat fee ($10 and up). Some judges cannot accept money. Ask. | Groom gives fee to best man who pays after ceremony. |
| Clergymembers (minister, rabbi, priest). | Usually a donation ($10 and up) depending on ceremony size. Ask. | Groom gives donation to best man who pays after ceremony. |
| Ceremony assistants (altar boys, sextons, cantors, organists). | Sometimes covered by church fee, or ask clergy what's customary ($5-$25). | Ceremony hosts pay church fee when billed; separate fees, tips after service. |

# YOUR AT-HOME WEDDING

*Your wedding is a time for family and all the cozy warmth you've always found at home. And home is exactly where you can hold your marriage ceremony and reception if you want to share that warmth with your guests.*

## YOUR INVITATIONS

You may invite as many people as your house or yard will hold. Or bring more indoor space outdoors by renting circus-sized tents or canvas marquees. A variety of tent shapes can fit together puzzle-fashion to span the quirks of any yard, and you can even rent high-ceilinged wedding tents that link up to porches to make house additions. It's a worthwhile investment if there's even a chance of rain. When your guest list includes more than 50 names, send engraved invitations. Try to order them three months in advance to allow time for engraving, addressing, and mailing. Here's how they might be worded if both ceremony and reception are at home:

> *Mr. and Mrs. John McNeal Smith*
> *request the pleasure of your company*
> *at the marriage of their daughter*
> *Mary Louise*
> *to*
> *Mr. James Park Warren*
> *Tuesday, the fourteenth of December*
> *at four o'clock*
> *911 Brookline Court*
> *Royal Oak, Michigan*

*R.S.V.P.*

If you plan to hold the ceremony in church and only the reception at home, then send standard combination wedding and reception invitations, substituting your home address for the name of a hotel, hall, or club. The most cordial invitation a guest can receive, of course, is a personal note. When fewer than 50 people will attend, your mother may send handwritten invitations at least two weeks before the wedding. Informal invitations, written on folded plain or initialed notepaper, read:

*Dear Jane and Howard,*

*Mary and Jim are being married here at the house, 911 Brookline Court, a week from Tuesday. That's December fourteenth at four. We do hope you can be with us.*

*Sincerely,*
*Marilyn*

## PRE-WEDDING PLANS

Your at-home wedding may range from formal to informal. Whatever the case, start your plans early. Arrange for a member of the clergy, or a judge who makes house calls; hire a pianist or orchestra to accompany your procession and reception conversation or dancing; speak to your police chief about overseeing parking. Hire a professional photographer to snap pictures of your ceremony and candid shots of all the reception guests too. Your florist can help you cordon off with garlands and ribbons a stairway or aisle for your procession and an area for the ceremony. Borrow or rent (check the Yellow Pages) folding chairs to flank the aisle. Or if space is scarce, the guests may stand, leaving the area free for unobstructed movement (maybe dancing) later on. Your receiving line may form right where the ceremony was or, if you're married at a church, station a brother or sister at the door to greet guests and take their coats as they arrive. (Rent coat racks.) Have a receiving line wherever your guests can move on to a cordial cup of punch or champagne for toasting. They also might like to freshen up in one of the bathrooms you've stocked well with toilet and first-aid supplies (soap, tissue, bandages, tampons).

## FOOD FOR FUN

If you haven't the facilities or can't face preparing food for a crowd, call a caterer. He'll provide everything from Swedish meatballs to bartenders. Even if you're doing the cooking, you may still need a caterer's services to provide enough matching china, flatware, glassware, linen. Whoever cooks, avoid sit-down dinners if your guest list exceeds 30. Instead, plan on tea and sandwiches, cocktails, or a buffet. (Remember that the earlier in the afternoon or the later in the evening the reception is, the less sustenance your guests are likely to need.)

If you're doing everything yourself, the morning of the wedding make sandwiches and canapes simple enough to serve without help (you might recruit extra hands anyway. Or start cooking weeks ahead, freeze everything, and just defrost it wedding morning). Experiment in advance with appetizing recipes from a basic cookbook, ones that can be easily increased to serve a crowd—cheese balls, *boeuf bourguignonne*, fresh fruit medleys. For a buffet, avoid foods that require knives and arrange everything on the serving table so guests move along it directly to the eating area. Place all beverages on separate serving tables.

And, if you've furnished tables for eating, designate two prominent ones for the bridal party and parents. Another attention-getter deserving of its own flower-festooned table far from the crowd is your wedding cake. Order it from the bakery or make it yourself. If you do bake your own but lack the skill to frost it with stars and rosebuds, loop fresh daisy chains around the edges. Or trim it with ribbons. Or just set it on an elaborate cake plate that's been in the family for years.

If you're offering some kind of punch, count on each guest drinking at least two 4-ounce cups every hour. So at a five-hour party, you'll need about 25 quarts for every 20 people. If it's mixed drinks, figure that each person will down two drinks the first hour, one every hour after that. You'll get about 17 drinks from a fifth of liquor. So for 20 guests at that five-hour party, you'll need seven fifths—two each of Scotch and vodka, one of gin, bourbon, and rum. Get half-gallons of red and white wine, some beer too. (Flip back to the "Bar Checklist" for more planning help here.) Feel free to adapt any of these suggestions to suit your own wedding, and your guests can't help but absorb and enjoy the happy, relaxed mood of your home.

## MARRYING OUTDOORS

Hoping to hold your ceremony, reception—or both—out in the sunshine? Pick a place that is private yet accessible, roomy, with ample parking. And, just in case the rain clouds come, arrange for shelter so your guests can continue celebrating indoors. Here's more to think about.

**Choose a site that you love—your guests will too!** That mountain you two climbed on your first date might be perfect if your clergymember and guests don't mind leaving their cars below, fording a small stream, and hiking up with the reception picnic baskets. Rent a house boat. Or consider your own backyard, country club, local inn, or a historic landmark. Check out state parks too. Some rent lodges (it's your rain shelter!) by the day for a small fee—but reserve early. Whatever place you select, ask the police to oversee parking if you're expecting a crowd and there's no adjoining lot.

**Pick the time of year and time of day that's best for you.** Gather statistics from your nearest weather bureau for the month with the sunniest days and most comfortable temperatures. Spend a day at the site you've chosen. Ask the inn-keeper when the garden will be in full bloom. And think comfort—will morning or late afternoon be cooler than noon? Time of day also determines how much your guests eat. Serve the most food if your reception is during lunch or dinner hours, the least amount of food around 2 p.m.

**Prepare for the elements.** The number of guests you invite will be influenced by your budget *and* by how many people will fit comfortably inside that lodge, inn, or your living-dining room should it rain. If you have the money (and a large patch of level, treeless ground), your caterer or local rent-a-tent company can keep everyone dry under a wedding marquee. Various sizes, shapes, and colors—striped or solid—are available. Fair weather? The tent won't go to waste. Set up your buffet tables there. Later, convert it to a disco-tent for dancing.

Once you know how many guests you can accommodate, mail out the invitations. Have your mother send personal, hand-written invitations if you're asking fewer than 50 people. Otherwise send printed invitations. Include a good map with parking instructions if your guests don't know the area.

**Line up all the professional help you'll need.** As soon as you set the date, arrange for a judge or member of the clergy who's willing to officiate outdoors. Before you hire a photographer, look at his portfolio of outdoor shots to make sure he can handle strong sunlight, deep shade, and wide open space. Choose musicians who can do both the ceremony and reception. Pianos don't travel well. But do consider flutes, portable organs, accordians (or a battery-operated cassette if you want to furnish your own music). Let your florist create an aisle for the processional with a white runner bordered by tubs of white geraniums. For an Orthodox or Conservative Jewish ceremony, order a flowered *huppah*. Some florists offer a package wedding plan for *all* the arrangements you need. Another money-saver: buy the flowers in bulk from your florist and arrange them yourself. Want your guests seated? If you can't borrow enough chairs, rent them. Try the Yellow Pages. Or call upon your caterer. Besides providing the food, he can recruit bartenders and waitresses, and conjure up all kinds of equipment, from crystal and teacups to coat racks and the bridal table. Have your caterer, florist, and photographer visit the wedding site in advance so they'll know where to set up their equipment on the big day.

**Enjoy your kind of wedding in your kind of dress.** A traditional ceremony? Float down the aisle in a cloud of chiffon. The shorter chapel-length train is easiest to manage outdoors. But if you've dreamed of a longer train, just hook it up for dancing. You also might look into the new wedding separates at your bridal salon—a lacy, long skirt paired, perhaps, with a sleeveless, blouson, or scoop-neck top. Pure white looks prettiest outdoors, a pastel underskirt lends a country air. More color ideas? Wear a shorter, peasanty, off-the-shoulder dress in dotted swiss; sash it in sky blue or sunny yellow satin. And pick up the color in your attendants' dresses. For your hair and theirs, how about white straw hats or garlands of flowers? Whatever style your wedding, select a cool, comfortable fabric. Some summer classics: breezy organza, heirloom cotton, crisp eyelet.

**Add a personal touch to the ceremony.** Say your vows in the shade of the sugar maple your grandfather planted. Or let a cascade of your favorite flowers (roses?) serve as a backdrop for the altar. Use cushions or hand-embroidered kneelers at a religious wedding. For a friendly feeling, have everyone stand behind you in a semicircle, then turn around after the vows and hold your receiving line right there. (Load up a nearby table with pitchers of iced tea and lemonade for guests waiting their turn.)

**Plan an easy reception—either catered or do-it-yourself.** Serve a buffet—you won't need waiters! Set up food tables in the shade if you don't have a tent. Keep everything covered till the last minute. Serve finger or fork foods—fewer spills. For appetizers: fresh fruit compote or crisp raw vegetables with a guacamole dip. Main dishes: ham and turkey, hot or cold, with rolls for dainty sandwiches. Or set out quiche, beef stroganoff, or Swedish meatballs in chafing dishes. Offer vinaigrette dressing with the salad. It won't spoil. Do try to arrange things on your serving table so everyone heads directly for the eating area. Have enough tables for everyone. Reserve two tables for the bridal party and families. Where to cool the champagne? In a new, ice-filled, plastic trash can! Beverages and the wedding cake get their own tables, a safe distance away from traffic. Clean-up? Hire one helper for every 25-50 guests.

If you want to do-it-yourself, and informally, have a cookout. Get a volunteer to man the grill. Use paper plates imprinted with your name and your groom's. Or pack up picnic baskets with cheese, sausage, bread, and fruit. Tuck in tablecloths so your guests can choose their own place to dine.

**Think of all the little things to insure everyone's good time.** Set up a game table for kids—one for adults too. Volleyball, croquet, even three-legged races add to the fun.

For an at-home reception, stock the bathroom with lots of toilet paper, soap, and towels. Mosquitos? Call in a professional sprayer . . . or do it yourself two hours before the guests come. Make special arrangements for your garbage man to cart away the party trash before the neighborhood dogs do.

What if, with all your planning, a cat joins the receiving line or a butterfly lands in the cake? *Laugh* at the unexpected—it's humor that will see you through your years together.

# LONG-DISTANCE WEDDINGS

You're in Chicago, the wedding's in Denver? Here's how to plan a long-distance wedding that's long on happiness.

**Firm up your plans early.** As soon as you get engaged, sit down with your fiancé to talk about the kind of wedding you'll want. Be sure you have a good etiquette book and some back issues of BRIDE'S to look at wedding clothes styles and colors. Decide whether you'd want a small, family wedding, or a large gathering of all your friends and relatives. Is an at-home reception more to your liking? Or a lavish seated dinner. As you're talking, write your ideas down on paper.

**Find help.** You'll need someone in your wedding town to act as a "go-between" for you—making all the necessary ceremony and reception arrangements. If you'll be marrying in your hometown or his, one of your mothers is the most likely candidate. But it could also be an aunt or a close friend. Send her a copy of your basic requirements along with a timetable (the "BRIDE'S Calendar" will help). Then follow up with the first of many telephone calls. Ask your go-between to poll family and friends for names of florists, photographers, caterers they recommend. Have her collect brochures, pictures, etc., then narrow selections down to two or three and send *you* the material. Meanwhile she can go ahead and book the church, order and send out invitations (make the R.S.V.P. address your wedding town).

**Do some work on your end.** Choose and order your dress and your maids' dresses (if your honor attendant's close by, ask her to help you decide on dresses your maids will love). Ask the store's consultants what measurements they need to have from each maid (some stores have forms for this). Send the forms to your maids, along with tips on taking measurements from any sewing book. When you get the cards back, order the dresses.

**Make things easy on yourself.** If your reception site offers a package deal—where food, flowers, music are provided for one price—take it! Ask maids and aunts to pool their shower guest lists to give you one large shower that's less of a hassle for everyone.

**Plan a trip home**—the two of you—a month or two before the wedding. Confirm preliminary reservations in person, work out final details (reception menu, music), see your clergymember to discuss vows and readings. Call up the local marriage license bureau for the re-quirements on marriage licenses, blood tests. Order the men's tuxedos from your local formalwear shop. Register your gift selections at stores where you know your friends and family shop (also make arrangements to get your wedding gifts home). Then arrive home at least a week before the wedding. Ask maids and ushers to arrive a few days early too so any necessary alterations in their outfits can be made. And do be sure to give your go-between a very special gift—you couldn't have done it all without her!

## DOUBLE WEDDINGS

A double wedding is happiness times two. It takes only a few special arrangements for a two-couple wedding.

**Did your best friend Kathy** recently get engaged too? Or is your future brother-in-law planning to marry soon? You might consider a double wedding. It's a way of celebrating the close bonds between friends. And in the case of two members of the same family, one double wedding can cut down on the expense of holding two separate weddings.

**In a double wedding** each couple has their own set of attendants. If you'll have three maids, three ushers, the other party should be that number too. You and the other bride can always be each other's maid of honor.

**What does everyone wear?** You and the other bride should wear similar style dresses (both in cathedral-length trains and veils, for instance). Your maids can wear different styles, as long as the colors harmonize (like mauve and aqua). Ushers, grooms, and fathers can dress the same for a formal wedding (daytime stroller outfit or evening black tie). For a less formal wedding, they could choose tuxedos in coordinating colors.

**If the two brides are sisters,** the parents often issue a joint invitation. The wording:
*Mr. and Mrs. Paul Jones/request the honour of your presence/at the marriage of their daughters/Sarah Ann/to/Mr. John Jay Henderson/and/Gloria Jill/to/Mr. Keith Scott Peters.*

**If the brides aren't related,** each family can send out separate invitations, or the two families can send out a joint invitation: *Mr. and Mrs. Jacob Smith/and/Mr. and Mrs. Benjamin Horowitz/request the honour of your presence/at the marriage of their daughters/Melissa Smith/to/Mr. Carl Burger/and/Kay Horowitz/to/Mr. Thomas Douglas.*

**To see that the ceremony goes smoothly,** decide which bride will walk down the aisle first. Traditionally, it's the older bride and her wedding party. If your church or synagogue has two aisles, each wedding party can use one side for the procession and recessional. Seat all the parents of the brides in the first row of the bride's side of the church, parents of the grooms in the first row of the groom's side. At a wedding of two members of a family, plan on only one receiving line with just the parents and couples in it.

A wedding of friends? Each family forms a line. At the reception, choose one bride's table or two—whichever will be more fun for everyone!

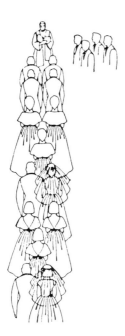

All ushers lead the procession. First party follows, then first bride on father's arm. Next, second party and bride (in a wedding of sisters, the younger goes second, escorted by another male relative).

At the altar, couples stand side by side with first bride and groom on left; fathers behind daughters. In a wedding of sisters, father stands behind eldest, then moves over to give younger daughter away.

Recessional order: first couple, second couple, honor attendants, maids and ushers (paired). When brides act as each other's attendant, best men escort maids, extra ushers bring up the rear.

# GUIDE TO WEDDING CLOTHES

| STYLE OF WEDDING | BRIDE | GROOM _and men of the wedding party_ | BRIDESMAIDS _and maid of honor_ | MOTHERS _or wedding hostesses_ |
|---|---|---|---|---|
| **VERY FORMAL EVENING** _200 guests or more; after 6 p.m._ | Dress with a long train. Veil to complement dress, often long or full. Long sleeves or gloves to cover arms. Shoes to match dress. Full bouquet or flower-trimmed prayer book. | Traditional: Full-dress tailcoat with matching trousers, white waistcoat, white bow tie, wing-collared shirt. (Optional: Black top hat, white gloves.) Contemporary: Black contoured long or short jacket, wing-collared shirt. | Four to 12. Long dresses, short veils, or other headpieces, gloves to complement sleeve length. Any style bouquet, shoes to match or harmonize. | Floor-length evening or dinner dresses. Small hats or veils. Shoes, gloves, and flowers to harmonize. |
| **VERY FORMAL DAYTIME** _200 guests or more; noon, afternoon._ | Same as very formal evening, but short train is also appropriate. | Traditional: Cutaway coat, gray striped trousers, gray waistcoat, wing-collared shirt, ascot or striped tie. (Optional: Top hat, spats, gray gloves.) Contemporary: Contoured long or short jacket, wing-collared shirt. | Four to 12. Same overall style as very formal evening, but dresses are often less elaborate. | Floor-length dresses, not so formal as those for evening. Same accessories as those worn for evening. |
| **FORMAL EVENING** _100 guests or more; after 6 p.m._ | Long dress with a chapel or sweep train. Veil of a length to complement dress. Accessories the same as those for very formal wedding. | Traditional: Dark dinner jacket with matching trousers, dress shirt, bow tie, vest or cummerbund. (Optional: White or ivory jackets in summery climate.) | Two to six. Similar to very formal, but dresses are sometimes short. Gloves are optional. | Dinner dresses, usually long. Small hats or veils, shoes, gloves and flowers harmonizing with dresses. |
| **FORMAL DAYTIME** _100 guests; morning, afternoon._ | Same as formal evening, but an elaborate, short dress worn with a bridal headpiece with short veil is also acceptable. | Contemporary for both: Groom may choose formal suit in white or light colors for summer, darker shades for fall; dress shirt, bow tie, vest or cummerbund. Groomsmen coordinate with similar ensembles. Traditional: Gray stroller, waistcoat, striped trousers, shirt, striped tie. (Optional: Homburg, gloves.) | Two to six. Dresses either long or street length, but not too elaborate. Matching or harmonizing accessories, including bouquet. | Elegant dress or suit, usually street length. Flowers to wear. Other accessories to match or harmonize. |
| **SEMI-FORMAL EVENING** _100 guests or fewer; home, chapel._ | Trainless, floor-length or shorter dress white or pastel. Veil, elbow length or shorter. Same accessories as for a formal wedding, but simpler bouquet is used. | Traditional: Favorite suit; white, colored, or striped shirt, four-in-hand tie. Contemporary: Dinner jacket or formal suit; dress shirt, bow tie, vest or cummerbund. | Seldom more than one, plus an honor attendant. Elaborate, street-length dresses. Small bouquets. | Elaborate, street-length dresses with appropriate accessories. |
| **SEMI-FORMAL DAYTIME** _100 guests or fewer; often home._ | Street-length dress, white or pastel color, short veil. Small bouquet or flower-trimmed prayer book. | Same as semi-formal evening. | Seldom more than one. Same as semi-formal evening, but dresses are simpler. | Same as semi-formal evening dress, but somewhat less elaborate. |
| **INFORMAL** _family; daytime._ | Suit or street dress. Hat, gloves, shoes, and bag. Nosegay or flowers to wear. | Same as semi-formal. | Maid of honor only. Dress or suit similar to bride's. Flowers to wear. | Dresses or suits similar to honor attendant's. |

_Brides marrying again may choose any option (omitting veil), as long as clergy approves._
_Guests dress as for any social event, except they do not wear all white or black._

# THE BEST DRESS FOR YOU

## Which wedding look will flatter your figure

No matter what your height, weight, or shape, there's a wedding dress that's perfect for you. You've just got to know what to look for. So when you head off to the bridal shop or the bridal salon in your department store, keep in mind the tips *below*, the sketches *right*.

**If you're short** (five-feet, four-inches or under) and want to look taller, shop for dresses with neat seams or lace appliqués that run up and down lengthwise. Consider empire, princess, or A-lines with small collars and cuffs, narrow belts (or maybe none), trim at the neckline and shoulders to draw an admiring eye upward. Do look for dresses specially made for you, the "petite" bride.

**If you're tall** (five-feet, nine-inches plus) and want to minimize your height, shop for dresses with trim that wraps *all* around, wide belts, large collars, big cuffs, raglan or butterfly sleeves, flared or tiered skirts, low necks.

**If you've a full figure**—think you could afford to lose about 20 pounds, choose a carefully fitted, solid-colored dress in a princess or loosely shaped style that just skims the body. Don't try clingy fabrics. Do go for slender sleeves, V-or shallow U-shaped necklines, and graceful skirts with gores or fullness at the front and sides.

**If you're slender** and feel you could put on a few pounds, do it with fabrics that have texture, sheen, nap, or horizontal ribbing. Good ones are satins, velvets, or jerseys that drape you softly. Choose them in a dress with a gathered or dirndl skirt, full long sleeves, a bloused-bodice top, a belt in a color different from the rest of the dress.

**Do you have thick midriff and waist?** Aim for the slimming effect of a lifted waistline and A-line skirt. Avoid tight waists, cummerbunds, and shaped midriffs in contrasting colors.

**Skinny midriff and waist?** Give yourself a little shape with well-defined midriffs, natural or sashed waistlines. You might add some contrasting color here (pastel pink, sunny yellow).

**Broad shoulders?** Look for dresses with smooth, set-in sleeves, low Vs or high covered necks. Stay away from puffed or leg-of-mutton sleeves, bare necklines, broad collars, haltered tops.

**Narrow shoulders?** Drape them with cape collars or capelets. Accent them with sleeves that gather at the top, necklines that are bare or widely curved.

SHORT    TALL    FULL-FIGURED    SLIM

**Big bosom?** Stick to V-, U-shaped, or high necklines with a keyhole yoke. Avoid cinched waists, empires that come up high under the bust, clingy jerseys.

**Wide hips?** Let an A-line or gently flared half-circle of a skirt skim them. Then balance yourself top and bottom by choosing a broad collar and puffy sleeve.

**Shop early for your wedding dress**— at least six months, —or even more— before the big day. Most dresses are special-ordered and take a couple of months between order and delivery. And you'll want extra time for last-minute alterations.

**Call ahead for an appointment** at your bridal salon, especially during the pre-summer and pre-holiday rush seasons, so you'll be assured of really personal service.

**Go shopping alone,** or with just one other person whose taste you trust. The fewer opinions you have to contend with, the better. And wear or take along appropriate shoes that are a good height and style for the dress you have in mind. No loafers or beach sandals!

**Duplicate your wedding-day measurements** when you have your fittings with the right underthings— padded or strapless bra if you'll wear one, a long slip. And since birth control pills may change your measurements too, start the pill (if you plan to take it) at least three weeks before you order your dress.

**Tell the bridal consultant your wedding plans**—the date, hour of day, degree of formality, the overall look you want, and approximately what you can spend—so she can guide you to the right dress. And do clip pictures of the dress styles you like (thumb through BRIDE'S) to show to the bridal consultant.

**Choose your wedding dress first,** then find the headpiece to harmonize. Wearing an heirloom veil? Shop for a dress to match *its* color.

# YOUR HEADPIECE

## *Suiting it to your dress, your looks*

**CHOOSE YOUR BRIDAL HAT** so it complements your wedding dress—whether it's a long, elegant satin, or a smart, street-length jersey—and flatters your hairstyle too—a short, curly bob or a long, silky mane. Before you shop, look over the headpieces here. The **face-framer,** an almost wreath-like cap, tops any wedding day style, particularly a traditional one with elaborate detailing. It's a good choice for round faces and hair-dos with bangs, or for long, smooth hair that's pulled off the face, The classic **mantilla** (this one with a half-cap "lift" under it for added height) goes well with almost any dress style, all hair lengths. But if your mantilla is elaborately designed with lace and pearls, keep your hair smooth and simple (your dress bodice and neck-line too), so there's some contrast between them. The **Juliet cap,** usually for more formal looks, sits snugly on the back of the head and sets off short hair nicely—especially a style that curls around the face. The **wreath** can be a band of flowers and pearls, as here, or an array of ribbons and lace. It's terrific for crowning long, shoulder-length or short, curly hair. The versatile **half-hat** can also be lavished with pearls and lace for more formal looks, or left plain for a less formal dress. Hair? Chin-length, wavy and fluffy. A brimming **picture hat** best suits casual, outdoorsy dress and scooped necklines. It's especially good with long hair swept back or curled around the shoulders. The **toque** is the perfect complement to a glamorous drape of chiffon. Placed on one side of your head, the toque needs a hairstyle with fullness on the other side (a chignon?). The **pillbox** can rest straight across the head or on a slant. Small brimless hats like the pillbox and toque are perfect for brides with glasses. The **derby** is best paired with a ruffly, old-fashioned dress, a twirly parasol. To go with a derby, hair that's pinned up, or in romantic, loose waves.

**MATCH YOUR HEADPIECE** with your dress by shopping for both at the same time and place. Try them on together. Then look at yourself in a series of full-length mirrors to see the total look from all angles. And re-member to match colors—a white headpiece with a white dress, ivory with ivory, maybe blue ribbons woven through a cap that tops a dress underlined in blue. To be sure you're getting the same fabric or lace, ask your bridal consultant to order half a yard that matches your dress, then let her take care of having the cap or hat made. Also fit the headpiece to your figure and face. Tall? Try a brimmed hat or close-fitting cap that's not too high on the head. Short? Choose a tiny cap, a narrow-brimmed hat. Full-figured? A neat, snug cap with a short veil. Round face or glasses? A trim, off-the-face style and a long smooth veil. Long face? A soft

face-framer, a poufy veil. A headpiece *must*—it has to be comfortable, feel secure so you're not afraid to turn your head or bend over. To help anchor it, use white hair-pins on either side, or at the point where the veil is attached to the hat. If it's a mantilla or wreath, wiggle pins through the lace or flowers. They'll never show.

**ADD A FINISHING TOUCH** to your headpiece with a floaty veil. Your choices? The four-yard **cathedral** for a very formal dress; a three-yard **chapel-length** veil for a formal, long-sleeved dress; the elbow-length **bouffant** or the three-tiered **fingertip** to set off a short-sleeved formal look or complement a face veil, show off a dress's pretty back; the **cascade,** an almost straight veil to flatter the now-styled jerseys; the **pyramid,** varying from fingertip to knee-length, for updating a traditional dress. Generally, the more formal the dress, the longer the veil.

As for matching headpieces with veils . . . Caps can take floor-length veils. Wreaths? Try elbow-lengths. Hats? A bit of veil behind. One idea: order a veil that can snap off from your headpiece when you take to the dance floor for all the reception festivities.

Half-hat

Wreath

Face-framer

Juliet cap

Mantilla

Picture hat

Toque

Pillbox

Derby

The easiest way to start "shopping" for your wedding dress is to thumb through several issues of BRIDE'S, then cut out the picture that comes closest to how you want to look. Paste it in the space below, then show it to the bridal consultant in your department store or bridal salon to help her help you find the perfect dress and headpiece for you.

---

**THIS IS HOW I WANT TO LOOK
ON MY WEDDING DAY**

*(Paste Picture Here.)*

## YOUR ATTENDANTS' DRESSES

Is one of your bridesmaids 5'0" and well-endowed, another 5'10 and very slender? Fortunately, bridesmaids' dresses are made with just this situation in mind, so with a little patience you're sure to find a style that looks perfect on everyone.

It's up to you to choose the dresses your maids will wear, but it's only right to let them have some say. Shop first for the dresses by yourself and narrow the selection down to three or four you like. Try to pick dresses that are within your maids' budgets and that can be worn again for other occasions. Once you've made your choices, round everyone up to try on all the dresses and make the final decision.

## What if your maids are scattered all over the country? These tips can help.

Ask the store's bridal consultant for measurement forms or a list of dimensions she needs from each maid (usually bust, waist, hips, height, weight, and dress size).

Send a measurement form to each maid, with a list of accessories she'll need (gloves, pearls). Enclose return envelopes, postage.

Pick adjustable headpieces like picture hats with elastic insets, stretchy turbans. Or order fresh nosegays from the florist.

Order dresses and headpieces and pay for them yourself. Collect when maids come for the wedding.

Ask maids to arrive a few days ahead so there's plenty of time to make alterations.

## THIS IS A GOOD WEDDING LOOK
## FOR ALL MY ATTENDANTS

*(Paste Picture Here.)*

# BRIDE'S WEDDING CLOTHES CHECKLIST

☐ VERY FORMAL    ☐ DAYTIME

☐ FORMAL    ☐ EVENING

☐ SEMI-FORMAL

☐ INFORMAL

COLORS

Bride _____

Maid and/or Matron of Honor _____

Bridesmaids _____

## Bride

|  | Style | Color | Fabric | Size | $ Cost | Store |
|---|---|---|---|---|---|---|
| Dress | | | | | | |
| Headpiece | | | | | | |
| Shoes | | | | | | |
| Pantyhose | | | | | | |
| Gloves | | | | | | |
| Lingerie | | | | | | |
| Jewelry | | | | | | |

Total cost of bride's clothes $ _____

Dates of fittings _____ time _____

_____    _____

Date ready _____    _____

**Maid and/or Matron of Honor**

Dress style _____ size _____ store _____ cost $ _____

Headpiece _____ cost $ _____ Jewelry _____

Gloves _____ size _____ cost $ _____ Shoes _____ size _____ cost $ _____

Total cost of honor attendant's clothes $ _____

Fitting dates _____ time _____

_____     _____

Date ready _____

**Bridesmaids**

Dress  style _____ store _____ cost $ _____

| | Dress color | Size | Headpiece | Price | Glove size | Shoe size | Cost | Jewelry |
|---|---|---|---|---|---|---|---|---|
| Name _____ | | | | | | | | |
| Name _____ | | | | | | | | |
| Name _____ | | | | | | | | |
| Name _____ | | | | | | | | |

Total cost of *each* maid's clothes $ _____

Fitting dates _____ time _____

_____

Date ready _____

# YOUR MAN'S WEDDING OUTFIT

What will your groom wear in his formal wedding? There are so many possibilities, it can be confusing. Should he stick with tradition and wear a classic cutaway, striped trousers? Or would a snappy, modern tuxedo, color-coordinated to your maids' dresses be more romantic?

Whatever wedding outfit your groom chooses, it should *feel* right to him. And if, like many grooms, he's wearing his first tuxedo on his wedding day, he may have no idea of what he likes. To find out, your groom can thumb through BRIDE'S for pictures of the traditional and contemporary type suits that are available. He can visit a formalwear store (do go along with him), where he'll slip into a cutaway, grin at himself in top hat and tails, get the feel of a velvety double-breasted tuxedo, a ruffly shirt, a four-in-hand tie. You can help him decide on his outfit, and whether or not he'll dress exactly as his ushers, best man, and your fathers do, or vary his shirt, jacket, or pants so he'll stand out from the rest of the wedding party as your leading man.

Before your groom buys or rents any formalwear, be sure his choice matches the style of your dress, the formality of your wedding. Flip back to our "Guide to Wedding Clothes."

## GOOD-GROOMING TIPS

Take along swatches from your and your maids' dresses to coordinate colors of the menswear.

Ask your groom to share your spotlight by wearing a white suit, a different color shirt or tie from that of his men if you prefer the contemporary to traditional look.

Make sure his formalwear fits. Shirt collar should hug neck; shirt cuffs should extend at least one-half inch beyond jacket sleeves; the trousers should touch shoe tops.

Match up the accessories: black or coordinating dress shoes and socks for dark suits (black, green, navy, brown); for pastels or white, light shoes and complementary socks. (Both black and white dress shoes can be rented at most formalwear specialty stores.)

Put the fathers in traditional black if they don't feel comfortable in the contemporary outfits your men may choose.

Ask about cards that the groom can fill out, listing styles of colors, names of groomsmen. Then each can stop by for a fitting at his leisure. The menswear shop may also have mail-order fitting cards so out-of-towners can be measured at their local shops.

Go through BRIDE'S till you find all the different ways you might want your groom to look. Then show him, and let him pick the wedding suit he and his men would feel most comfortable wearing, and paste its picture opposite.

## THE SIX BIGGEST QUESTIONS GROOMS ASK ABOUT HOW TO RENT A TUXEDO.

**Q** *How soon should I start looking around for my wedding tuxedo?*
**A** You can start "window shopping" as soon as you and your fiancée talk about the kind of wedding you want (see "Guide to Wedding Clothes"). To get an idea of what's new and what's available, thumb through BRIDE'S. Circle suit colors and styles you like. Then six to eight weeks before the wedding, go with your fiancée to a formalwear specialist to make your final choice and to be fitted.

**Q** *How do I know if the store I go into is a formalwear "specialist?"*
**A** Any store which has a wide variety of tuxedos, colors, and accessories *in stock* is a specialist. Of course, you can also rent tuxedos through your florist, a tailor, or department store, but you may find the selection of tuxedos limited and the prices higher.

**Q** *A couple of my ushers don't live in town. How can I get them fitted?*
**A** Ask your formalwear salesperson for a "mail measurement card" for your out-of-towners. Your friends can take these cards to their local formalwear shop, get measured, then send the cards back to you. With all the necessary information right on the cards, *your* formalwear store can then tailor tuxedos to fit each usher. Make sure ushers arrive at least a day before the wedding for the final fitting.

**Q** *About how much should I figure on spending to rent a tuxedo?*
**A** Prices vary depending on the area where you live (a rented tux in Des Moines will probably cost less than in New York City), on the style tuxedo you choose, on the store you rent from, and on the selection. Generally, you'll spend around $25 to $45 on your tuxedo.

**Q** *What exactly do I get with a rented tuxedo? Do I have to buy a lot of "extras?"*
**A** No. When you rent a tuxedo, you rent a complete package—everything you need to look like the dashing groom (except socks and underwear)! Included is the jacket, a vest (or cummerbund), trousers, suspenders, shirt, studs, cufflinks, and a tie. You can even rent shoes at most formalwear stores.

**Q** *How soon before the wedding should I pick up my tuxedo?*
**A** Two or three days before. And when you do, make a point of trying everything on right down to the cufflinks. If you're missing a shirt stud or the trousers are a tad too long, there'll be time for adjustments. And plan on the best man returning your tux the first working day after the wedding.

# MY GROOM AND HIS MEN WANT TO WEAR SOMETHING LIKE THIS

*(Paste Picture Here.)*

# GROOM'S WEDDING CLOTHES CHECKLIST

☐ VERY FORMAL          ☐ EVENING                    ☐ STROLLER

☐ FORMAL               ☐ WHITE TIE AND TAILS        ☐ DARK SUIT

☐ SEMI-FORMAL          ☐ BLACK TIE                  ☐ CONTEMPORARY

☐ INFORMAL             ☐ DINNER JACKET

☐ DAYTIME              ☐ CUTAWAY

Men's formalwear store _____ fitting date _____ time _____

Date ready_____

## Groom

|  | Size | Cost |  | Size | Cost |
|---|---|---|---|---|---|
| Trousers_____ | | $ _____ | Neckwear_____ | | $ _____ |
| Shirt_____ | | $ _____ | Collar _____ | | $ _____ |
| Coat _____ | | $ _____ | Gloves _____ | | $ _____ |
| Waistcoat_____ | | $ _____ | Jewelry_____ | | $ _____ |

Total cost of groom's clothes $_____

## Best Man

|  | Size | Cost |  | Size | Cost |
|---|---|---|---|---|---|
| Trousers_____ | | $ _____ | Neckwear_____ | | $ _____ |
| Shirt_____ | | $ _____ | Collar _____ | | $ _____ |
| Coat _____ | | $ _____ | Gloves _____ | | $ _____ |
| Waistcoat_____ | | $ _____ | Jewelry_____ | | $ _____ |

Total cost of best man's clothes $_____

## Ushers

|  | Shirt size | Trouser size | Coat size | Waistcoat size | Jewelry |  |
|---|---|---|---|---|---|---|
| Name _____ | | | | | | $ _____ |
| Name _____ | | | | | | $ _____ |
| Name _____ | | | | | | $ _____ |
| Name _____ | | | | | | $ _____ |

Total cost of *each* usher's clothes $_____

# 8 CONSUMER TRAPS TO WATCH OUT FOR WHEN YOU PLAN YOUR WEDDING

## by Elinor Guggenheimer

*Each year hundreds of newlyweds file complaints at New York City's Department of Consumer Affairs. Here, former Commissioner Elinor Guggenheimer tells you how to avoid getting ripped off during the happiest time of your life.*

Here it is—the most exciting day of your life! ... the day you've been planning for months! ... dreaming about for years!

—So how come your attendants' dresses are flaming fuchsia instead of daffodil yellow? And where's that "famous" orchestra you hired? And why on earth are the waiters serving Chicken Fricassee when you ordered Beef Wellington? And why, oh why, does the inscription on your cake read "Congratulations Birthday Boy?"

Because it's one of the cruel ironies of life that just when you believe nothing could possibly go wrong, something does. You'll probably be spending more money during the next few months than ever before. When you buy more, it stands to reason that you must be more careful about buying. Here's how and why.

### 1 What you don't see is what you might get.

Carol and Joe decided to have an old-fashioned garden wedding at Carol's parents' home. Carol made catering arrangements with the same reliable firm that had been catering her family's parties for years.

On their wedding day, you would have sworn the caterer was using the same equipment he used 30 years earlier at Carol's parents' wedding. The table settings weren't old-fashioned—they were just plain old! The chairs he supplied were soiled and tattered. The plates were dull and chipped.

Carol was furious. When she returned from her honeymoon, she called the caterer and demanded, "Why didn't you warn me?" His reply: "You didn't ask."

Clearly, it was unfair of the caterer not to warn Carol about the condition of his equipment. But then Carol had purchased the use of it without bothering to inspect its condition. Would she have ever bought a dress that way? Never!

The same rules that apply to your everyday purchases apply even more so to the purchases you make for your wedding. Shop around. Check for quality. Put everyting in writing. Understand the ins and outs of any contract before you sign away on the dotted line.

### 2 Mystery music.

Lucy and Mike were dazzled by a band they heard play at a friend's wedding. They immediately obtained the band's name—the "Dee Ception Orchestra"—and hired it to play at their own wedding three months away.

Well, the big day finally arrived—and so did a completely different band. When Lucy asked the guitarist what had happened to the Dee Ception Orchestra, he said, "But we *are* the Dee Ception Orchestra."

Many people like Lucy and Mike have no idea of how orchestras operate. Often the name of a band merely indicates the name of a *bandleader* who may have a number of orchestras working out of his office. There might have been ten Dee Ception Orchestras playing at ten different receptions on Lucy and Mike's wedding day.

What's more, Mr. Dee Ception himself could have taken the day off—even though a standard contract might have said that the orchestra would be "under the leadership of Dee Ception Music." The word "leader" can be used to indicate the name of the person who *contracted* for the musicians—not necessarily the person who'd physically *lead* the music. To make sure you get the musicians you want, ask for an "in person" clause on your contract. Specify, in writing, any leader, musician, or group of musicians you want—by name, if possible.

### 3 Such a deal!

When Jesse and Beverly went to buy a diamond engagement ring, they had only two requirements: the price of the ring could not exceed $600, and the stone had to be good enough to represent a sound investment.

After weeks of searching, Jesse and Beverly found the ring of their dreams—but it cost $900, and the jeweler absolutely refused to lower his price.

Just as they turned to leave, the jeweler softened. He told them to take the ring to an appraiser whose card he gave them. He said he'd be willing to accept *whatever* the appraiser felt the ring was worth—even if it meant he'd lose money on the deal.

Upon examining the stone, the appraiser proclaimed it a *perfect* diamond— worth about $1,500. The couple quite naturally rushed back to the jeweler and took him up on his original $900 offer.

Quite a bargain . . . or so they thought, until a year later when Beverly decided to get a new setting. She went to a *different* jeweler this time, and asked to see a setting that would complement her "perfect diamond."

One look at the stone and the jeweler said. "I'm sorry to have to break the news to you, but this diamond is extremely flawed. I don't think you could get more than $200 for it."

Beverly was shocked. She took the ring to several appraisers.

All gave the same sorry diagnosis.

When Beverly paid a visit to the jeweler she'd originally purchased the ring from, he acknowledged that yes, she did indeed buy *a* ring from him—but not *that* ring. He refused to refund her money.

That's when Beverly finally turned to the New York City Department of Consumer Affairs for help. The investigation that ensued revealed a very interesting pattern of fraud.

The jeweler would warn his friend the appraiser that someone was coming over to price a ring. He'd instruct the appraiser to quote a certain price—usually about $500 more than his own. When the buyers made their purchase on the basis of the phoney appraisal, the jeweler would give a piece of the profits to the appraiser in return for his "cooperation."

Even the most careful consumer would have had no way of knowing this kind of operation was going on. But he might have had reason to *suspect* it. Because *any* reputable dealer will allow you to take an expensive piece of jewelry to an appraiser of your *own* choosing.

The Federal Trade Commission (FTC) has issued a set of rules to regulate the jewelry industry. If you think you've been "had," file a complaint with the FTC.

Your city may also have local laws regulating the sale of jewelry. New York City's Consumer Protection Laws, for example, require that a jeweler specify detailed information on a receipt for jewelry costing over $75. The receipt must list: the material of which the jewelry is composed; whether or not any material is synthetic; the price; the weight if it's a diamond.

You'd be wise to get this kind of written receipt from your jeweler. At the very least, you should be aware of the jeweler's policy on returns. *Always* insist on a written guarantee.

**4 The high cost of un-planning.**

Karen and Bob, a couple who became engaged last May, decided to plan their February wedding well in advance. They contracted for a room in a catering hall, and put down a $600 deposit toward a $2,000 reception.

In August—*six months* before the wedding—Karen and Bob realized they'd never be able to afford such an extravagant reception.

When they called the catering hall to cancel, the manager told them not to worry. Since they'd cancelled so far in advance, he'd certainly be able to fill the room with another party. When he did so, Karen and Bob would be released from any financial liability. The manager said they could expect the return of their $600 sometime after the cancelled date.

March came, and so did a bill for an additional $400. As it happened, the manager hadn't been able to fill the room. And under the terms of the particular contract they'd signed, Karen and Bob were liable for 50 percent of the cost of the reception—$1,000.

Laws regulating size of contract cancellation fees vary from state to state. New York's provides that companies with contracts offering "package deals" (flowers, limousines, music, photography, etc.) can charge only up to 20 percent of the original contract price.

Find out from your state's Attorney General's office what your liabilities might be if you cancel a contract (some states just set a ceiling—the caterer might charge less). Make sure your financial liability is spelled out in writing.

**5 There must be some mistake!**

It's a basic fact-of-consumer-life that *everyone* makes mistakes sometimes. You've got to be on your guard to catch them.

Wedding clothes, for example, may arrive in the wrong size, color, even in soiled condition. Be sure to order yours well in advance, and to insist on a delivery date that allows for corrections. (Proofread your wedding invitations too. Have a friend double-check.)

## 6 Photo play.

Wedding photography is an expensive, one-shot investment. When it comes to hiring your photographer, you'd be wise to use one who's been recommended to you by a *good* friend. If that's impossible, be sure to interview a number of photographers before you settle on one. Ask all to supply you with at least two references, and plenty of samples of their work.

If you plan to use a studio that has more than one photographer on its staff, make sure the one whose samples you liked will be the one sent to your wedding. Get a written promise.

Be straightforward with the terms of your contract. Specify: 1) the date the photographs are to be delivered; 2) the number of photographs you're obligated to buy above and beyond the basic cost; 3) the cost per album; 4) the types of pictures you want—color, black and white, formal, candid; 5) the location of the photography—just at the church and reception?

## 7 "Just leave your honeymoon to us."

Travel agents operate *independently* of the hotels and airlines for whom they book reservations. Though they're given the right to sell tickets (for which they make a commission), their services are *free* for the consumer.

The Air Traffic Conference (ATC) in Washington, D.C., oversees the domestic air ticket operations of travel agents. If you book a flight to Miami, and end up in Duluth, file a complaint with them. They can prohibit any consistently fraudulent agent from selling tickets. For international flight foul-ups, contact the International Air Traffic Association located in Washington, D.C.

Avoid honeymoon travel problems by getting your entire itinerary in writing— time plans, costs, dates, meal plans, any extras.

## 8 "What happened to my bag?"

What do you do when your luggage falls into the Atlantic (or from the looks of it, might as well have)? Under a ruling by the Federal Aviation Administration, you're entitled to collect damages from the airline for each piece of luggage that's lost or damaged. The *amount*

depends on the weight of the luggage, whether it was checked or carried on, and whether the flight was domestic or international. Airlines are *not* liable for more than $500 per bag—unless you've indicated *beforehand* (when you check in) that it contains or is worth more than that amount. What's wisest, of course, is to avoid packing *any* valuables in luggage you check. Carry them right with you in a tote.

If your bags are lost, stolen, or damaged, file a claim with the airline representative *before* you leave the airport. Do *not* surrender any claim check until a lost bag has been returned. The Civil Aeronautics Board publishes a pamphlet which outlines the ways you can avoid common problems in dealing with airlines. Send for "Air Travelers Fly Rights" from the CAB at JFK International Airport, Federal Bldg., Jamaica, N.Y. 11430.

What if your honeymoon hasn't lived up to what your travel agent *told* you—and *sold* you (for example, coffee in the A.M. instead of the promised full American breakfast)? *Misrepresentation* is a serious consumer abuse. Try obtaining financial redress from the travel agency itself. If this fails, file a formal complaint with your local consumer protection agency.

You have every right to expect your wedding day and honeymoon to be perfect. But "perfect" takes planning. The outcome will depend not only on dollars and cents, but on consumer sense in spending your dollars too.

# YOUR WEDDING ANNOUNCEMENT

It's customary to publish the pertinent details of a formal wedding in the couple's home town newspaper. So don't forget to contact the society editors of your and your fiancé's local papers (you may already know them if they published your engagement announcement). A morning wedding is sometimes written up in an evening paper the same day, but most wedding stories are published the day after the ceremony. Check with your newspaper in advance to learn its exact requirements and deadlines. Some, for example, require the bride to fill out a standard form and submit it to the society editor a week or two before the wedding. Others want telephoned confirmation that the wedding has actually taken place before they will allow publication of the story.

If your paper does not supply wedding announcement forms, just type the information double-spaced on one side of plain white paper, 8½ × 11 inches. Be sure to put your name, address, and telephone number (or that of someone else in the community who can be called for verification and additional details) in the upper right-hand corner. The date you'd like the announcement published should appear in the upper left-hand corner.

If you want a photograph published with your wedding story, send an 8 × 10 glossy print of your bridal portrait along with the announcement details. A typed line of identification should be attached to the photo in case it gets separated from the story. Enclose the picture, announcement, and a piece of stiff cardboard in a manila envelope and address it to the society page editor. If you send photographs to more than one paper in the same city, you may want to submit different poses to each one. In some communities, newspapers will print portraits of the bride and groom together. If you choose this option, you'll have to make suitable arrangements with your photographer before your bridal portrait is taken.

A typical wedding announcement reads:

*Miss Mary Clark Butler, daughter of Mr. and Mrs. Willard T. Butler of South Orange, was married this afternoon to Emile Claude Pomeroy, son of Mr. and Mrs. James C. Pomeroy of Short Hills. Msgr. Patrick Flynn of Englewood, uncle of the bride, performed the ceremony at Trinity Church in South Orange.*

*The bride, escorted by her father, wore an ivory dress of organza trimmed with rows of Venise lace. Bands of matching lace trimmed her chapel train and fingertip veil. She carried a cascade of white roses and stephanotis.*

*Miss Carla Butler, sister of the bride, was the maid of honor. The bridesmaids were Misses Gloria Smith and Linda Kerr of South Orange, Mrs. Alexander McGinnis of Teaneck, and Mrs. Kenneth Brophy of Buffalo, New York.*

*Thomas Buckley of Newark served as best man. The ushers were Richard Butler, brother of the bride, John Allison of Short Hills, and Edward Lyons and Francis Grayson of New York City.*

Some newspapers also publish descriptions of the bridesmaids' and mothers' dresses and flowers, the location of the reception, details of the newlyweds' respective educational backgrounds, professional affiliations, grandparents' names, honeymoon plans and other information. Use published stories in your paper as your guide to the type of detail to include. A prior marriage is sometimes mentioned in a line saying, "The bride's previous marriage ended in divorce."

If your parents are divorced, the announcement would read: *". . . the daughter of Mrs. Clark Butler of South Orange and Mr. William T. Butler of New York City."* If one of your parents is widowed, the correct phrasing is *". . . the daughter Mrs. William T. Butler and the late Mr. Butler."* If your mother has remarried and you have been adopted by your stepfather, this information appears later in the story, perhaps in reporting that your stepfather gave you away.

Filling out this form will help you prepare a wedding announcement for your newspaper.

To appear: _____    _____
                    (Date)                              (Your parents' names)

                                         _____
                                                      (Street address)

                                         _____
                                                    (City, state, zip code)

                                         _____
                                                (Area code, telephone number)

Miss _____ , daughter of Mr. and Mrs. _____
            (Your full name)                                      (Your parents' names)

of _____ , was married this _____ to
         (Your parents' home town)                    (Morning, afternoon, evening)

_____ , son of Mr. and Mrs. _____ of _____
      (Your fiancé's name)                          (His parents' names)              (His parents' home town)

_____ of _____ performed the ceremony
      (Clergymember or official)              (Address, if necessary)

at _____ in _____
        (Church, hotel, etc.)              (Location)

The bride, escorted by her father, wore _____
                                              (Description of your dress)

_____

_____ She carried a bouquet of _____

_____
                        (Description of your flowers)

Miss _____ was the _____ of honor. The bridesmaids
         (Honor attendant's name)              (Maid or matron)

were _____ of _____ , _____ of
          (Maid's name)                (Her home town)              (Maid's name)

_____ , and _____ of _____ .
      (Her home town)              (Maid's name)                (Her home town)

_____ of _____ served as best man. The ushers
        (Best man)                  (His home town)

were _____ of _____ , _____ of _____ ,
         (Usher)                   (Home town)                  (Usher)                  (Home town)

and _____ of _____ .
        (Usher)                   (Home town)

# 3

# Parties! Parties! Parties!

From the moment you decide to marry, life becomes a whirl of parties. Some, like the traditional maids' luncheon or dinner, you'll give yourself. But most—showers, the rehearsal dinner—other people will give for you, your groom too. What *can* you do? Let your pleasure show. Smile. Thank the host or hostess with a note, flowers, tickets to the theater or a sports event. Write to any gift-givers. Subtly, tactfully see to it that no guest is invited to so many parties he or she feels pinched for time or money. Something to remember: parties for the bride and groom are often just what the hosts and guests have been waiting for to let loose and have a little fun themselves.

# SHOWER GUIDE

## Hints to the hostess on gifts and guests

Of all the party occasions that go along with being engaged, showers are some of the best. Not only for all the really needed little gifts they supply, but because, quite simply, they're always fun—whether you go for the traditional "ladies only" get-together or choose a mixed group of men and women friends to honor both bride and groom.

At heart, a shower is really just like any other party. Though the bridal attendants often make the plans, any good friend of the couple may host one. But never a member of the immediate family (bride's mother, groom's sister). That's too much like asking for gifts. (A note to honor attendants: Every bride deserves at least one shower. And it's up to you to give it if no one else volunteers.)

When you—office colleague, school friend or member of the wedding—sponsor a shower, choose your own favorite party style, from a pot luck supper to poolside splash, at home or in a restaurant, with cake and punch, drinks and nibbles, or a full meal for all. Play traditional shower games, spin your best disco tunes, or make good old-fashioned talk the main entertainment. Anything goes—as long as the highlight of the party comes with the bride (or couple) opening gifts.

**THE GIFTS.** What makes a suitable shower gift? Just about anything the bride and groom might want, need, or enjoy—from a new broom to a potted palm. But this is the time to keep the price down; the couple will get more expensive needs as wedding gifts.

If your wedding couple long for something really special (that crystal decanter? an Italian desk lamp?), ask everyone to chip in a few dollars toward a group gift you'll buy. Otherwise, set a theme for guests to follow in choosing their own gifts, doing your best to pick up any hints dropped by the bride or groom ("I sure wish we had some decent cookbooks"). Some ideas to consider: kitchen or bath needs; tools and a tool chest; plants and gardening aids; a basic medicine cabinet; books and magazine subscriptions; travel helps; bar gadgets and liquor; season tickets to the theater or ballgame; herbs and spices; and lingerie or sewing accessories for a women-only shower. Just for fun, you might decorate around your theme—for that travel shower, hang up brightly-colored posters of faraway places; for a gardening shower, put ivy and geraniums on the table.

**THE GUESTS.** Once you've picked your theme decide on a date that's convenient for both you and your couple. (Forget surprise showers; they backfire all too often.) About four to six weeks before the wedding should suit everyone. And an evening or weekend assures your biggest turnout. Then telephone or mail your invitations to all the guests with an R.S.V.P. to you. Include your suggestions as to colors, sizes, appropriate gifts. You needn't be acquainted with everyone as long as you ask only good friends of the bride or groom that you know for sure will be invited to the wedding. So do ask the bride's mother, best friend, or groom for help with your guest list (they'll have addresses, phone numbers too). Figure ten or fewer couples for a mixed group, maybe a dozen or so if it's women only.

It's always polite to invite the wedding couple's parents to come along, at least for the gift opening and a drink. Members of the bridal party are traditional guests too. Just make sure no one gets overwhelmed by invitations; too many showers can bankrupt the bridesmaids. If yours is but one of several parties being given for the same couple, you might even schedule the opening ceremony for early in the evening, and ask the bridal party to drop by for the fun later on.

**THE GOOD TIME.** When shower-hour finally arrives, try to arrange to have guests appear about 30 minutes before the bride and groom so you can collect gifts at the door and arrange them nicely on a special table. (Or ask everyone to drop their gifts off with you ahead of time.) Allow a little while for everyone to exchange greetings before presenting the presents. Then have a roomy trash can ready for wrappings and ribbons. Ask a special friend to assist with recording gifts and givers, tucking things back into boxes along with their cards so the bride's thank-you noting will run smoothly. And do supply a few shopping bags or boxes to help the couple tote their new possessions away.

**MY SHOWERS**

Theme: _____

Hostess: _____

Date: _____ Time: _____

Place: _____

| Guests | Gift | Date thank-yous sent |
|---|---|---|
| 1 _____ | _____ | _____ |
| 2 _____ | _____ | _____ |
| 3 _____ | _____ | _____ |
| 4 _____ | _____ | _____ |
| 5 _____ | _____ | _____ |
| 6 _____ | _____ | _____ |
| 7 _____ | _____ | _____ |
| 8 _____ | _____ | _____ |
| 9 _____ | _____ | _____ |
| 10 _____ | _____ | _____ |

**MY SHOWERS**

Theme: _____

Hostess: _____

Date: _____ Time: _____

Place: _____

| Guests | Gift | Date thank-yous sent |
|--------|------|----------------------|
| 1 _____ | _____ | _____ |
| 2 _____ | _____ | _____ |
| 3 _____ | _____ | _____ |
| 4 _____ | _____ | _____ |
| 5 _____ | _____ | _____ |
| 6 _____ | _____ | _____ |
| 7 _____ | _____ | _____ |
| 8 _____ | _____ | _____ |
| 9 _____ | _____ | _____ |
| 10 _____ | _____ | _____ |

**MY SHOWERS**

Theme: _____

Hostess: _____

Date: _____ Time: _____

Place: _____

| Guests | Gift | Date thank-yous sent |
|--------|------|----------------------|
| 1 _____ | _____ | _____ |
| 2 _____ | _____ | _____ |
| 3 _____ | _____ | _____ |
| 4 _____ | _____ | _____ |
| 5 _____ | _____ | _____ |
| 6 _____ | _____ | _____ |
| 7 _____ | _____ | _____ |
| 8 _____ | _____ | _____ |
| 9 _____ | _____ | _____ |
| 10 _____ | _____ | _____ |

## THE MAIDS' LUNCHEON

Just before the wedding, you and your attendants can unwind at a bridesmaids' luncheon. Hoping to surprise you with the wedding presents there, your maids might give this party. But you might do it too. Then you'll have an excuse to introduce out-of-town maids, schedule final dress fittings, display your gifts, and distribute wedding mementos. The right site? A favorite restaurant or your home. If lunch conflicts with work, you instead might plan Saturday tea or dinner the night of the bachelor's party—whatever's timely for all.

*Tradition promises a rosy future to one of the attendants at the bridesmaids' luncheon. When she bites down on the thimble or ring baked inside the pink lady's cake that arrives with dessert, she becomes the person to marry next.*

## THE BACHELOR'S PARTY

Your groom, the best man, and all the ushers deserve a release from pre-wedding tensions. So see they pack themselves off to a bachelor's party. If his men don't volunteer to give it, suggest your fiancé play host. Then advise him to pass out his attendants' thank-you presents there. You might even help him draw up a guest list that includes close male friends and relatives who won't participate in the wedding. But the entertainment he can plan himself. Since it's likely to be liquid, you however might ask that the party be held any time but the night before the wedding. That way you'll assure everyone a pleasant and sober ceremony.

*At the end of the bachelor's dinner, the groom customarily proposes a champagne toast to the bride. Then each man smashes his glass, so it can never serve a less worthy purpose.*

## OUT-OF-TOWN GUESTS

**INVITING YOUR FAR-FLUNG FRIENDS.** The college roommates, all scattered now; the aunt who moved away when you were ten but always sent the best birthday gifts—if you love them, invite them—no matter where they live. It's your way of telling them they are still important to you and your fiancé. Send off your invitations to them six weeks ahead, instead of the usual four. Then your guests can arrange time off from work if they need to, and you'll have an edge on getting responses back. After all, you want to make sure the caterer gets an accurate head-count on schedule.

Other ways of getting the answers to flow in? If your groom is from another city, ask his mother to let you know as soon as possible how many guests to expect from their area. (It would also be helpful if his family could send copies of plane and train schedules to their hometown friends who'll be coming to the wedding.) Though it's not traditional, you could insert response cards with the invitations.

Anyone who hasn't replied ten days before the wedding and who lives over two hours away could be counted as an automatic "no." To find out for sure, your mother can call and be direct, "We'd love to have you at the wedding. Will you be able to come?"

**PUTTING THEM UP.** Recruit friends to house the guests. Or have your groom scout out hotels and motels near the reception or ceremony site a month in advance. Ask about group rates and whether rooms can be reserved in a block. It's more fun if everyone stays together. More convenient too. Those with cars can drive the others to the ceremony and reception. As acceptances roll in, mail your guests the name and address of the hotel. Unless they're members of the wedding party, usually everyone pays his own way. So send the rates too.

**GETTING THEM TO THE CHURCH ON TIME.** Mail anyone not familiar with your town an easy-to-follow map with hotel, reception, ceremony sites—parking lots too. Label important roads with names *and* route numbers; the turns, with landmarks (gas stations, buildings). Draw to scale. Include a North arrow. Some sources of help: your American Automobile Association, Chamber of Commerce, the area outline map in front of the phone book. Have your map photo-copied or printed to match the invitations.    If your guests won't be staying over, enclose the map with the invitations. Otherwise include it with the lodging information.

**GIVING THEM THE ROYAL TREATMENT.** Not enough cars to transport everyone to the wedding events?

Rent a school bus. Or pair each visiting guest with a guest from your area. Let your "ambassador" meet the visitor at the airport or hotel, drive him to the wedding, sit with him, introduce him all around. Your uncle flying in from Genoa will bubble over if he has someone fluent in Italian by his side. Thank your substitute hosts with a gift or a tankful of gas.

It's a very warm idea too to brighten up the hotel rooms with bouquets from the florist, welcoming notes from you or your parents, and schedules of party and wedding events with necessary names, addresses, and phone numbers. So everyone can get acquainted before the wedding, invite the visitors to the rehearsal dinner. Too many? Ask the aunt whose shower offer you declined to host a buffet. After the last of the rice has been swept away, a supper back at the house (specially prepared ahead of time, perhaps by your wedding caterer) will allow your parents one last visit with the friends and relatives they haven't seen for so long. Being surrounded by people at that time will help chase away those feelings of loneliness after you and your groom leave for your honeymoon. Everyone can kick off his shoes and talk about what a wonderful wedding *your* wedding was.

# GUEST ACCOMMODATIONS CHECKLIST

Host or hotel _____

Address _____ Phone _____

## Guests

1. Name _____

   Address _____ Phone _____

   Date arriving _____ Date leaving _____

2. Name _____

   Address _____ Phone _____

   Date arriving _____ Date leaving _____

3. Name _____

   Address _____ Phone _____

   Date arriving _____ Date leaving _____

Host or hotel _____

Address _____ Phone _____

## Guests

1. Name _____

   Address _____ Phone _____

   Date arriving _____ Date leaving _____

2. Name _____

   Address _____ Phone _____

   Date arriving _____ Date leaving _____

3. Name _____

   Address _____ Phone _____

   Date arriving _____ Date leaving _____

# GUEST ACCOMMODATIONS CHECKLIST

Host or hotel _____

Address _____ Phone _____

**Guests**

1. Name _____

   Address _____ Phone _____

   Date arriving _____ Date leaving _____

2. Name _____

   Address _____ Phone _____

   Date arriving _____ Date leaving _____

3. Name _____

   Address _____ Phone _____

   Date arriving _____ Date leaving _____

Host or hotel _____

Address _____ Phone _____

**Guests**

1. Name _____

   Address _____ Phone _____

   Date arriving _____ Date leaving _____

2. Name _____

   Address _____ Phone _____

   Date arriving _____ Date leaving _____

3. Name _____

   Address _____ Phone _____

   Date arriving _____ Date leaving _____

# WEDDING REHEARSAL

## SETTING UP

**Schedule your rehearsal** two or three nights before the wedding. That way everyone can party all night at the rehearsal dinner, sleep late the next day, and show up at the wedding without a hangover or dark circles. But if one family or wedding party members are from out-of-town and can't arrive till the last minute, set the rehearsal for 5:30 the night before or if it'll be an evening wedding, sometime the same day.

**Invite your maids, honor attendant,** ushers, best man, parents, flower girl and ring bearer with their parents, clergymember, organist, soloist—and *you* be there! (No, it's not bad luck to participate in the rehearsal— it's worse luck to have something go wrong at the wedding.) Ask people by phone or send postcards. Do request that everyone be prompt. And have your best man spread the word to save any cocktails for later. You'll need everyone sober enough to pay attention.

**Dress up.** Slacks, jeans, and anything too bare are out of place at church or temple. Wear what will look pretty at the rehearsal dinner—a day-into-evening dress or a softly gored skirt and silky blouse. And do your re-hearsing in your wedding shoes, especially if they're high-heeled or strappy. (Get used to scaling any church steps now.) A nice pair of pants and a shirt are fine for the men—with a tie and jacket if the rehearsal dinner will be held outside the home, at a restaurant or club.

## HINTS FOR THE USHERS

Ask their help in keeping the wedding on time. The guests should be seated as soon as a crowd gathers in front. Decide how you want your guests seated—the bride's family on the left, the groom's on the right, or everyone together. This is an easy way to even out the church if one family has more guests than the other. Draw up a list of guests who'll need special seats or help and give to the head usher. Remind your ushers to offer their right arm to a woman, have her escort follow behind. Assign two ushers to show your mother and your groom's to and from their seats; two ushers to lay the pew ribbons if you are using them; and two ushers to help unroll the white aisle runner.

**Figure out how you want the church emptied** . . . by having the ushers bow out each row or letting your guests exit themselves. Ask your ushers to stay and help collect mass books from pews, clear out dressing rooms, and direct guests to the reception. Printed maps make it easy. Bring them along as well as any wedding programs to store till wedding day. And finally, tell the ushers to arrive at the church at least an *hour* early wedding day.

## SOME DO'S AND DON'TS

Rehearse the processional with music provided by your organist. (Remember to bring along his or her fee, you may forget to do this on wedding day.) Everyone starts up aisle on the left foot, walks naturally, keeping a distance of four pews from the preceding couple. Make sure each person knows where to stand for the ceremony; whom to pair with for the recessional.

**Don't over-rehearse your flower girl or ring bearer.** Show them where to go after they walk up the aisle, then send them home. Do sew a fake ring in your size onto the ring cushion just in case the best man forgets the real thing.

**Watch your clergymember for signals.** Although he won't read the actual ceremony, he will indicate where you and your groom make your responses and when your best man gives the ring. The clergymember might tell you to enter on your father's left—but if you'll be wearing a long train, ask to enter on your father's right. That way he can return to his left front pew without stepping over your gown. Writing your own ceremony? Give everyone copies so they'll know what happens when—like singing, for instance.

**Practice bouquet-passing** with three fake ones made from gift-ribbon bows. At the point in the processional where you reach the front of the church, your honor attendant hands her bouquet to the maid on her left. Then you pass yours to her so your hands are free to manage your skirt. Your attendant returns the bouquet to your *right* hand after the benediction so you can slip your left arm through your husband's for the recessional. And she retrieves her bouquet on the way up the aisle.

## REHEARSAL DINNER
## WHO'LL PLAY HOST?
Though almost anyone can host the rehearsal dinner, it's usually the groom's parents who do the honors. But keep in mind that it's perfectly correct for the bride's parents, any set of grandparents, another relative, or a close family friend to give the dinner if the circum-stances seem right. Maybe your groom's family is from out of town, and won't be arriving until the day of the rehearsal. And your older sister offers to have the dinner at her house to spare the groom's mother the bother of long-distance planning and last-minute prepa-rations. In a case like this, your sister's suggestion might work out best all around.

## IT'S A PARTY!
Don't let the name fool you—a rehearsal dinner doesn't have to be a "dinner" at all. It can be any kind of party that suits your style and puts everybody in the mood for celebrating. If the rehearsal's early in the day and

it's warm enough, you might want to have a poolside barbecue or picnic. If you prefer a formal setting, plan a seated meal in a restaurant or club. Or if you'd like a cozy buffet supper at home, the menu can feature anything from cold meats and salads to wine and cheese to a potluck reminiscent of your "roots."

Traditionally, the rehearsal and rehearsal dinner are held the night before the wedding. But you may want to rethink this customary timing. Sometimes it's smarter to have your rehearsal dinner two or three nights or so before the wedding, particularly if your ceremony is in the morning or early afternoon. This way, you can party as long as you'd like without worrying about getting up for a wedding the next day, or about any tipsy ushers missing the ceremony. (If members of the wedding are coming a long distance an early rehearsal is probably impossible. End the party early enough for everyone to get a good night's rest.)

## YOU'RE INVITED
As a rule, almost everyone who takes part in your rehearsal is invited to the rehearsal dinner. That's you and the groom, your bridesmaids, ushers, and both sets of parents. You should also ask the spouses of any of your married attendants, and the parents of any children in the wedding (the children themselves are not invited, and even the parents may decline the invitation so they can take the youngsters home from the rehearsal). If the clergymember is a family friend or has come quite a way for the wedding, he or she should be invited, along with spouse. Beyond that, the guest list is up to you. You and your groom may want to extend an invitation to grandparents, sisters and broth-

ers, aunts and uncles. And if there are friends arriving from out of town, it might be wonderful to include them, especially if they haven't seen each other in ages. Whatever you do, be consistent. If you're going to invite your grandparents, ask his too—the same goes for brothers and sisters, other relatives, and friends. Once you've decided who'll be invited to the rehearsal dinner, give the list of names to your hostess. If the party's small, she might want to contact everybody by phone to let them know the time and place. Otherwise a card or brief note written on informal stationery make nice invitations.

Suppose the groom's parents are planning the rehearsal dinner from far away. You or your mother can help by suggesting a place, engaging a caterer, reserving a room. Then his mother can discuss the menu, plan the seating, and finalize the arrangements by mail or phone.

## THE LAST-MINUTE DETAILS
Your rehearsal dinner is probably the last chance you and your attendants will have to be together before the wedding, so it's both a practical and sentimental occasion. If you've got to double-check any wedding details—like transportation to the reception or receiving line instructions—now's the time. It also may be a good time to take care of signing your marriage license, and to give your bridesmaids and ushers gifts that will thank them for being in your wedding.

There's a great spirit of warmth at a rehearsal dinner—you'll wine and dine and toast each other on and on. Everyone has a good time—and what a happy wedding memory for the two of you to look back on!

## OUR REHEARSAL DINNER

Host and hostess: _____

Date: _____ Time: _____

Place: _____

Menu

_____

_____

_____

_____

_____

Guests

1 _____      7 _____

2 _____      8 _____

3 _____      9 _____

4 _____     10 _____

5 _____     11 _____

6 _____     12 _____

# 4

---

# Your Wedding Gifts

Around wedding time, you *will* give a few gifts—to your groom, your attendants, maybe even your parents in appreciation for all the love they've shown you now and as you were growing up. But it's almost guaranteed you'll never *get* more gifts in your life. And there's only one very small thing you have to do in return: say thank-you. Say it out loud when you see the giver at the office, then when he or she passes through the receiving line. Say it in writing the day the present arrives, no later than a month after the honeymoon. What *not* to say? "Gosh, we'd really like . . ." (when asked you *can* tell where you're registered, of course) or "Oh, you shouldn't have . . ." or "Could I return this for . . ." Each gift *is* for you. But more than that, it's an expression of someone's very own thoughts and feelings. Someone special.

# GIFTS FOR ATTENDANTS

**FOR THE BRIDESMAIDS:** Your gifts to them should be identical, with the exception of the honor attendant's, which may be a little more important. As these are members of your wedding, choose something of lasting value such as a silver bangle bracelet, leather or silver picture frame, disc charm, or circle pin. Have them monogrammed, if you can, and allow time for this when you buy them.

**FOR THE USHERS:** Whether or not your fiancé gives them some of the accessories for formal wedding attire, he also gives the ushers identical presents. A silver key ring or bar jigger, a leather stud box are all appropriate and even better when they are initialed. The best man may receive the same present or something different.

## SOMETHING DIFFERENT FOR ATTENDANTS

Plant cuttings in little silver or bright ceramic pots (include tips on plant care). Sturdy vacuum bottles and stadium blankets. Tickets to an upcoming sports event (reserve adjoining seats well ahead of time). Winged corkscrews; their favorite wines.

Samples of your handicraft—maybe needlepoint pillows or découpage pin trays. Leather, pocket-size address books.

Pretty picture frames (fabric, silver, enamel) with photos of you and your fiancé. Monogrammed pewter shot glasses.

Deluxe shower heads with spray controls. Auto emergency kits (flares, scrapers, fire extinguishers, first-aid supplies).

Unusual brass, wooden, or glass candlesticks holding tapers you just made.

A pocket-size tool or manicure kit.

I know my attendants would like _____

_____

Final choice for maid or matron of honor_____

Store _____

Pick-up date _____

Choice for bridesmaids_____

Store _____

Pick-up date _____

My fiancé's attendants would appreciate _____

_____

Final choice for best man _____

Store _____

Pick-up date _____

Choice for groomsmen _____

Store _____

Pick-up date _____

# WHO SENDS WEDDING PRESENTS?

It is customary for guests who attend the reception to send gifts. Those who regret and those invited only to the ceremony may, but need not, send presents. And if it's you or your fiancé's second wedding, those who sent a gift before may not give another. You and your groom should not feel uncomfortable about asking relatives and friends to your wedding even if they live a long distance away and will be unable to come. They are not obligated to send gifts if they regret the invitation, although some will anyway. You may also receive packages from persons you don't even know, since it is customary for all gifts, even those from relatives of the groom, to be sent to the bride.

Then there are the extra-special presents that will come . . .

**FROM THE BRIDESMAIDS:** They may give you individual presents or a joint one. The latter is usually something you can use and display with pride in your new home. It might be the engraved plate for your invitations worked into a small silverplate tray with all your attendants' names inscribed on the back. Your honor attendant may contribute to a joint present or give you an individual one.

**FROM THE USHERS:** Like the bridesmaids, they may give a joint present to your groom. It too might be a silver tray engraved with facsimiles of all the ushers' signatures, a classic bowl, a carving set with horn and silver handles. The best man may contribute, or give the groom an individual present.

**THE GROOM'S PARENTS** also may give the bride a handsome present, although it is not mandatory. A silver tea service is the classic gift, but it is more apt to be a set of fine stemware today, good china, or other table appointments. Sometimes the groom's parents pay for the honeymoon as a wedding gift.

**THE BRIDE'S PARENTS** customarily give her a very special present for her new home. Traditionally, it is silver flatware but it might be china, a silver coffee set, or furniture or part of a downpayment toward a house.

**THE GIFTS YOU NEED AND WANT** can be yours for the choosing. Look over the lists in the "At-Home" chapter at the end of this book, then go to the Wedding Gift Registry in your favorite store and talk to the Wedding Gift Registry Consultant there. She will advise you about patterns, help you to coordinate your table accessories, and assist you in choosing everything else you like. All will be listed and filed with the Registry. Then you simply pass along the word through your immediate family and close friends—about this sure-fire way to track down the presents that will please you most. People *want* to know. They can ask the consultant about your list at any time; the Registry will keep it up-to-date so that you won't receive any duplicates.

**PRETTY AND PRACTICAL PRESENTS** are equally important, but almost everything can be both. (Even a kitchen knife may combine a sharp cutting edge with a graceful handle.) Your selection can, and probably will, run the gamut from saucepans to silver. Go over every inch of your new home in your imagination; think carefully about its functions and its looks. If you're still vague about your decorating plans, opt for accessories of pure, classic design that will go with everything. You don't have to wait to file your gift list until you've chosen your table patterns. Table accessories and serving pieces make popular wedding presents, and are as effective when they harmonize as when they match your patterns.

**COVER A WIDE PRICE RANGE** so everyone can buy you something you want—at his or her price. And remember that people have their preferences in *giving*. Some, particularly among your parents' friends, may feel rather strongly that silver makes the only suitable wedding gift. So list a sugar spoon and pickle fork as well as a handsome tray! You will need them all.

# THANKS!

*Which wedding gifts do brides appreciate most? That's what we recently asked BRIDE'S married staffers and friends. And though there were a few answers like "asparagus-cooker," an amazing number agreed on the following gifts, which we've ranked here according to popularity.*

Money

Silverware (either sterling or silverplate serving pieces and holloware)

Toaster-ovens

Candlesticks (silver, crystal); Automatic coffeemakers; Vacuum cleaners

Cookware; Carving sets; Oven-to-table casseroles

China; Crystal; Linens; Toasters; Water pitchers (pewter, silver, crystal)

Decanters; Crystal bowls; Blankets; Slow-cookers; Table lamps; Blenders and Food Processors; All-in-one salt and pepper shakers

## YOUR WEDDING GIFTS

The gifts you receive as a bride not only provide a nucleus for equipping and decorating your new home, but are wonderful tokens of friendship as well.

Your fiancé, your mother, your honor attendant, and your bridesmaids may all want to join in the fun and help you open your gifts. Just be careful that no cards or essential details get lost in all the excitement. Keep accurate records to avoid mixing up gifts or omitting thank-you notes.

As you open each package, list it immediately in the record on the following pages. Include an identifying description of the gift, the name and address of the donor, the store from which it came (in case you want to exchange it later), the date it arrived, and the date your thank-you note is mailed. If you expect a lot of gifts, it's best to attach a number corresponding to the listing on each one—then you'll know which silver candy dish came from your fiancé's great-aunt Susan.

You may want to enlist your maid or matron of honor's help to keep your gift record.

### PRESENTS ON DISPLAY

Wedding presents are usually displayed in some part of the house that is not in constant use. Rows of card tables covered with fine white tablecloths or snowy sheets may be used to hold the gifts. You will probably start your display as soon as you have six or eight gifts, rearranging them as more come in. Group gifts into categories, with silver on one table, glassware on another, electrical appliances on a third. Display only token place settings of your tableware patterns. Scatter similar gifts so that it's not obvious to anyone that you received twelve sets of salt and pepper shakers. If you file the gift cards elsewhere, you can display just one set of exact duplicates and each donor will think you've received only his own. Modest gifts should not be made to suffer comparison next to extravagant gifts. Do not display money gifts, though you might put out a small white card, saying, "Mr. and Mrs. Thomas Brown, check." Garlands of greens, small bowls of flowers, or clusters of ribbon from the packages may make your display more festive.

It's always wise to take out a temporary floater policy insuring your gifts while they are on display. If you receive many valuable presents, you may also want to ask a neighbor to guard them during the ceremony and other times when the house will be empty.

If your reception is held in your home, your guests will see the gifts at that time. Receptions in other locations do not include a gift display. You may ask friends to come over informally to see the gifts or give a special luncheon, tea or bridesmaids' party to show them. Gift displays are often left intact for a week after the ceremony so friends and relatives can drop by to see them.

## DAMAGED GIFTS

Gifts that arrived damaged must be handled with great tact. If you receive one from a local store, return it for replacement. If it comes from an out-of-town store, write a letter of explanation and wait for their instructions. Be sure to ask them not to mention the breakage to the donor. More than one bride has neglected to make such a request, only to learn that the store did call the donor after she'd sent a thank-you note with no mention of the damage. If a broken gift was mailed by the giver, check the wrappings to see if it was insured. If so, you may return it with a note of explanation so the donor can collect the insurance and make the replacement. You should never mention damage to an uninsured or nonreturnable gift, however, as it may make the donor feel obliged to send another. Damaged gifts are never displayed unless they can be arranged so the damage is not obvious.

## EXCHANGES

No matter how careful you are about registering your gift preferences, you'll probably receive at least a few presents you can't use. Some duplicates—especially of breakable items—are nice to have, but no bride really needs more than one silver candle snuffer. It's both proper and practical to exchange duplicates, but no one likes to think his gift was one of the ones returned. If you received exact duplicates or other items that can be exchanged without the giver's knowing, go ahead. Otherwise, it's only right to keep the gift so your Aunt Agatha won't be hurt to discover that the silver candlesticks she so carefully selected never found a place in your new home. Never ask where a gift was purchased so you can exchange it, and don't mention duplication or exchange in your thank-you notes.

# WEDDING GIFT LIST

| NAME AND ADDRESS | DESCRIPTION | STORE | DATE REC'D. | DATE ACK'D. |
|---|---|---|---|---|
| 1. | | | | |
| 2. | | | | |
| 3. | | | | |
| 4. | | | | |
| 5. | | | | |
| 6. | | | | |
| 7. | | | | |
| 8. | | | | |
| 9. | | | | |
| 10. | | | | |
| 11. | | | | |
| 12. | | | | |
| 13. | | | | |
| 14. | | | | |
| 15. | | | | |
| 16. | | | | |
| 17. | | | | |
| 18. | | | | |
| 19. | | | | |
| 20. | | | | |
| 21. | | | | |
| 22. | | | | |
| 23. | | | | |
| 24. | | | | |
| 25. | | | | |

# WEDDING GIFT LIST

| NAME AND ADDRESS | DESCRIPTION | STORE | DATE REC'D. | DATE ACK'D. |
|---|---|---|---|---|
| 26. | | | | |
| 27. | | | | |
| 28. | | | | |
| 29. | | | | |
| 30. | | | | |
| 31. | | | | |
| 32. | | | | |
| 33. | | | | |
| 34. | | | | |
| 35. | | | | |
| 36. | | | | |
| 37. | | | | |
| 38. | | | | |
| 39. | | | | |
| 40. | | | | |
| 41. | | | | |
| 42. | | | | |
| 43. | | | | |
| 44. | | | | |
| 45. | | | | |
| 46. | | | | |
| 47. | | | | |
| 48. | | | | |
| 49. | | | | |
| 50. | | | | |

# WEDDING GIFT LIST

| NAME AND ADDRESS | DESCRIPTION | STORE | DATE REC'D. | DATE ACK'D. |
|---|---|---|---|---|
| 51. | | | | |
| 52. | | | | |
| 53. | | | | |
| 54. | | | | |
| 55. | | | | |
| 56. | | | | |
| 57. | | | | |
| 58. | | | | |
| 59. | | | | |
| 60. | | | | |
| 61. | | | | |
| 62. | | | | |
| 63. | | | | |
| 64. | | | | |
| 65. | | | | |
| 66. | | | | |
| 67. | | | | |
| 68. | | | | |
| 69. | | | | |
| 70. | | | | |
| 71. | | | | |
| 72. | | | | |
| 73. | | | | |
| 74. | | | | |
| 75. | | | | |

# WEDDING GIFT LIST

| NAME AND ADDRESS | DESCRIPTION | STORE | DATE REC'D. | DATE ACK'D. |
|---|---|---|---|---|
| 76. | | | | |
| 77. | | | | |
| 78. | | | | |
| 79. | | | | |
| 80. | | | | |
| 81. | | | | |
| 82. | | | | |
| 83. | | | | |
| 84. | | | | |
| 85. | | | | |
| 86. | | | | |
| 87. | | | | |
| 88. | | | | |
| 89. | | | | |
| 90. | | | | |
| 91. | | | | |
| 92. | | | | |
| 93. | | | | |
| 94. | | | | |
| 95. | | | | |
| 96. | | | | |
| 97. | | | | |
| 98. | | | | |
| 99. | | | | |
| 100. | | | | |

# WEDDING GIFT LIST

| NAME AND ADDRESS | DESCRIPTION | STORE | DATE REC'D. | DATE ACK'D. |
|---|---|---|---|---|
| 101. | | | | |
| 102. | | | | |
| 103. | | | | |
| 104. | | | | |
| 105. | | | | |
| 106. | | | | |
| 107. | | | | |
| 108. | | | | |
| 109. | | | | |
| 110. | | | | |
| 111. | | | | |
| 112. | | | | |
| 113. | | | | |
| 114. | | | | |
| 115. | | | | |
| 116. | | | | |
| 117. | | | | |
| 118. | | | | |
| 119. | | | | |
| 120. | | | | |
| 121. | | | | |
| 122. | | | | |
| 123. | | | | |
| 124. | | | | |
| 125. | | | | |

# WEDDING GIFT LIST

| NAME AND ADDRESS | DESCRIPTION | STORE | DATE REC'D. | DATE ACK'D. |
|---|---|---|---|---|
| 126. | | | | |
| 127. | | | | |
| 128. | | | | |
| 129. | | | | |
| 130. | | | | |
| 131. | | | | |
| 132. | | | | |
| 133. | | | | |
| 134. | | | | |
| 135. | | | | |
| 136. | | | | |
| 137. | | | | |
| 138. | | | | |
| 139. | | | | |
| 140. | | | | |
| 141. | | | | |
| 142. | | | | |
| 143. | | | | |
| 144. | | | | |
| 145. | | | | |
| 146. | | | | |
| 147. | | | | |
| 148. | | | | |
| 149. | | | | |
| 150. | | | | |

# WEDDING GIFT LIST

| NAME AND ADDRESS | DESCRIPTION | STORE | DATE REC'D. | DATE ACK'D. |
|---|---|---|---|---|
| 151. | | | | |
| 152. | | | | |
| 153. | | | | |
| 154. | | | | |
| 155. | | | | |
| 156. | | | | |
| 157. | | | | |
| 158. | | | | |
| 159. | | | | |
| 160. | | | | |
| 161. | | | | |
| 162. | | | | |
| 163. | | | | |
| 164. | | | | |
| 165. | | | | |
| 166. | | | | |
| 167. | | | | |
| 168. | | | | |
| 169. | | | | |
| 170. | | | | |
| 171. | | | | |
| 172. | | | | |
| 173. | | | | |
| 174. | | | | |
| 175. | | | | |

# WEDDING GIFT LIST

| NAME AND ADDRESS | DESCRIPTION | STORE | DATE REC'D. | DATE ACK'D. |
|---|---|---|---|---|
| 176. | | | | |
| 177. | | | | |
| 178. | | | | |
| 179. | | | | |
| 180. | | | | |
| 181. | | | | |
| 182. | | | | |
| 183. | | | | |
| 184. | | | | |
| 185. | | | | |
| 186. | | | | |
| 187. | | | | |
| 188. | | | | |
| 189. | | | | |
| 190. | | | | |
| 191. | | | | |
| 192. | | | | |
| 193. | | | | |
| 194. | | | | |
| 195. | | | | |
| 196. | | | | |
| 197. | | | | |
| 198. | | | | |
| 199. | | | | |
| 200. | | | | |

# WEDDING GIFT LIST

| NAME AND ADDRESS | DESCRIPTION | STORE | DATE REC'D. | DATE ACK'D. |
|---|---|---|---|---|
| 201. | | | | |
| 202. | | | | |
| 203. | | | | |
| 204. | | | | |
| 205. | | | | |
| 206. | | | | |
| 207. | | | | |
| 208. | | | | |
| 209. | | | | |
| 210. | | | | |
| 211. | | | | |
| 212. | | | | |
| 213. | | | | |
| 214. | | | | |
| 215. | | | | |
| 216. | | | | |

**YOU AND YOUR GROOM** may exchange gifts if you wish to, or he alone may want to give you a wedding present. Traditionally, this can be anything but clothing. Jewelry is an ideal choice, especially the classic piece that won't become out of date. A string of cultured pearls or stud earrings, a gold bracelet or pin are all good. So is an initialed brief case, a traveling clock, a leather jewelry box. You might give your groom a good pen and pencil set, a silver picture frame. Or you two might exchange similar presents such as fine watches or luggage.

I think my groom would like _____

_____

_____

Final choice _____

Store _____

Pick-up date _____

I'll hint around to him for _____

_____

_____

# WRITING WARM THANK-YOUS

Send off a personal, handwritten thank-you note for each gift you receive—even if it's from a close friend you've thanked in person and see every day. You don't have to send written thanks to your fiancé or your own parents, though they might love finding a surprise note in a pocket or on their pillows.

Keep up with your notes by writing as each gift comes in. And do try to send a thank-you off within two weeks after a gift arrives—no later than one month after your honeymoon. Traditionally, thank-you notes are written in blue or black ink on white or off-white folded notepaper—four- by five-and-one-half-inches. You may send decorated or imprinted notes too. If they'll be monogrammed, your maiden name initials are correct before marriage, your new ones (if you're changing your name) after marriage.

Incidentally, it has long been the custom for brides only to write thank-you notes. But especially if gifts came addressed to you and your husband at or after the wedding, or from people only he knows, your groom can do the honors.

## FIVE QUICK STEPS TO THE PERFECT THANK-YOU NOTE

**1.** Address the note to the person who gave you the gift. Traditionally, you write the woman if it's a married couple: *Dear Mrs. Nelson.* Or you can address both husband and wife. It's a joint gift from more than four people? Address the group as a whole: *Dear Friends.*

**2.** In the first sentence, say thanks—and make sure to name the gift: *Thank you so much for the sporty plaid blanket you and Mr. Nelson sent.* (Notice how you mention the husband). If you aren't sure what the gift is, simply describe it: . . . *the lovely etched crystal piece.*

**3.** Mention something more about the gift—like how perfect it is for your home: *Since we'll be moving to Vermont, the blanket is sure to keep Bob and me warm through those long winters ahead.* If it's money, tell what you'll put it toward. Slip your groom's name in too!

**4.** Add another thought—maybe a comment about the wedding plans or a visit that will involve the gift-giver: *So glad you'll be at the wedding— you two always get everyone dancing!* Then say thanks again.

**5.** Sign off. Use your maiden name before the wedding, your new married name after—both first *and* last if you don't know the giver well.

Dear Miss Martin,

Thank you for the beautifully engraved silver piece. You can be certain John and I will give it a place of honor in our new apartment. I hope that someday our home will be as warm and personal as I've always remembered yours. Thank you again.

Sincerely,
Ann Brown Smith

**If you aren't really sure what the gift is, simply describe it.**

Dear Co-Workers,

Thank you, thank you for the place setting of China! Now John and I have service for twelve — just what we need to host the annual partners' dinner. How did you *ever* guess? Seriously, we do appreciate it — and I can't wait to get back with our honeymoon snapshots for you to see.

With much affection,
Ann Smith

**If it's a joint gift, write a group note, then thank everyone in person.**

Dear Uncle Ed,

Thank you so much for the generous wedding check. It was a wonderful surprise. John and I have added it to savings earmarked for a car — and thanks to you, we're almost there. We'll be driving around to see you soon!

Love,
Ann

**If it's a gift of money, let the giver know how you'll be using it.**

June 17th

Dear Mrs. Robins,

Thank you very much for the blender you and Mr. Robins sent. John tells me you always served the thickest milkshakes in town— and now we can too! I can't wait to meet you both at the wedding. Again, many thanks.

Sincerely yours,
Ann Brown

**If you haven't met the gift-givers yet, mention a time when you might.**

Dear Bob and Jan,

Thanks so much for the lamp that's a gum machine too! John and I haven't stopped talking about it — and it's sure to be a conversation piece whenever we have people over. You two are always so clever and fun, we hope you'll be among our first guests. Thanks again.

Love,
Ann

**If it's a gift you don't like, say how clever it is. Returning it? Don't tell!**

124

# 5

# Just For The Two Of You

Who's all the celebration for? YOU! So do take time out now and then from the wedding planning to pamper yourself. Indulge in a "makeover" that'll leave you both beautiful and relaxed. Take stock of your clothes— mend your old things, send them to the cleaners. And while you're certainly not going to buy a whole new wardrobe, you might budget for a few "trousseau" nighties and dresses to make you *feel* like a bride. Don't forget to get appointments for health check-ups, to notify people of your name-change. And don't forget HIM. Talk about religion, money, birth control—marriage—not just the wedding. And continue "dating." (You might even splurge on a fancy restaurant lunch the day you pick up the license.) Throughout the flurry of pre-wedding activity, it'll keep you in touch. Loving and close.

# BEAUTY COUNTDOWN

*In order to look and feel your very best for the wedding, you should start a beauty and health routine six months ahead. The list here will help you plan your time, remember what's to be done, shape up your body from head to toe.*

### SIX MONTHS BEFORE:
Try that new hairstyle or cut you want for your wedding day so there's time to get used to it, change it, or let a too-short cut grow. Plan too to suit your headpiece to your hairstyle.

Make time for exercising, sleeping, eating right so you're not run down by wedding day. Diet if you must (ask a doctor first), but don't lose or gain weight once you have your dress.

See a dermatologist about any skin problems.

### THREE MONTHS BEFORE:
Get checkups: dentist; doctor; gynecologist (Choose birth control. The pill? Start it now—you may gain weight, feel nauseous, need to switch); ophthalmologist (budget in an extra pair of glasses or contacts in case you lose, break one during the festivities).

Treat yourself to a professional manicure; keep up the nail-care routine at home.

Experiment with a new makeup look if you're ready for a change. Seek out free makeover demonstrations at cosmetic counters. Go home and try each look with your wedding hat, veil.

### ONE MONTH BEFORE:
Buy any new makeup you've decided on; learn to apply it yourself.

Make a wedding-day salon appointment for a shampoo and set if you're not having your hair done at home or doing it yourself.

Shape unruly eyebrows now so any bare spots can grow in, redness can fade.

Test any new hair removal methods—waxing, depilatory, electrolysis—you want to use.

### TWO WEEKS BEFORE:
Pamper yourself all over. If you can spare one day ($50 and up), do it at a salon. Get a massage, facial, defuzzing, manicure, pedicure, hair trim, set, last-minute advice on wedding-day makeup. Or indulge in all this at home.

Stock up on cosmetics for your honeymoon.

### THE DAY BEFORE:
Plan to have (or give yourself) a manicure, pedicure. Tweeze stray eyebrow hairs. Remove hair from legs, arms, underarms, bikini line, face. Eat sensibly. Get eight hours' sleep!

### ON YOUR WEDDING DAY:
Soak in warm, scented bath.

Powder and moisturize all over. Use a deodorant. Mist on fragrance.

Shampoo and set hair (at salon, home). Soften it with a cream rinse, instant conditioner.

Touch up your manicure.

Snack on a light meal so there's something in your stomach.

Relax; lie down for 30 minutes with a facial mask that you've used before.

Apply makeup: foundation, blusher, eye shadow, mascara, lip color, gloss.

Slip into your wedding dress, shoes, headpiece.

## YOUR TROUSSEAU

| | COLOR ON HAND | COLOR TO BUY | COST |
|---|---|---|---|
| **COATS** | | | $ |
| Warm | | | |
| Lightweight | | | |
| Raincoat | | | |
| Dressy coat | | | |
| **SUITS** | | | |
| 1. | | | |
| 2. | | | |
| 3. | | | |
| 4. | | | |
| Blouses | | | |
| 1. | | | |
| 2. | | | |
| Sweaters and short jackets | | | |
| 1. | | | |
| 2. | | | |
| 3. | | | |
| **WORK DRESSES** | | | |
| 1. | | | |
| 2. | | | |
| 3. | | | |
| 4. | | | |

|  | COLOR ON HAND | COLOR TO BUY | COST |
|---|---|---|---|
| **DRESSY DRESSES** | | | |
| 1. | | | $ |
| 2. | | | |
| 3. | | | |
| 4. | | | |
| **SPORTSWEAR** | | | |
| Pantsuits | | | |
| 1. | | | |
| 2. | | | |
| Jackets | | | |
| 1. | | | |
| 2. | | | |
| Slacks/jeans | | | |
| 1. | | | |
| 2. | | | |
| 3. | | | |
| 4. | | | |
| Shorts | | | |
| 1. | | | |
| 2. | | | |
| 3. | | | |
| Skirts | | | |
| 1. | | | |
| 2. | | | |
| 3. | | | |

|  | COLOR ON HAND | COLOR TO BUY | COST |
|---|---|---|---|
| Shirts | | | |
| 1. | | | $ |
| 2. | | | |
| 3. | | | |
| 4. | | | |
| Sweaters | | | |
| 1. | | | |
| 2. | | | |
| 3. | | | |
| **ACTIVE SPORTSWEAR** | | | |
| Tennis dress | | | |
| Swimsuits | | | |
| 1. | | | |
| 2. | | | |
| Beach cover-ups | | | |
| 1. | | | |
| 2. | | | |
| Ski pants | | | |
| 1. | | | |
| 2. | | | |
| Parka | | | |
| 1. | | | |
| 2. | | | |
| Other | | | |

| | COLOR ON HAND | COLOR TO BUY | COST |
|---|---|---|---|
| **LINGERIE** | | | |
| Bras | | | |
| 1. | | | $ |
| 2. | | | |
| 3. | | | |
| 4. | | | |
| strapless | | | |
| Girdles (if needed) | | | |
| panty | | | |
| regular | | | |
| Panties | | | |
| 1. | | | |
| 2. | | | |
| 3. | | | |
| 4. | | | |
| 5. | | | |
| 6. | | | |
| 7. | | | |
| Slips | | | |
| 1. | | | |
| 2. | | | |
| 3. | | | |
| 4. | | | |
| full length | | | |

|  | COLOR ON HAND | COLOR TO BUY | COST |
|---|---|---|---|
| Half slips | | | |
| 1. | | | $ |
| 2. | | | |
| Nightgowns | | | |
| short | | | |
| short | | | |
| long | | | |
| long | | | |
| Robes | | | |
| short | | | |
| long | | | |
| Hostess outfit | | | |
| **ACCESSORIES** | | | |
| Shoes | | | |
| 1. | | | |
| 2. | | | |
| 3. | | | |
| 4. | | | |
| 5. | | | |
| boots | | | |
| 1. | | | |
| 2. | | | |
| sandals | | | |
| 1. | | | |
| 2. | | | |

|  | COLOR ON HAND | COLOR TO BUY | COST |
|---|---|---|---|
| Gloves/mittens | | | |
| 1. | | | $ |
| 2. | | | |
| 3. | | | |
| 4. | | | |
| Hats | | | |
| 1. | | | |
| 2. | | | |
| 3. | | | |
| Belts | | | |
| 1. | | | |
| 2. | | | |
| 3. | | | |
| Scarves | | | |
| 1. | | | |
| 2. | | | |
| 3. | | | |

|  | COLOR ON HAND | COLOR TO BUY | COST |
|---|---|---|---|
| Hosiery | | | |
| pantyhose | | | $ |
| knee-hi's | | | |
| sport socks | | | |
| Handbags | | | |
| 1. | | | |
| 2. | | | |
| 3. | | | |
| Luggage large suitcase and/or wardrobe | | | |
| weekender | | | |
| cosmetic case and/or tote bag | | | |
| other | | | |

TOTAL COST OF NEW TROUSSEAU CLOTHES $ _____

# GUIDE TO BIRTH CONTROL

*Whether you and your husband choose to have children now, next year, or never, in all likelihood you will practice some form of birth control during the course of your marriage. And as your needs change through the years, you may want to vary the method you use as well. Because it's so important that you find the right contraceptive for you, we recommend that you research the various methods available today. Weigh the advantages and disadvantages, discuss them with your fiancé, then seek the advice of your own physician. To help you, we have worked with Planned Parenthood Federation of America Inc. to prepare this introductory chart of the choices open to you and your groom.*

| METHOD | AVAILABILITY | RELIABILITY | HOW IT WORKS | ADVANTAGES | DISADVANTAGES |
|---|---|---|---|---|---|
| **HORMONE PILLS** | Requires a doctor's prescription. Yearly checkup, including Pap test, breast exam, and blood pressure test recommended. In addition to fees for initial examination and regular checkups, pills cost about $2 to $4 per one-cycle supply. | Combination pills virtually 100 percent effective when taken according to directions. Mini-pills (no estrogen) slightly less effective. | Most regimens require one pill taken orally for 21 consecutive days each month to suppress ovulation. During the next seven days no pill (or an inert pill that maintains routine) is taken. Mini-pill is taken every single day. | Complete separation of pill-taking from sex so pleasure of both partners is unaffected; ease of use by most women. Other than mini-pill, nearly 100 percent effective. | Possibly nausea, headaches, weight gain, or breakthrough bleeding. There's a link between the pill, blood clots, and heart attack. Risk increases after age 30—especially for heavy smokers. |
| **INTRAUTERINE DEVICE (IUD)** | Available only through doctor. Device insertion and follow-up visit can range from $25–$65. Annual checkups are also necessary. Hormone releasing device, and IUDs using copper must be replaced periodically; check with doctor. | About as effective as mini-pills, as long as the device remains in place. | Presence of an IUD in the uterus prevents pregnancy—apparently by making it impossible for implantation of the egg to occur. | Second most effective method. Once inserted, an IUD requires user to check only occasionally to make sure device is in place. Does not affect sexual pleasure of couple. | IUD may be expelled, cause discomfort, bleeding. Some risk of perforation of uterus, tubal pregnancy, spontaneous abortion, or infection that in rare cases may cause infertility also possible. |
| **DIAPHRAGM** | Requires a doctor's, prescription and fitting. In addition to the physician's fee, you pay $3–$8 for the diaphragm and 10¢–20¢ per application for the spermicidal jelly or cream used with it. | Very effective when used regularly and properly. (Jelly or cream protects if diaphragm is displaced during sex.) Must be refitted every year, or after pregnancy, gain or loss of ten pounds. | A flexible rubber dome is inserted into the vagina prior to intercourse to cover the cervix and prevent sperm from entering the uterus. Sperm are immobilized by jelly or cream. Diaphragm must be left in place six hours after intercourse. | High level of protection with virtually no risk to health or interference with sexual pleasure (insertion can be a bedtime routine) of either partner during intercourse. | Some women have pelvic conditions that rule out use. It may become dislodged during sex if woman's on top. The need to add more cream or jelly during sex can inhibit spontaneity. |
| **CONDOM** | No prescription necessary. Varies in cost from about 25¢ each (for rubber sheaths) to $2 (for lubricated animal skin prophylactics). | About as effective as a diaphragm when used carefully, consistently. Some failures from slippage, puncture. | A thin sheath worn by the man during intercourse keeps sperm out of the vagina. A spermicidal barrier in the vagina can give extra protection. | High degree of protection against pregnancy and sexually transmitted diseases. No health hazards. | Interrupts sexual foreplay for some. Less direct genital contact may interfere with sex. Allergy to rubber in rare cases. |
| **AEROSOL FOAM** | No prescription or examination necessary. Complete kit, for 20–30 applications, costs about $5 in drug stores ($2–$3 for refills). | Less effective than prescription methods; fairly reliable when used consistently and according to instructions. | A pre-measured amount is injected into vagina no more than an hour before intercourse; the foam acts to immobilize the sperm. | Good degree of pregnancy prevention without a prescription or danger to either partner's health. | The need to use at time of intercourse and before each act may inhibit spontaneity, tends to be messy. |

| METHOD | AVAILABILITY | RELIABILITY | HOW IT WORKS | ADVANTAGES | DISADVANTAGES |
|---|---|---|---|---|---|
| **OTHER VAGINAL INSERTS** | No prescription necessary. Cost of different products ranges from about 10¢–20¢ per application. | Varies with type of product and brand, but all are less effective than foams. | Spermicidal jellies, creams, suppositories, or tablets are placed in the vagina shortly before intercourse to immobolize the sperm. | Relatively low cost and freedom from health hazards to either partner. | Sensitivity to chemicals sometimes causes irritation. Tablets and suppositories must dissolve in vagina. Like aerosol foams, only less effective. |
| **FERTILITY AWARENESS METHODS (FAM)** | Available to anyone at no cost (except for ovulation and temperature calendars, basal thermometer). Must learn to accurately calculate fertile period (variations in cervical mucus, body temperature will help). Consultation with doctor advised. | Varies with system used and with accuracy and consistency of records kept; generally less effective than other methods mentioned above. | Couples abstain a certain number of days each cycle—before, during, and after woman's ovulation usually amounting to about one week of cycle. | No health risks or side effects for either partner. Only birth control method officially sanctioned by the Roman Catholic Church. | Continuous recording of dates of menstrual cycles, and/or mucus consistency, and temperature required. Must note conditions (stress, illness) that may change cycle regularity. Risk of abnormal offspring due to fertilization of aging ovum. |
| **STERILIZATION** | Male: Vasectomy is a minor operation usually performed in doctor's office under a local anesthetic. Fees range from $75–$250. Female: Traditional tubal sterilization with hospital stay costs $500 and up. Newer procedures not requiring hospitilization cost $250–$500. | Male: Virtually fail-safe once the doctor has confirmed the absence of sperm in the ejaculate. Female: Virtually safe from pregnancy at all times. | Male: The tubes (vas) which carry sperm are blocked. Female: Tubes through which egg travels to uterus are closed off. For both, there is no impairment of sexual functioning. | Contraception is separated from the sexual act. The only method designed to provide permanent and complete birth control. | Reversal of male or female operation is difficult and fertility often is not restored. Female: Standard tubal ligation may be performed shortly after childbirth or abortion, or combined with other surgery; must be arranged well in advance. |
| **ABORTION** | The 1973 Supreme Court decision makes abortion legal in all 50 states. Operations must be performed by a physician and cost about $200 for a pregnancy under 12 weeks, $400 for hospitalization and abortion for a pregnancy 15–20 weeks. | Ends the present pregnancy but does not prevent future ones from occurring. | For a pregnancy under 12 weeks, vacuum aspirator is used. Past 12 weeks, the procedure may be done by stimulating the uterus to contract and empty, or by a mechanical evacuation method. | A pregnancy that might pose a physical, mental, or economic threat can be safely terminated, particularly if done early. | Complications occur least often with abortions before 12th week, but vaginal bleeding, infection, uterine perforation may occur. Repeated abortions may lessen ability to carry future pregnancy full term. |

## BIRTH CONTROL

### *Choose what's right for you*

No birth control method available today is perfect for every couple. So once you've read our "BRIDE'S Guide to Birth Control," you and your husband will have to choose what best meets your needs. Here's help.

Keep all newspaper and magazine articles that make you ask questions—books too. Your daily newspaper as well as women's magazines and books for women will publish recent findings on birth control.

Show them to your husband. Also show them to your doctor so you can get complete answers.

Shop for a gynecologist who *will* take you seriously, *won't* "push" his pet method. Don't be afraid to switch. Get names from your friends or County Medical Society. Or visit a Planned Parenthood or women's clinic (check "Clinics" in the Yellow Pages).

See the doctor three months before the wedding (TODAY, if you're having sex unprotected). Allow time to change methods.

Note before going to the gynecologist: the age you began menstruating; your history of cramps, spotting, missed periods, vaginal infections, pregnancy, serious illness; the dates your last period started and ended; the number of days in your last six menstrual cycles (count the first day of each period as "Day 1"); who in your family has had diabetes, heart disease, blood pressure problems, phlebitis, and breast, cervical, or uterine cancer; the brand and/or size of any pill, IUD, or diaphragm you've used; the name of any medication you're on.

Discuss friend's likes, dislikes—your husband's too. Does he turn on to the scent of foam? Rule out abortion in case of birth control failure? Remind him, however, that unless you choose condoms or vasectomy, *you and your body* bear any risk or nuisance.

Vow to share what responsibilities you can: put his condom on for him; assign him to dole out your pill; pay for foam out of the grocery—not your pocket—money; invite him to hear what the doctor says.

Match your method and temperament. Compulsive? You'll remember the diaphragm, foam and/or condom. Forgetful? Consider an IUD. Fastidious? The pill.

Have a back-up method on hand—perhaps foam for the month you miss two pills, a diaphragm to dam the IUD's heavier menstrual flow, so you don't have to skip sex.

Return to the doctor every six months to a year. Ask for pelvic and breast exams, Pap smear, blood-pressure check, urinalysis, and VD tests, as well as any needed pill prescription renewal or IUD or diaphragm refitting. Also go back any time some unfamiliar symptom (migraine, lower back pain, discharge, etc.) bothers you.

Reevaluate your birth control method as your needs change. Can't possibly risk a pregnancy? The pill may be best for you right now. Want to start a family soon? You may feel more comfortable with a diaphragm.

Use birth control faithfully, exactly as directed. Nothing works better than you.

## WHAT'S YOUR NAME?

## Here's everything you need to know about keeping it, changing it, living with it!

### ALL YOUR OPTIONS

What's in a name? A lot! Your name is uniquely personal—one of the things that make you *you*. So explore the options here, and make sure the married name you choose fits you and makes you feel proud!

**ADOPT HUSBAND'S NAME:** This is the most popular choice. If you're Mary Anne Smith and you marry John Jones, you become Mrs. Jones—also known as Mary Smith Jones (replacing middle name with maiden name) or Mary Anne Jones (swapping last names).

**KEEP YOUR OLD NAME:** How? Just continue to use it. Becoming Mrs. "His-Name" is custom, not generally the law. As long as more people know you as Mary Anne Smith than as Mrs. Jones, it's accepted as your legal name. Why keep your maiden name? Maybe you just can't imagine calling yourself anything else. Or maybe it's a matter of professional pride—you tried your first case as "Mary Smith," and it's a name you want to keep.

**BE MS. *AND* MRS.:** You may choose to lead a double life—Ms. (or Miss) Mary Smith in the office, Mrs. Mary Jones after hours. Lots of women do. Both names are legally recognized, as long as you have dual identification (like a birth certificate and marriage license). It's even possible to open your own bank account, maintain separate charge accounts, and apply for credit under your maiden name.

**HYPHENATE YOUR NAMES:** You and your husband might combine your surnames into one hyphenated last name, such as Smith-Jones. You're Mary Smith-Jones, he's John Smith-Jones, together you're Mr. and Mrs. Smith-Jones. Put his name first or your name first, depending on which sounds better. (If you have children, you can either have them adopt the hyphenated name or pick one last name for them to use.) It's not necessary to go through court proceedings to have a hyphenated name officially recognized—just start using it, and it will become accepted.

## "CALL ME"

MRS. JOHN OR MRS. MARY? Strict etiquette would call you "Mrs. John Jones" if you're married or widowed, "Mrs. Mary Jones" if divorced. Today, many women would rather be Mrs. Mary Jones, in any case.

WHAT DO YOU CALL YOURSELVES? Let your friends know by sending "at home" cards with your wedding announcements: "Mr. and Mrs. John Jones (or Mary Smith Jones and John Jones, or Mary Smith and John Jones)/will be at home/after May 1, 1980/12 Oak Avenue, Anytown, New York 12345." To business associates, send a card saying: "Ms. Mary Smith/announces she has adopted the surname of/Jones."

AT WEDDING TIME . . . Sign your maiden name to thank-yous written before the wedding—after, it's your married name alone, *never* "Mary and John Jones." Honeymooning with a passport in your maiden name? Bring your marriage license along for I.D. If you receive gift checks made out to "Mr. and Mrs. John Jones," sign your married name on the back.

## THE NEW YOU . . .

*Here is a convenient list for you to clip out and check off as you put your new married name on important papers and cards.*

- ☐ **Driver's license**—fill out a name change form at the Motor Vehicle Bureau, and they'll send you a new driver's license by mail.
- ☐ **Car Registration**—take your "pink slip" and your car registration to the Motor Vehicle Bureau.
- ☐ **Social Security**—notify your local social security office of the change, so they can send you a new card.
- ☐ **Income tax (Federal)**—use your new name and the same social security number on your next tax return.
- ☐ **Voter's Registration**—register your new name with

the County Clerk's office or your local polling place.
- ☐ **Passport**—fill out a new application form at your passport agency.
- ☐ **Bank accounts**—go to your bank and sign new signature cards. You can also change a single account to a joint account, if you wish.
- ☐ **Credit cards**—notify stores and companies; they'll issue new cards with your new name. To prevent theft, be sure to destroy your old cards.
- ☐ **Insurance**—get in touch with your insurance agent to make the necessary changes on life, health, automobile insurance policies.
- ☐ **School and Empoyer's Records**—notify the personnel office or registrar of the change so they can change mailing lists, etc.
- ☐ **Post Office**—have the post office list your old and new names with your new married address. Put both on your mailbox, if necessary. Also ask them to hold any mail that might be sent to your old address with your old name.

## GIVE YOURSELF SOME CREDIT!

Did you know that—single or married—it's important for you to establish credit in your own name? If all your new accounts read "Mr. and Mrs.," you may have no identity of your own in the eyes of creditors. A bank doesn't know that "Mrs. Jones" is the same person who paid off a college loan and managed five charge accounts as "Mary Smith." So if you ever need money (to start your own business, to put toward a house), it helps if you've earned your own credit rating. How do you do it?

**Use one name in all your financial dealings.** It might be Mary Smith or Mary Smith Jones. It should not be Mrs. John Jones.

**Maintain your own bank and charge accounts.** Expect to be treated as an individual—if a bank or card issuer wants to know about your husband's income or credit standing, tell them it's irrelevant since the account is yours, not his.

**Insist that creditors keep separate files on you and your husband both,** if you open any kind of joint account—it's your legal right. And make sure a credit card issued to you is your card, not just an "authorized user" card for his account. Want to know more about your own credit? Send all your questions to the Center for a Woman's Own Name, 261 Kimberly, Barrington, Illinois, 60010.

# HOW WELL DO YOU REALLY KNOW EACH OTHER?

Well enough to know you want to marry! But to make sure you haven't forgotten to discuss anything major (Does he _really_ expect to houseclean? Would you _gladly_ move if he got a job transfer?), answer True or False to the following statements. Ask your fiancé to do the same. Then check over each other's responses and talk about any surprises.

|  | YOU | HIM |
|---|---|---|
| **MONEY MATTERS** | | |
| You and your partner will share all assets, debts, and major financial decisions. | | |
| Each of you will have some money of your very own. | | |
| You expect to be chief bookkeeper in your home. | | |
| There's a certain standard of living you expect to achieve in a few years time. | | |
| You have worked out a budget you know you'll both be able to stick to. | | |
| You worry sometimes about your partner's spending and saving habits. | | |
| **JOBS** | | |
| You both plan to have full-time jobs. | | |
| Household chores will be divided up fairly between the two of you. | | |
| Your partner's job will probably outrank yours in real importance. | | |
| If your partner was offered a promising job elsewhere, you'd be willing to move. | | |
| **CHILDREN** | | |
| You both want children, and you agree on how many and when. | | |
| If you do have children, you'd expect to quit your job. | | |
| You're content with the contraceptive you've decided to use. | | |
| If you found you couldn't have children of your own, you'd consider adopting. | | |
| You will probably be more responsible for child-raising than your partner. | | |
| You do not totally object to abortion. | | |
| Someday you might consider sterilization. | | |
| **SEX** | | |
| It's easy to discuss sex with your partner. | | |
| You feel largely responsible for your partner's sexual pleasure. | | |
| There's a right time and place for sex (like only at night or only in bed). | | |
| You'd feel obliged to have sex even if you weren't in the mood. | | |
| If you ever had a sex problem, you'd consider going for professional help. | | |
| **LEISURE TIME** | | |
| You expect to spend almost all of your free time together. | | |
| It's important to spend some time away from each other. | | |
| You'd give up your favorite activity if your partner didn't share your interest. | | |
| You plan to take annual vacations away from home together. | | |
| If you have children, you wouldn't feel obliged to do everything as a family. | | |
| **FRIENDS** | | |
| Now that you have each other, you really don't need friends as much as before. | | |
| You expect friends to give you ample warning before dropping by for visits. | | |
| You'd object to your partner having a close personal friend of the opposite sex. | | |
| You should share each other's friends, whether you really like them or not. | | |
| You tell your best friend _everything_. | | |
| **RELATIVES** | | |
| You plan to see your family regularly, and certainly on holidays. | | |
| If you ever were in need, you'd expect parents to help out. | | |
| You wouldn't mind having a parent live with you someday. | | |
| **RELIGION** | | |
| You plan to attend religious services regularly. | | |
| If you have children, you'd raise them in a particular faith. | | |
| You'd prefer sending any children to religious-affiliated schools. | | |
| Religious traditions will be observed in your home. | | |
| You will make regular religious donations. | | |

## YOUR MONOGRAM

Once you've chosen the name you'll use after you marry, you may also want to select a monogram to personalize such things as your silver, towels, stationery.

There was a time when almost every wedding gift—from pillowcases to crystal stemware—bore a monogram. Today, many gifts come without, since many brides prefer no monogram. Or if they do want something monogrammed (maybe just one set of "company" towels or a special silver tray), they have it done themselves after the wedding. This way, you can avoid the "no exchange" rule that usually applies to monogrammed gifts, and make sure your monograms will read as you want them to (especially if you are keeping your own name after marriage, but your friends and relatives don't know it yet). Another way to get the monogram style you want: list it at the Wedding Gift Registry so gift-givers will know.

The letters of the customary three-part monogram are the bride's initials—that of her first name, maiden name, and new last name, in that order, provided the letters in the monogram design are all the same size. But if one letter is larger than the others, it's the new married name initial. You also may want a combination of your first name initial, your husband's first initial, and your married initial above or below the other two. Whichever you prefer, caution: if your initials spell a word, like BAD or JAR, choose a monogram design in which the last initial is in the center and larger than the other two, bDa, or jRa.

Where to put your monogram? Simple silver is a "natural" for marking. Many patterns even have a monogram shield. Very ornate silver is sometimes marked on the back although this can't be done with knives that are decorated all around. Some silver styles have their own alphabets specially designed to harmonize with them. And often the silver monogram most easily engraved is a single initial—that of your married last name. Plain linens make the most of a monogram. Patterned linens usually don't show off a monogram well unless the pattern is limited to a narrow border—printed, woven, or embroidered. Some jacquard towels have plain areas in the design where a monogram may be placed to advantage.

Your monogram design might vary to suit the item that'll carry it. Styles range from traditional to contemporary, from ornate to tailored. Four popular ones are sketched here. 1. Elaborate intertwined initials: handsome for everything but very modern silver and linens. 2. Block capitals in a triangle—centered with a star: great for simple silver and stationery. 3. Tailored oval or diamond shapes: good for pretty much anything (and there are similar triangles best suited to linens, stationery). 4. Three letters not contained in a shape, with either the middle letter or the last one the largest; pretty for linens or stationery; ideal for silver if the center letter is largest.

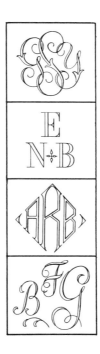

## YOUR MARRIAGE LICENSE

Apply together for your license at the city clerk's office two or three weeks before your wedding. You will need proof that you are of age or that you have your parents' consent to marry and proof of citizenship if you were not born in the United States. And you will both need doctor's certificates verifying the results of your blood tests and physical examinations.

There is usually a waiting period (perhaps two to three days) to get the results, and the certificate is good for a maximum time limit (usually about 30 days). Keep this limit and the valid period of your marriage license (usually 30 days) in mind when you make a date to get the license. Your groom usually pays the fee.

## MARRIAGE LICENSE CHECKLIST

Date we go for the marriage license _____ Time _____

Office of City Clerk _____

        Building _____

        Address _____

        Phone _____

Fee $ _____

We both need

_____ Identification (Driver's license, birth certificate)

_____ Proof of age

_____ Citizenship papers

_____ Doctor's certificates

_____ Proof of divorce

Waiting period _____ License is valid _____ days

# 6

---

# Your
# Wedding
# Ceremony

At last, the BIG DAY. By now, you should have nothing to think about—nothing but your groom. You won't if you and your wedding party run through the procession, ceremony line-up, and recessional at the rehearsal. Then after a good night's sleep (you couldn't?), try to eat a little something. Dress with the help of your maids. Review the ceremony schedule (relax—if you forget, someone *will* be there to help). And even if it means a tear or two on your wedding makeup, spend a few moments alone with your parents. It's a day for families, a day for love.

## YOUR WEDDING CEREMONY TIMETABLE

Worried you'll get to the church to find chaos? The ushers haven't arrived, guests aren't seated, the aisle canvas is still bundled up. That won't happen if you follow this schedule. Figure out when "two hours to go," "one hour to go," etc., is for you, write up your timetable, and give copies to everyone concerned. This schedule is for a formal wedding 15 minutes' drive from the bride's home. Live further away? Allow yourself extra time for unexpected traffic jams.

**TWO HOURS TO GO** Start dressing with the help of your mother and honor attendants. If any maids are dressing at your home, they put on their outfits now.

**ONE HOUR TO GO** Attendants who've gotten ready elsewhere join you at your home to have pictures taken and to pick up flowers. Your parents should finish dressing too, so family photos can be made.

**45 MINUTES TO GO** Ushers arrive at the ceremony site, pin on boutonnieres, place massbooks and wedding programs in pews. They also collect seating plans from head ushers, wait for guests to arrive.

**30 MINUTES TO GO** Organist starts playing introductory music in the church. Meanwhile ushers show guests their places, starting with the main aisle pews behind those kept for family. Your attendants and mother leave home for the church.

**20 MINUTES TO GO** Groom and best man arrive and await the bridal party in the vestibule. Clergymember checks marriage license, receives his fee, gives any last-minute instructions to the groom and ushers. You and your father leave for the church.

**TEN MINUTES TO GO** Your attendants show up, followed by your mother, groom's parents, other close family members. Wedding party and family wait in the vestibule. Relatives are shown to reserved pews.

**FIVE MINUTES TO GO** Groom's parents are seated in the front pew on the right of the main aisle. You and your father arrive about this time, and join the wedding party. Any late-coming guests who are waiting are seated. The last person to take her place is your mother. Musical solo begins.

**ONE MINUTE TO GO** Two ushers lay the aisle canvas. If white ribbons are being used to rope off the pews, the same two ushers should do this after the bride's mother is in her seat. They then return to the vestibule for the procession.

**CEREMONY TIME** Clergymember takes his or her position at the front of the church. Groom, accompanied by best man, stands ready. The procession music begins and, "Here Comes the Bride"—you!

The procession for a formal wedding traditionally lines up like this:

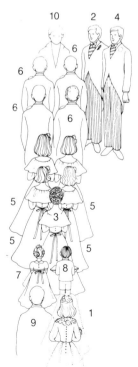

PROCESSION: 1) Bride, 2) Groom, 3) Maid or Matron of Honor, 4) Best Man, 5) Bridesmaids, 6) Ushers, 7) Flower Girl, 8) Ring bearer, 9) Father of the Bride, 10) Clergymember. (Junior Bridesmaid would precede maid or matron of honor.)

A longer procession that includes the bride's and groom's parents and grandparents, if desired (a Jewish custom), lines up like this:

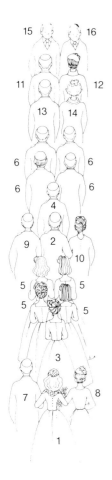

FAMILY PROCESSION (TRADITIONAL JEWISH): 1) Bride, 2) Groom, 3) Maid or Matron of Honor, 4) Best Man, 5) Bridesmaids, 6) Ushers, 7) Father of the Bride, 8) Mother of the Bride, 9) Father of the Groom, 10) Mother of the Groom, 11) Bride's Grandfather, 12) Bride's Grandmother, 13) Groom's Grandfather, 14) Groom's Grandmother, 15) Cantor, 16) Rabbi. (Flower Girl and Ring Bearer, if any, precede bride and her parents.)

The procession stands at the altar like this:

AT THE ALTAR: 1) Bride, 2) Groom, 3) Maid or Matron of Honor, 4) Best Man, 5) Bridesmaids, 6) Ushers, 7) Flower Girl, 8) Ring Bearer , 9) Father of the Bride, 10) Clergymember.

When parents are included—as in many Jewish weddings—it's like this:

JEWISH WEDDING: 1) Bride, 2) Groom, 3) Maid or Matron of Honor, 4) Best Man, 5) Bridesmaids, 6) Ushers, 7) Father of the Bride, 8) Mother of the Bride, 9) Father of the Groom, 10) Mother of the Groom, 11) Rabbi.

After the ceremony, everyone pairs up for the recessional:

RECESSIONAL: 1) Bride, 2) Groom, 3) Maid of Honor, 4) Best Man, 5) Bridesmaids, 6) Ushers, 7) Flower Girl, 8) Ring Bearer .

## SPECIAL VARIATIONS

*If your father has died,* you may ask your brother, uncle, cousin, mother, or a close relative, a family friend, or an usher to escort you down the aisle. Then your mother may give you away. In some ceremonies, she merely nods or says "I do," from her place in the first row at the appropriate time. When the bride's right hand is placed in the clergymember's hand, the best man usually escorts the bride's mother to her side.

*If your parents are divorced,* your father may still give you away. Instead of sitting down with your mother, however, he takes his place in the third row. If you prefer, your stepfather or another male relative to whom you feel very close may walk you down the aisle. If divorced parents are included in the Jewish procession, only the parent and stepparent who raised the bride or groom takes part. In this case the multiplicity of grandparents may be overwhelming and they may all, properly, be seated.

## SEMI-FORMAL WEDDINGS

Most formal wedding procedures also apply to semiformal weddings. A smaller wedding party seldom includes children, unless they are the children of a bride or groom marrying again. There are usually fewer guests at a semiformal wedding, and pew ribbons, aisle carpets, and canopies are usually omitted if you don't wear a long wedding dress and train.

## INFORMAL WEDDINGS

Guests at an informal wedding seat themselves as soon as they arrive. When it's time for the ceremony to begin, you and your groom, the honor attendant and the best man all take your appointed places in front of the judge or clergy. At the end of the short ceremony, without a recessional, you'll turn to greet your guests.

# 7

# THE RECEPTION

WOW! It's a party, just about the best one you've ever been to. And it's *your* reception. Make sure it's as happy a time for everyone else as it is for you two. Do up a schedule of what's to come, give it to your mother (the official hostess), the banquet manager, the orchestra leader, and a friend or family member who can see things go smoothly. Greet all the guests in the receiving line. Circulate, try to speak again to each person during the party. Ask the photographer to snap those closest to you. Let them all laugh with you when you cut the cake, toss the bouquet and garter, "escape" under a shower of rice. It's fun. Especially when your date for the party is your husband!

# YOUR WEDDING RECEPTION

Fun—that's what your wedding reception is for. So here's a timetable for the most common kind of wedding reception—a buffet lasting about three hours—that'll give you plenty of time to greet each guest, do a little eating and dancing, see that everyone enjoys himself. Of course, there's no reason the party can't go on longer and the schedule adjusted to suit your needs. Fill in the times you want everything at *your* wedding reception to happen.

_____ Cars arrive with you and all members of the wedding party at the reception site.

### The first half-hour:
_____ Bridal party gathers for a few quick photos, while any musicians start to play.

### The second half-hour:
_____ Bridal party forms the receiving line, guests begin to pass by. Drinks or punch cups are poured, guests mingle, pick up table-seating cards, if any.

### After one hour:
_____ Buffet is announced. Wedding party are seated. Guests line up for buffet. Wedding party are served. Best man proposes first toast. Musicians continue playing.

### After one and one-half hours:
_____ First course is cleared from head table. Musicians strike up dance music; traditional first dance begins.

### After two hours:
_____ Tables are cleared. Musicians signal time for cake-cutting ceremony. Cake is cut. Dancing music resumes. Dessert is served.

### The last half-hour:
_____ Bride and groom throw bouquet and garter.

_____ Bride and groom slip away to change, say good-bye to parents. Honeymoon time!

_____ Bride and groom run out to their car in a shower of rice.

_____ Parents signal musicians to stop playing, bar, if any, to close, bid farewell to guests.

# YOUR RECEIVING LINE

*The receiving line at your wedding will be as much fun for you as it is for your guests—if you take the time to plan it.*

Left to right: Bride's mother, groom's mother, groom's father, bride, groom, honor attendant, maids.

One of the nicest ways for you, your groom, and both families to meet all the wonderful people at your wedding is in the receiving line. Just think, you'll finally get to shake hands with his zany Uncle Charlie—your maids can get a look at your two handsome cousins. When's the best time to have the receiving line? It's usually formed as wedding guests arrive at the reception hall. But some brides prefer it right after the ceremony in the church vestibule. Your mother should head the line. As the host, your father usually circulates among the guests. The rest of the traditional line-up is shown above. Ushers, flower girls, ring bearers are not included. If you're having a reception of 200 or more, you can streamline things by including your honor attendant, but omitting bridesmaids. What if your situation's special? Divorced parents who host the wedding *together,* line up the same way. If your stepmother's the hostess, though, she would greet guests. Your groom's stepmother would stand in line if, for some reason, his real mother can't attend. Marrying again? Unless your reception's very small, you'll *want* the families to meet and, for this, the receiving line's perfect!

Keep the party going and the receiving line flowing smoothly. Set up a buffet table not far from the end of the line. You might serve just simple little tea sandwiches and punch if you're planning a sit-down meal to follow. That way, after the guests have a chance to say their personal hellos, they'll just naturally move on and mingle. A refreshment table is also a good way guests can meet *other* guests. "Excuse me, I overheard you saying that you went to school with the bride. I'm her Aunt Betty." More helpful suggestions for a successful receiving line listed *below.*

● Go over the guest list with your mother and his, so names will be fresh in your minds.
● Introduce yourself if you don't know a guest. Chances are the person will take the hint and offer his or her name in return.
● Smile at everyone, shake hands, and say just a few words of welcome.
● Present each guest to the person standing next to you, in the receiving line
● Don't panic if you forget a name or two. Just give a friendly smile and ask.
● Take rings off your right hand to avoid painful handshakes (for guests too).
● Take off your gloves—skin contact is much friendlier when you shake hands.
● Rub a little cream anti-perspirant on your palms to keep them from sweating.
● Visit the bathroom before you form the line. Suggest that your maids do too.
● Set a small table behind the receiving line to hold the wedding party bouquets.
● Ask ushers to bring thirsty hand-shakers some refreshments (a glass of champagne?).
● Don't smoke in the receiving line.

# Reception seating the easy way

*How to make sure everyone at the wedding sits in the "right" place, so they'll be sure to have a good time!*

At the Bride's Table, notice how seating is on one side, so that guests can see you. (any centerpiece should be low for the same reason). You and your groom sit in the middle of the table. He's on your left, on your right's the best man. The maid of honor is on your groom's left. Groomsmen, bridesmaids alternate on each side of the table.

At the Parents' Table, your mother and father sit opposite each other (here, far left and right). Your groom's mother, a guest of honor, sits on your father's right. On your mother's right put the clergymember or your groom's father. If it's the clergymember, your groom's father goes on your mother's left (shown here). In other seats: grandparents, out-of-town relatives, clergymember's spouse or assistant.

**Mix family and friends together at the guest tables.** Place people next to "strangers" you know they'll like. Keep in mind interests, occupations. Your Aunt Agatha, a volunteer at the city zoo, is a natural next to your groom's friend George who just returned from an African wildlife preserve. As at any party, alternate men and women at the tables. They'll all have more fun this way. Seat husbands and wives at the same table, but *not* next to each other (though you might put engaged couples together). Put spouses of married attendants at guest tables, *not* at the Bride's Table (but do seat them there if the wedding party is small). You'll want your relatives sitting next to his family members. After trading stories about the two of you, they'll feel like old friends!

**Consider creating special tables for special people.** If your parents are divorced, have two parents' tables. That way the parent who is not hosting your wedding can sit with good friends, favorite cousins and really feel at home. Small, informal wedding? You and your attendants can sit with both sets of parents, some relatives too at one big head table. Children at your reception? Do seat them next to their parents, but after they've finished eating, have a game table set up in a corner of the room for quiet play. Lots of young adults, single friends? Have a "singles table"—your friends will feel more at ease, and who knows, may just meet their future bride or groom.

**Let your guests know where to sit.** Small reception? Placecards will do. For a larger gathering, you might number tables, put a seating chart ("Martha Jones— Table 9") on a table near the entrance to the reception hall, or near the guest book so guests can find their way easily.

**Plan on having a few tables at a stand-up reception.** Everyone will need a place to rest glasses, hors d'oeuvres (especially if food is hot). Do circulate among guests, introduce them to new people so that they will all have a good time, and your reception will be a celebration!

# THE FIRST DANCE

The traditional "first dance" is your first as bride and groom. But there's no reason why your guests shouldn't begin dancing as soon as they have cleared the receiving line and the music starts playing. After you've caught your breath from greeting the guests, there is a pause in the music—or the strains of "Here Comes the Bride"—the floor clears, and dancing resumes with you and your groom circling the floor alone. You are next claimed by your father while your groom dances with his new mother-in-law. The best man and the father of the groom are your next two partners, while your husband takes your maid of honor and his own mother around the floor. The order of these traditional dances is optional, but they are usually completed before the guests join in again. You'll probably dance with each usher and your groom with each bridesmaid before the dancing ends. It's also customary for each man in the wedding party to request a dance with each bridesmaid and both mothers.

# THE CAKE-CUTTING CEREMONY

**THE CAKE-CUTTING IS A CEREMONY IN ITSELF.** The time: an hour after the receiving line disbands at a tea or cocktail reception, or at a dinner, before dessert. The band might signal with "The Bride Cuts the Cake." A friend or the banquet manager can also tell you when to go over to the cake table, or to get ready for the waiters to carry it in. If the maids and ushers line up on either side of the table, the guests *will* gather. Then, hand over hand, you two can cut into the bottom layer.

(Do feed each other the first slice—it's a great snapshot.) Serve peices to your parents next. The caterer or friends can take over from there, cutting the cake according to the baker's instructions. Don't forget to see that the top gets saved for your first anniversary. Tape it in heavy paper and freeze, or if it's a fruitcake, wrap in a brandy-soaked cloth and bury it in a tin of powdered sugar.

**A PRETTY CAKE TABLE SHOULD BE ALL SET UP**—complete with be-ribboned knife—before the cake is delivered. A long, lacy cloth, maybe covering a pastel liner, or a creamy linen one (borrow, or ask the caterer to bring it) makes a perfect table-topper. So do flowers. Order a special arrangement, or plan on displaying your bouquet there. Most important: make sure the table stands in a spot where people can admire the cake—but far enough out of the way (*not* near the receiving line) where it won't get toppled.

Along with the cake at your wedding should come something to toast with—real champagne, bubbly sherbet and ginger ale punch, or that classic accompaniment of sweets—just a bit of sherry. It's nice if a full cup is waiting for each guest at the end of the receiving line. Then the best man can propose the first toast—you two stay seated (if you are). In return, your groom (you too) can raise his glass and thank all pres— your mother next, and on as long as you wish. Another idea: serve a beverage reminiscent of your heritage—Spanish sangria, Japanese plum wine. If you're Jewish, you already may have sipped two wines during the ceremony—one dry to represent the sorrows in life you'll share, one sweet to symbolize the joys. A French custom: the couple drink first from a big bowl of wine, or "marriage cup," then carry it around together, serving everyone as a gesture of community sharing.

## THROWING THE BOUQUET AND GARTER

Just before you change into your going-away clothes, word is passed to the bridesmaids and other single women to gather at the bottom of a stairway, under a balcony or at some other convenient spot. If your going-away flowers are part of your bridal bouquet, remove them first. If you carry a prayerbook instead of a bouquet, you may throw the floral and ribbon streamers. Some brides turn and toss the bouquet over a shoulder, but if you'd like to aim at your sister or dear friend, you'll probably face the group as you throw. Tradition says that the woman who catches the bouquet will be the next bride.

The bride's garter (usually blue satin) may be thrown to the ushers and other bachelors. The groom removes it from your leg and you toss it, as you tossed the bouquet, with the man who catches it destined to be the next to marry.

# 8

# Your Honeymoon

The thing nobody ever tells you is how tired you can get from all the wedding activity. How little chance you two may have had to be alone. You *need* a honeymoon (even if you've slept together before). To unwind, to get reacquainted. So talk now about what you'd really like to do (just sleep? bat a tennis ball around?), where you've *always* imagined it would be (Hawaii? your grandmother's cottage?). Shop the travel agents. Get brochures. Budget carefully. Pack carefully—then GO!

# HASSLE-FREE HONEYMOON PLANNING

The beckoning brochures, the welter of fare facts, the confusion of friendly advice have a way of making travel planning look difficult to impossible at the start. But the sorting, the choosing, the dreaming ahead become part of the fun when you take things step-by-step. To start with . . .

**Talk things over** as early as you possibly can, and as honestly. Early is important because the more time you have, the better your chance of getting exactly the space in the place at the time you want instead of having to settle for almost perfect or pay more for accommodations because the rooms in your price range are all taken. "Honestly" means each of you being clear how you— personally—would really like it to be. Resist the temptation to white-lie just a little for each other's "sake"—it can only confuse things. Instead . . .

**Get specific.** Even though you're sure you know, double-check each other on basics. How do you want to spend your time? Doing the Big Town? Playing the sport game? Lazing away on a beach? Next, focus in on specific activities: beaching, tennis, golf, skiiing, other sports, shopping, sightseeing, museuming, scenery-rambling, gourmet eating, night-clubbing, and so on. Then store these in your memory place while you . . .

**Write away** for full information about destinations that seem likely to fit your dream patterns. BRIDE'S booklet listings are a good starting point; a single coupon can bring response from so many different directions. To learn more about travel in foreign countries, consult government tourist offices (check your nearest big city phone book, or write us for addresses of the ones that appeal to you). For travel facts about cities, contact the appropriate Convention & Visitors Bureau (e.g., New York Convention & Visitors Bureau, San Francisco Convention & Visitors Bureau, etc.). Write to airline tour departments or call at their ticket offices for timetables, fare facts, package tour booklets. Write hotel chain headquarters, individual resorts or their local representatives (listed in the Yellow Pages) for brochures, rate sheets, and honeymoon package details; to train and bus lines for info on all-American touring. Now, getting all your facts together . . .

**Balance time and money budgets.** Timing makes your dollars go further whenever you take advantage of night-flight savings, weekday, excursion, and special fares on land and in the air. Always ask about these. And investigate off-season travel too. Europe's best-buy months are in winter and spring when you can take advantage of bargain-priced eight-day GIT

packages to see the lively sites. In mid-April the savings shift to the Bahamas, the Caribbean, and Mexico's sunny coast resorts where hotel rates drop a dramatic 30 to 50 percent below winter highs and stay there till half past December.

In the timing-for-its-own-sake department, try to strike a reasonable balance between the hours you'll spend in transit and total days away. Make four hours' travel time your maximum one-way trip limit if you're going to be away less than a week. For longer stays and good place reasons (like a chance to see Europe or Hawaii), you can lengthen train and plane time spent. But be easy on yourselves: don't over-program your first few days away.

When it comes to money budgeting, transportation, transfers (between home and airport, airport and hotel), hotel room, and meals are clearly the big basics. Prices depend on so many variables that no "overall average" figures have much meaning. Costs for two might run anywhere from $30 to $50 a day in a National Park or a Mexican village that's really away from it all to $150 and up at a luxury resort without being out of line. Generally, you can count on city stays costing more than countryside rambling and Modified American Plan rates (including breakfasts and dinners) saving lots compared to the total cost of meals bought separately. Packaged trips often mean worthwhile economy as well as easier planning and cost estimating. Finally, allow for: tipping (about 15 percent of your total budget), shopping, personal expenses (like beauty salon and barber shop visits), bar bills, and airport taxes (up to $10 per person). With the figures in mind and brochures in hand, you're now ready to . . .

**Narrow the field** and start corresponding with hotels, resorts, and air, cruise, bus, or railroad lines. There is no reason on earth why you can't make your own reservations—especially if transportation and a hotel stay are all that's involved. However, if it's your first big trip or arrangements are at all complex, we strongly recommend that you . . .

**Consult your friendly neighborhood travel agent**— who can supply first-hand insights that can make final decision-making a lot easier, clarify fare situations, and answer last-minute queries, then take over all the arrangements-making chores—from hotel reservations to visa applications (not passports) and issuing traveler's checks. Here's where friends' recommendations can be a real help. Also reassuring: a seal that indicates membership in the American Society of Travel Agents, the national association that sets professional standards for the industry. Ideally, you should talk with the agency person who's most recently been where you're going. For all this expert care, you'll probably pay little or no extra since agents are paid commissions by carriers, tour operators, and hotels whose services they sell.

Approximately ten days before take-off you'll be presented with an all-important envelope containing your itinerary, tickets, transfer coupons, hotel confirmations, sightseeing vouchers. At which time you pay and . . .

**Double-check the details**—more to get them fixed in your mind than to unearth agency errors (though if there are any of those, you've still got time to mend them).

**Finally, promise yourselves** you'll try to keep your luggage count down to two bags per person—one to carry on, one to check (and both properly tagged with names and address, or the airlines won't accept them); remind each other to reconfirm flight (24 hours ahead of time is the domestic rule; it's 72 hours overseas), or you might find yourselves left seatless; keep your things about you by making and keeping a packing list, using as few hotel drawers as possible, never vacating a hotel room without taking one last look at the back of the bathroom door; leave yourselves plenty of check-out and getting-to-the-airport time (then slight hitches won't make you jittery); and hide enough money in the depths of a suitcase for the airport head tax (times two), for coffee, and a taxi home. And that you'll plan on a beautiful time because, you know, you will.

# HONEYMOON TRAVEL CHECKLIST

Travel Agent _____

Address _____ Phone _____

Cable address _____

Agent's representative at destination site _____

Address _____ Phone _____

Cable address _____

## TRANSPORTATION

Air, Rail, Ship, or Bus Line _____

Ticketing Address _____ Phone _____

|  | Departure | Return |
|---|---|---|
| Date | _____ | _____ |
| Ticket Number | _____ | _____ |
| Airport or Station | _____ | _____ |
| Flight or Route Number | _____ | _____ |
| Class | _____ | _____ |
| Take-off Time | _____ | _____ |
| Arrival Time | _____ | _____ |

Confirmation date_____ Transportation cost $ _____

Car Rental Agent _____

Address _____ Phone _____

Make and model of car reserved _____

Pick-up and Drop-off site _____

Terms of charges _____

Estimated car rental cost $_____

## YOUR ROOM

Hotel or motel _____

Address _____ Phone _____

Phone for reservations (800) _____

Cable address _____

Manager or assistant manager _____

Check-in Date _____ Time _____ Check-out Date _____ Time _____

Description of room _____

Daily rate _____ Total room cost $_____

## MEAL PLAN

European (none)_____Continental (just a light breakfast)_____

Modified American (breakfast, dinner)_____American (breakfast, lunch, dinner) _____

Other_____

Total meal cost $_____

## HONEYMOON PACKAGE ACTIVITIES

1. What _____

   Where _____

   Date_____ Time _____

   Reserved _____ Optional _____ Voucher:Yes _____ No _____

2. What _____

   Where _____

   Date_____ Time _____

   Reserved _____ Optional _____ Voucher:Yes _____ No _____

3. What _____

   Where _____

   Date_____ Time _____

   Reserved _____ Optional _____ Voucher:Yes _____ No _____

4. What _____

   Where _____

   Date_____ Time _____

   Reserved _____ Optional _____ Voucher:Yes _____ No _____

5. What _____

   Where _____

   Date_____ Time _____

   Reserved _____ Optional _____ Voucher:Yes _____ No _____

6. What _____

   Where _____

   Date_____ Time _____

   Reserved _____ Optional _____ Voucher:Yes _____ No _____

## POCKET MONEY

| Form | $ | Amount or Limit |
|---|---|---|
| Single dollar bills ($10-15 is good) | | |
| Other cash | | |
| Traveler's checks | | |
| Bankbook checks | | |
| Credit cards (American Express, Bank America, Diner's Club, Master Charge, oil company cards) | | |
| Foreign currency, if any | | |

Total pocket money _____

Total cost of honeymoon _____

## TO CARRY

_____ Driver's license

_____ Proof of age, citizenship (birth certificate, voter registration card)

_____ Marriage license

_____ Passport or visa, if needed

_____ Names, addresses, phone numbers of all parents, with notation of time difference between their homes and your honeymoon spot

_____ Hometown doctor's name, address, phone number

_____ Copies of any prescriptions (for eye glasses, contraceptives, etc.)

_____ List of all credit card numbers

_____ List of all traveler's check numbers

_____ Checking account number

_____ Name, address, phone number, and cable address of home banker (in case you run out of money)

_____ Shopping and gift list with everyone's sizes

_____ Names, addresses, phone numbers of local friends, relatives to call

_____ List of recommended restaurants, sights, etc. in honeymoon area

_____ List of luggage contents (needed for claiming any losses)

You may know where you're going to honeymoon. But do you know what to take, and in what bags? Probably not. Begin by making two lists—what you're likely to be doing each day, then all the clothes you'd need for those activities. Now rate each item. Is the fabric good for travel? Can you wear it more than once? Does it fit into a basic color plan? "Yes" votes go on your packing list. Here are sample lists for three different honeymoons.

## FOR A TENNIS WEEKEND

1 all-weather coat or jacket

1 sporty, daytime outfit (jeans and T-shirt?)

1 pair of casual sandals

1 long evening outfit

1 slip (if needed)

2 pairs of pantyhose (if needed)

1 pair dressy sandals

1 evening bag

1 cardigan sweater

1 cotton bandana

2 tennis outfits

1 tennis hat or visor

2 pairs of tennis socks

1 pair of tennis shoes

1 nightgown

1 travel robe

1 pair packable slippers

3 sets of underwear

1 tennis racket

1 can of tennis balls

1 bathing suit, cover-up, cap, beach towel (if needed)

## FOR A WEEK IN THE SUN

1 all-weather coat

1 blazer

1 cardigan sweater

2 pairs of casual slacks

1 pair of dressy slacks

1 pair of shorts for bicycling

3 washable tops

1 sun hat or cotton bandana

1 pair comfy, casual sandals

2 long evening outfits

1 slip (if needed)

2 pairs of pantyhose (if needed)

1 pair of dressy sandals

1 evening bag

1 nightgown

1 travel robe

4 sets of underwear

2 bathing suits

1 beach cover-up

1 bathing cap (if needed)

1 beach towel

1 travel robe

1 pair of packable slippers

## FOR TWO WEEKS ABROAD

1 all-weather coat

2 three-piece suits (interchangeable blazers, pants, skirts)

4 washable T-shirts and/or blouses

1 cardigan sweater

2 pairs of walking shoes

2 long evening outfits (a shawl too?)

1 pair of dressy shoes

1 evening bag

3 pairs of pantyhose

2 slips

6 sets of underwear

1 nightgown

1 travel robe

1 pair of packable slippers

1 folding umbrella

*if summer, add:* bathing suit, beach cover-up, beach towel, sandals, shorts, sneakers.

*if winter, add:* boots, gloves, scarf, two wool tops

# HONEYMOON BEAUTY BAG

Check off which beauty aids *below* (you won't need them all) to pack for your trip.

- ☐ foundation makeup
- ☐ blusher
- ☐ powder
- ☐ under-eye coverup
- ☐ eyeshadow
- ☐ mascara
- ☐ eyeliner
- ☐ eyebrow pencil
- ☐ lipstick
- ☐ lip gloss
- ☐ facial moisturizer
- ☐ toner or astringent
- ☐ blemish cream
- ☐ shampoo
- ☐ cream rinse/ conditioner
- ☐ electric rollers
- ☐ blower dryer
- ☐ hair clips or bobby pins
- ☐ hair brush
- ☐ comb
- ☐ shower cap
- ☐ wash cloth
- ☐ nail brush
- ☐ body moisturizer
- ☐ body powder
- ☐ deodorant
- ☐ razor or depilatory
- ☐ razor blades
- ☐ toothbrush
- ☐ toothpaste
- ☐ purse-size breath freshener or mouthwash
- ☐ emery boards
- ☐ nail polish
- ☐ polish remover pads
- ☐ nail clippers or scissors
- ☐ tweezers
- ☐ cotton swabs
- ☐ prescription medicines
- ☐ aspirin
- ☐ first-aid kit
- ☐ extra contact lenses or glasses
- ☐ contact lens solution
- ☐ contraceptives
- ☐ sanitary napkins tampons
- ☐ sun screen or tanning lotion
- ☐ needle and thread
- ☐ safety pins
- ☐ travel-size clothes detergent
- ☐ bottle opener

# HONEYMOON PACKING

## The Inside Story

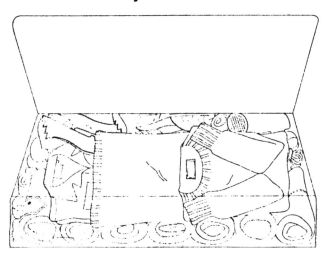

**1** Pack all your bulky things first—shoes, hairdryer, travel iron. Lay shoes heel to toe against hinge side of bag, place the other items there too. You want heavyweights nearest the ground when you're carrying the bag, so lighter-weight items on top can't get crushed.

**2** Make a layer of all no-wrinkle separates next—jeans, T-shirts, sweaters, beach towel, underwear. Roll them up tightly (this is especially smart if your bag is soft-sided— rolled up clothes will move with the give-and-take, still stay neatly pressed). Fill up all the empty spaces—put a padding of panties around hairdryer. Snugly packed clothes can't move around, rumple.

**3** Now put in everything that requires careful folding—linen slacks, cotton jackets, silk dresses. The secret is to make as few folds as possible. Lay slacks out flat, lining up creases, then fold in half. Fold each dress at the waist and pack lengthwise, skirt on bottom. Alternate collars and waistbands at opposite sides of the suitcase. Put plastic between layers to act as a cushion against wrinkles. (Plastic dry cleaner bags are economical, yet plastic trash bags can also tote your dirty laundry and wet swimsuits later on.)

**4** Find extra space for belts and fun jewelry inside your shoes.

**5** Consider packing a collapsible suitcase you can fill later on with mementos, gifts.

**6** Save for packing *last* anything you want to get at *first*—your swimsuit, or your nightgown.

**7** Keep all crucials (birth control, camera, travelers' checks, travel tickets, good jewelry) in a tote bag at your side—in case your suitcase gets lost.

# TIPS
## a honeymoon budget guide

*Tips—how much, for what, and to whom—aren't all that confusing when you take them step by step. Let's begin when you're:*

**1. Starting out:** Add 15% to the taxi meter fare, 25¢ for each bag the driver stows in the trunk.

**2. At the Airport:** Pay the sky cap $1 for up to four pieces of luggage, 25¢ for each extra bag.

**3. Aboard Ship:** $3 to $5 per day per couple to the cabin steward and the table steward. If you wish, tip the dining room captain a few dollars too. $2 a week for the deck steward if you take chairs. Pay each the day before the cruise ends by placing cash in an envelope marked with the steward's name and your cabin number.

**4. On a Train:** Give the sleeping car porter a dollar each time he makes up your berth.

**5. At a Resort:** With the exception of the bellhop (25¢ per bag) and the doorman (25¢ to hail a cab), it's customary to tip personnel directly (in an envelope) at the end of your stay: your waiter gets $3 to $5 a day, chambermaid, $1 a day. Check the assistant manager about who else to tip.

**6. In a Restaurant:** Tip 15% of the bill, $1 to the wine steward if you consult him. In Europe a service charge may be automatically added to your bill; if so, no tip is expected.

**7. On a Package Tour:** Though tips are often included, check your travel agent to make sure.

**NOTE:** A tip is a bonus for good service. If what you get is poor, say so; tip accordingly.

# HONEYMOON CATASTROPHES THAT NEEDN'T BE

*They call it the Trip of a Lifetime—don't they? And that means day after dreamy day of carefree bliss—doesn't it? Well, yes. Probably. And almost. But the fact is that honeymoon plans—like plans for mortal vacations—can sometimes get derailed. Luggage can stray, rain can fall, and the king-sized bed you requested can turn out to be skinny twins. Disaster? Not necessarily. Even on a honeymoon, a little applied common sense can minimize troubles that look monumental. Here's how to make quick work of some of the classic problems.*

**You lose your tickets.** If there's time, call your travel agent and he/she will either cope or tell you whom to contact at the airline/ship company/railroad. In a last-minute spot, airlines will ask you to file a lost-ticket claim, buy new tickets, and—if no one finds and uses the originals—will refund your money within 90 days. Or if you have proof of purchase, they'll simply reissue when you sign a pledge of responsibility in case of fraud. On the pier, find the cruise company representative in charge; there should be minimum hassle if you have proof of identity since a stateroom has been set aside in your name. At the AMTRAK station, the Station Manager will remake your tickets if you fill out a form; if you hold reserved space, the computer (in this case, it's a good guy) should have a record of your payment and all the information he needs.

**You miss the plane (boat, train).** Phone ahead to release plane or train space or warn the ship line if you possibly can. An airline will rebook you on the next available flight (even another line's), accept the tickets you hold. AMTRAK will put you on the next train, charge 5 percent penalty (minimum $5 per ticket) if you haven't cancelled. The agent of the cruise line or the local port authority will advise you about chartering a launch (if the ship's in sight) or flying to meet it.

**Your luggage disappears.** Occasionally it happens. Hold onto your claim checks, and notify an airline agent immediately. Do not leave the airport without filing a loss report (or your claim may not be honored later). If you're left luggage-less in a strange town, the airline will give you up to $25 each to buy necessities, after 18 to 24 hours will reimburse you 50 percent for reasonable clothes purchases (snuggies in Iceland, cool things in the tropics, etc.). After about 40 days, they'll settle claims up to $500 worth, allowing for depreciation.

**There's no room at the inn.** Try to keep your cool: though Right is on your side, to make things happen you need a hotel person on your team too. Calmly produce your confirmation slip or letter. Ask to speak to the senior hotel staff person on duty. If it's a matter of there being no rooms left in your category, but there are higher priced accommodations available, you'll be upgraded. If guests haven't moved out on time or through some other major foul-up there are no rooms at all, most hotels make it a policy to pay for overbooked guests' night at an equivalent hotel and round-trip taxi fare to same. If you ask, they'll also allow you a free long distance call to let the folks at home know where you'll be. And of course they give you top priority for the next available room. Some even add $$$ worth of certificates good for complimentary hotel food, drink, and activities. So hang in there. It could be worth your while.

**Your double bed is twins** (singles, that is). Reconfirming a week before your arrival and making sure your reservation is marked "HON. CPL." is the best insurance against this sort of thing happening. If it does, call the Assistant Manager or Front Office Manager, and ask for a change. If he possibly can, he will make it. If he can't move you immediately, he'll have your twins joined and the mattress changed; and he'll give you top priority for a switch to the next available double-bedded room.

**The room is rotten.** Don't leave in a huff. Give the management a chance to make things right. Again, the Assistant Manager or Front Office Manager is your man. Call him from the room, and explain what it is you don't like. He'll do his best to fix things up.

**You're embarrassed.** You'd like to play it suave, but you don't feel that way—about registering at the hotel, about undressing together, about who gets the bathroom first—about *anything*. It really is the exceptional couple who don't feel a little that way. Even if you've lived together, it all seems so *public*. Which is really kind of funny when you think about it. Gradually the problem will disappear by itself. But if you can laugh about it—together—it will go away faster.

**They find out you're honeymooners.** In coy times past, couples worried about this a lot. Today you should realize it's to your advantage to have them—i.e. the hotel or ship's staff—recognize that you're newlyweds. All over the travel world, there are standing orders to give honeymooners the very best, even extra special treatment. And it would be a shame to miss the champagne.

**You're too tired to. . . .** Or too excited. Or too nervous. Even couples who've slept together before find the fatigue, the pressure to perform are just too much. So they put off wedding-night lovemaking. If you feel that way too, you're in the majority. Sweet dreams and happy morning.
Incidentally, one thing "they" hardly ever remember to

mention in advance is the fact that many brides and grooms *are* terribly tired those first few wedding-trip days. It's a natural reaction to the last-minute rush and whirl that precede even the best-ordered weddings. So leave yourselves plenty of recovery and catchup time before scheduling sight-seeing trips or special events. Cancelling or postponing at the last minute is always a bore and a bother. And it can be costly too.

**Your old college roommate turns up.** And what's more, is honeymooning at the same hotel. Not to worry. Remember that (a) neither one of you wants to double-honeymoon, but (b) you're still friends. So (c) make a date for drinks or dinner next Tuesday.

**You get sick.** Call the desk and ask for the house physician—there's one on call 24 hours a day in most hotels. If you're going abroad and don't speak the language, an organization called the International Association for Medical Assistance to Travelers puts its members in touch with local, English-speaking physicians in 70 countries around the world. A donation to IAMAT, Empire State Building, 350 Fifth Avenue, New York, 10001 will get you a membership card, a directory, and relevant brochures about its work.
If you have a persistent or potential health problem—an unusual blood type, an allergy to penicillin, or a chronic disease like asthma or diabetes—you should know about the Medic Alert Foundation. It provides its members with a bracelet or dog-tag that identifies such a condition even when—in case of accident or trauma—you're unable to make it known yourself. There's even a label for wearers of contact lenses. A letter to Medic Alert, Turlock, California 95380, will bring you a brochure that describes its services.

**. . . or homesick.** You won't be the first. A telephone call can do wonders. Just make sure that it's not 3 a.m. at home when you decide to ring up. If you're watching pennies, the time at the calling end determines the going rate for long distance phoning.
**You're allergic—to the bugs, the sun, the food.** Go prepared. If you're seriously hypersensitive to bee stings, be sure you have serum with you. For everyday warm-weather bug bites, pack a counterirritant lotion or anesthetizing spray, and ask your doctor for an antihistamine to reduce the itch. Be cautious about sun the first two or three days in the tropics, and have supplies of suntanning or blocking lotion handy. Two home remedies: ammonia (to take the sting out of bites) and vinegar (to stop sunburn sizzle) are usually available from the housekeeper or kitchen even when drugstores are closed.
In the food department, take it easy the first few days—especially if you're changing climates or altitudes drastically. When in doubt, avoid milk and unpeeled fruit and vegetables; drink bottled water. And

ask your doctor to recommend medication just in case.

**You've smashed your glasses.** Always travel with a copy of your prescription and an extra pair of specs if you can. In a crunch, ask the manager to recommend a local optician and to use his influence to get you a new pair in the shortest possible time.

**You don't want to do the same things at the same time.** There's no law that says you have to. If he wants to go to the bull fights (which you'd hate) and you want to climb a pyramid (which he'd hate), split for the afternoon, and have your own kinds of good times. You'll be lots happier to see each other at dinner.

**You run out of things to talk about.** Don't strain yourselves. As a bride in Acapulco once explained it, "It takes a while to get used to the fact that you're not dating anymore." You don't *have* to amuse each other every minute of every day. Read a book. Take a walk. Take a nap. And enjoy the fact that you really don't need words.

**It rains . . . and rains . . . and rains.** Hideous, but it happens. Hotels plan rainy day parties, horse races, scavenger hunts—get in there and participate. And make sure your own emergency kit includes a *choice* of paperbacks, a crossword puzzle book, a portable chess or backgammon set, playing cards, ballpoints, score pads ("options" is the key word). In case of acute boredom, ask about local movies, a fortune teller. Whatever you do, don't stay indoors for the duration. Get into your rain gear; or take off your shoes and go for a barefoot walk. You won't melt, and fresh air does wonders to lift even the dampest spirits.

**Your passports turn up missing.** Search thoroughly, then report the loss at once to the nearest U.S. Consulate. They'll tell you what to do from there. Keep a record of passport number, date and place of issue with your list of travelers check numbers in a safe place—not a wallet—just in case. Two good places to keep "can't lose" papers are in your carry-on bags or zipped into the lining of your suitcase.

**You run out of money.** Try not to go completely broke in a foreign country. But remember, if it happens, you won't be the first. If it's a matter of paying the hotel bill, talk to the manager; he may very well be willing to bill you at home for part or all of what you owe. If you see a shortage coming, call or cable home for an international draft in the currency of the country you're in; your hometown bank can arrange it. And if you should lose all your money, the American consulate will do all it can to help until you can get refunded.

# 9

# At Home

Home. There's no place like it. Efficient, economical but, above all, comfortable. That's how you want it to be. Start by going over dozens of lists—what the two of you need now, what can wait till later—from spoons to towels to the number of all-night grocery stores near the apartment you'll rent. Decide what you like in terms of furniture and colors. Clip pictures from magazines, really *look* at your friends' houses, talk about them, browse through department store showrooms. And remember, it doesn't have to be a designer's dream, just your own.

# YOUR DINNERWARE

## *How to choose the kind, pattern, price for you*

You'll do plenty of good eating off your dinnerware—the guests you entertain will too. So you'll want to take your time when you buy, go to different stores, and choose carefully in order to get exactly what pleases you and your fiancé most. To help, here are some guidelines on what dinnerware's available to you and how to shop for it.

**China/Porcelain** This very durable dinnerware is thin, light in weight, and chip-resistant. Check its translucency by holding it up to the light; you'll be able to see your hand through it.

**Bone China** This type of porcelain china contains about 40 percent bone ash and is distinguished by its pure white color and, in most cases, by its delicate translucency.

**Stoneware** This ceramic is made of coarser clays than porcelain, yet is fired at high temperatures to make it chip-and-stain-resistant.

**Earthenware** Made of even coarser clays, earthenware must be fired at lower temperatures which makes it slightly less durable. It is often glazed and decorated in bright colors for a pottery look.

**Ironstone** This earthenware is heavy, and most often glazed white—with or without decoration. It may absorb moisture when chipped.

**Oven-to-tableware** This category ranges from porcelain to other types of clay, but it is distinguished by the manufacturers' guarantee that it will not break, chip, crack, or craze (develop fine cracks in the glaze) within a specified number of years under normal home use. (Be sure to read instructions before you subject any dinnerware to sudden temperature changes.)

**Plastics** This plasticware is durable and chip-resistant, and most often brightly decorated. Melamine, the best quality, is both stain- and heat-resistant.

**CONSIDER YOUR WANTS AND NEEDS** before you choose dinnerware. Naturally, you'll want something you both like a lot, so if blue's his favorite color and you love flowers, you'll probably start right off looking for blue floral patterns. Since the design of your dinnerware will help determine your final tablesetting, you'll also want to consider whether you want an elegant look, a more casual one—or both. Here definitions are difficult: elegance can mean an intricate design combining gold with several colors or a plain plate adorned with one perfect blue line. Similarly, casual dinnerware can be simple and rustic or a riot of color and pattern. Should you choose to have both sets (a good idea if you like to entertain), they *can* be used all at once if you choose them now to mix and match.

Also consider your glassware and flatware. A convenient rule: mix two patterned and one plain, one patterned and two plain; stay away from three of one type.

**DECIDE HOW MUCH YOU'LL NEED** before you shop for dinnerware. You'll want enough plates to get you through breakfast, lunch (on weekends) and dinner each day without running the dishwasher after every meal. Or if you're washing by hand, you'll want enough to serve his parents and yours, or a few friends (say, six or eight) who'll be coming for dinner after you're married. In either case, plan for at least eight 5-piece place settings to start (there's a dinner plate, salad plate, small bowl for dessert, soup, etc., tea cup and saucer in one place setting). Bread and butter plates are also useful for hors d'oeuvres or cheese. Add extra dinner plates, component pieces, serving pieces (platters and soup tureens are nice to get for Christmas, anniversary) until you've reached your goal (12? 18? 24?). You might also start off with a complete 20-piece set (four place settings) or 45- or 53-piece set which has eight 5-piece place settings plus vegetable plate, platter, sugar, creamer (and eight soup bowls in the 53 piece set).

**GO TO YOUR WEDDING GIFT REGISTRY** at your favorite department or jewelry store to list your dinnerware preferences so your wedding guests can help you get started on your first set. Since registering for a specific pattern means you'll be collecting it over the years, select carefully. Be sure, for example, that you both like the way the dinnerware *feels* and *looks* when you hold it. Check the shape of the cup. Is it evenly balanced and comfortable? Notice the shape of the plate. Is it a spacious *coupe* (rimless) or deeper *shouldered* (rimmed) design? Hold fine china up to the light to check translucency. Tip the plate at an angle. Does it reflect light brightly, look smooth? Is it free from waves, bumps, or pinholes? Next check price, quality, and availability. "Open stock" dinnerware is available—even one plate at a time—as long as the pattern's being manufactured. And fine dinnerware, made by a reputable company, should have certain standards, or in some cases, guarantees of performance. Price will depend upon the quality of the dinnerware *and* the decoration, and is likely to remain fairly constant. (Although some jewelry and department stores will notify their customers if and when their registered patterns go on sale.) A closeout sale, on the other hand, can save you money, but you won't be able to replace any pieces that break, or pick up more settings if you want them.

**TAKE CARE OF YOUR DINNERWARE** and it will look new years from now. When washing by hand, line the sink with a rubber mat or use a plastic pail to prevent any chipping. Rinse dishes in hot water, then let them air-dry, standing upright in a plastic drying rack. If you're washing them in a dishwasher, stack them *carefully* so they won't touch. Just piling dishes in a dishwasher not only doesn't get them clean, but risks chips and breakage. (Most dinnerware made today is dishwasher-proof, but if you're not sure about washing instructions, ask your salesperson about proper care.) To prepare for washing, scrape leftovers off plate with a paper towel or dish brush or rinse off under running water; don't use a knife or other sharp utensil. Always rinse coffee or tea from cups to prevent the possibility of staining. (If you do have a stain to remove, rub it gently with a borax cleaning compound, never use steel wool pads or scouring powder.) To store dinnerware, stand cups up straight or hang them from round hooks, don't stack them. Fine china plates are best stacked with felt protectors or paper napkins between them to prevent the bottom of one plate from scratching the top of another. To prevent cracking, never put a very cold dish in the oven unless it's oven-to-tableware. And don't cook in dinnerware over a flame unless you *know* it's flameproof.

# DINNERWARE CHECKLIST

PATTERN NAME    Fine china _____ Everyday dinnerware_____

MANUFACTURER    Fine China_____ Everyday dinnerware_____

| | FINE CHINA | | | EVERYDAY DINNERWARE | | |
| --- | --- | --- | --- | --- | --- | --- |
| | Quantity on hand | Quantity desired | Price | Quantity on hand | Quantity desired | Price |
| Dinner plates | | | | | | |
| Salad plates | | | | | | |
| Bread and butter plates | | | | | | |
| Cups and saucers | | | | | | |
| Fruit and cereal bowls | | | | | | |
| Soup plates | | | | | | |
| Cream soups | | | | | | |
| Demi-tasse cups and saucers | | | | | | |
| Vegetable serving dishes | | | | | | |
| Platters | | | | | | |
| Salad or serving bowl | | | | | | |
| Gravy boat | | | | | | |
| Butter dish | | | | | | |
| Sugar bowl and creamer | | | | | | |
| Teapot | | | | | | |
| Coffee pot | | | | | | |
| Tureen | | | | | | |
| Salt and pepper shakers | | | | | | |

# YOUR SILVERWARE

## *How to find the metal, pattern, and price for you*

Unless you plan to eat out for the next who-knows-how-many years, you've got to buy **flatware** (knives, forks, spoons, serving pieces). And you'll never get tired of looking at yours if you choose it with care. Here's a very brief rundown of the different kinds of flatware and **holloware** (bowls, pitchers, trays) you can choose from in most stores in your area today.

**Sterling Silver.** Flatware and holloware of solid silver (925 parts per 1000 by law—look for the word "sterling" stamped on every piece). To hold the price down, handles are sometimes hollow.

**Vermeil.** Flatware and holloware of sterling silver electroplated with pure gold.

**Silverplate.** Flatware and holloware of a non-ferrous metal (durable, rust-proof, heavy) electroplated with pure silver.

**Pewter.** Flatware and holloware of a soft, silver-gray metal made of a variety of tin alloys. Comes with either polished or satin (antique-like) finish. Polished eventually takes on the satin finish.

**Pewterplate.** Holloware of a base metal electroplated with pewter.

**Sterling II.** Flatware with hollow, sterling silver handles and stainless steel tines, bowls, and blades. (Sterling silver knives have always been made this way.)

**Stainless Steel.** Flatware and holloware of a non-precious metal (an alloy of steel, chromium, and in some cases nickel). Available with satin (the most popular), mirror, and new pewter finish (stainless steel brushed to look like pewter). Also comes in bronze or gold tone (stainless steel electroplated with bronze- and gold-looking materials). Quality is very important when buying stainless steel. Ask for 18/8 or 18/10 chrome-nickel steel (the toughest, also the legally set standard for the best). Check fork tines (too blunt or sharp?). Pay attention to weight; as a rule, the heavier the stainless, the better its quality.

**Special Alloys.** More and more manufacturers are developing their own special alloys (mixtures of various metals) to answer the growing consumer cry for practicality (price, versatility, durability). Some of these products look like silver, pewter, and stainless, but they should not be mistaken for them. Always ask the salesperson exactly what it is you're looking at, how it can be used (is it oven-proof?), and how it should be cared for (can it go in the dishwasher?).

**YOU MIGHT START** with a complete set of durable everyday flatware. But you may also want to begin collecting the more formal flatware and holloware that dresses up any meal—from pheasant under glass to just hamburgers and corn on the cob.

**MOST SILVERWARE IS OPEN STOCK**—you can buy any amount from one spoon to service for 50, and you can always order more. How much you'll need depends on the kind of entertaining you plan to do—buffet dinners may call for lots of serving spoons but no carving set; sit-down dinners will probably require soup spoons and butter spreaders. You might aim to complete eight or 12 six-piece place settings of main course soup spoons, dinner forks, meat knives, salad forks, butter spreaders, and teaspoons right away. Then you might add extra place settings, serving pieces, and special items like demi-tasse spoons, serving pieces, holloware, and a salad set as you find you need them.

**ONCE YOU'VE DECIDED ON THE METAL** you want, keep looking at patterns until you and your groom find one that suits your tastes and dinnerware. Don't feel you have to match up metals to any silver or gold rim around your china or glassware. In general, one of your three tableware patterns (in glassware, dinnerware, and flatware) should convey a different mood than the other two. So if you two have already chosen elaborate dinnerware and cut crystal, you might pick a simple, classic flatware pattern. Or if you lean toward ornate flatware, you might choose china and crystal in an unadorned style. Let your own tastes be the final rule; if you like all plain or all fancy, that's fine too.

**COLLECTING FINE FLATWARE AND HOLLOWARE** takes time—and money. Here are six economical ways to do it:

1) Shop at a store that offers a "club" or "special purchase plan" for sterling silver flatware. You agree to a minimum outlay, put down about ten percent, then pay off the rest in monthly installments over two or three years—with no interest or carrying charge.

2) Don't settle for two or four, four-piece place settings (knife, dinner and salad forks, teaspoon); buy six, eight, or 12 smaller settings. For example, you might buy the two-piece dessert setting (salad/dessert fork and teaspoon).

3) Start with just the serving pieces (a vegetable spoon, meat fork, gravy ladle). Use them alongside your everyday flatware as you collect everything else.

4) Watch for seasonal sterling silver reductions—especially in February and October.

5) Consider buying antique as well as new holloware.

6) List your preferences with the Wedding Gift Registry at your local department or jewelry store, so your wedding guests can add to your collection.

**HOW TO CARE** for your flatware and holloware? Wash all metals in hot soapy water; dry promptly with a soft cloth. Anything but ceramic- or wood-handled flatware and pewter can go in the dishwasher (pewter is too soft a metal for high temperatures, it also tends to darken). But to prevent spotting, remove *silver* before washer reaches dry cycle; dry your silver by hand.

Sterling silver and silverplate do tarnish (gold, stainless, and pewter don't). But your silver won't tarnish as much if you use it daily. In fact, use makes it even more beautiful, the "patina" of tiny scratches mellowing and warming its surface. If you don't plan to use yours daily, store it away from the open air, in a chest or drawer lined with special, tarnish-preventing cloth. Then polish your silver when you feel it needs it; this is usually once or twice a year.

PATTERN NAME   Silver_____ Everyday flatware_____

MANUFACTURER   Silver _____ Everyday flatware_____

# SILVER CHECKLIST

| FLATWARE | STERLING | | | EVERYDAY | | |
|---|---|---|---|---|---|---|
| | Quantity on hand | Quantity desired | Price | Quantity on hand | Quantity desired | Price |
| Teaspoons | | | | | | |
| Soup spoons | | | | | | |
| Luncheon knives | | | | | | |
| Luncheon forks | | | | | | |
| Salad forks | | | | | | |
| Butter spreaders | | | | | | |
| Dinner knives | | | | | | |
| Dinner forks | | | | | | |
| Cream soup spoons | | | | | | |
| Demi-tasse spoons | | | | | | |
| Iced drink spoons | | | | | | |
| Cocktail or oyster forks | | | | | | |
| Steak knives | | | | | | |
| Serving forks | | | | | | |
| Serving spoons | | | | | | |
| Salad servers | | | | | | |
| Soup ladle | | | | | | |
| Cream or sauce ladle | | | | | | |
| Sugar tongs | | | | | | |
| Sugar spoon | | | | | | |
| Jelly server | | | | | | |
| Butter server | | | | | | |
| Pie or cake server | | | | | | |
| Carving set | | | | | | |

# SILVER CHECKLIST

| HOLLOWARE | STERLING | | | EVERYDAY | | |
|---|---|---|---|---|---|---|
| | Quantity on hand | Quantity desired | Price | Quantity on hand | Quantity desired | Price |
| Tea Service | | | | | | |
|   teapot | | | | | | |
|   coffee pot | | | | | | |
|   sugar and creamer | | | | | | |
|   waste bowl | | | | | | |
|   tray | | | | | | |
| Large platter | | | | | | |
| Smaller platter | | | | | | |
| Vegetable serving dishes | | | | | | |
| Gravy boat and tray | | | | | | |
| Sauce bowl and tray | | | | | | |
| Bread tray | | | | | | |
| Butter dish | | | | | | |
| Water pitcher | | | | | | |
| Salt and pepper shakers | | | | | | |
| Bowls for flowers, candy fruit, etc. | | | | | | |
| Compotes | | | | | | |
| Candlesticks (high) | | | | | | |
| Candlesticks (low) | | | | | | |
| Cigarette urns | | | | | | |
| Ash trays | | | | | | |
| Coasters | | | | | | |
| Cocktail shaker | | | | | | |
| Ice bucket | | | | | | |
| Trivets | | | | | | |

# YOUR GLASSWARE

## *Buying glass tableware, cookware, accessories*

Once you start picking out glassware for your new home, you'll be amazed at how much more you'll choose than just a few drinking glasses. You'll want glass casseroles and baking dishes for cooking, pitchers and carafes for serving, canisters and jars for storage, and vases and bowls for fresh flowers, fruit. In other words, glassware for just about every table, kitchen, and household use. So here are the basics that'll help you choose it.

Glassware is either hand-blown or machine-made. When glass is **hand-blown,** it's created one piece at a time by a skilled glassblower. The result is a very fine, delicate, uniquely shaped piece of glass. **Machine-made** glass is either blown or molded mechanically, many pieces at a time, into uniform shapes. **Cut glass** is decorated by machine- or hand-cutting by means of moving steel or stone wheels. Typical decorations? Leaf or flower motifs, diamond designs. **Etched glass** has fine-line, lacy patterns made by a wax and acid process. **Pressed glass** is formed in patterned molds to give the glass dimensional, raised designs. The types of glass you'll use everyday? **Lime glass,** which has lime and soda or other alkalis, makes up most of the durable drinking glasses and jars you'll buy. **Lead glass,** with lead oxide and potash or other alkalis, is found in more of the fine goblets, vases, or pitchers you'll use. **Crystal** is a glass that has a high degree of brilliance. **Lead crystal** has superior brilliance and weight because it contains more lead than ordinary crystal. **Cased glass** is clear glass coated with layers of colored glass to give it a two-tone effect. **Milk glass** is opaque white, smoothly polished glass. **Colored glass** is made by mixing various kinds of mineral salts (such as copper to get green glass) with the basic glass materials.

**COLLECT GLASSWARE THAT INCLUDES** plain glass tumblers (glasses without stems), finely etched crystal, stemmed champagnes, monogrammed water goblets, beer mugs and steins, or whatever you'll use most. But don't stop when you have enough drinking glasses. Go on to meet your household needs with a pie plate or two, some custard cups, mixing bowls, coasters, etc. Most glassware you'll use all the time, like spice jars and measuring cups. Other, more fragile items you may be tempted to save for company. But try not to limit your use of fine glassware to just special occasions. Let a crystal goblet enhance the tang of freshly squeezed orange juice some mornings. Or have a handsomely faceted glass bowl dish up your favorite weeknight Caesar salad. For romantic table touches,

set the mood with candles flickering in tall, sparkling holders. Then bask in the warm glow of candlelight as it shines on glass tableware. Delight in the beauty of red wine swirling in radiant stemware. And tap a crystal glass with your fingertip to hear that impressive, resonant ring. Enjoy your glassware every day. And take pride in all your tablesettings by selecting glassware with your total table look in mind. If you've already chosen very plain dinnerware and flatware, either contrast it with elaborately cut or etched glassware, or stick to the same lines with smooth, simple glass. Just be careful about matching too many overly ornate tableware pieces. Remember that they'll all go together on the same table and the result may be too overwhelming. Ideas: Pick up a color in your dinnerware with tinted glass. Let a gold or platinum band on plates repeat itself on goblets.

**SIGN UP AT THE WEDDING GIFT REGISTRY** in your nearby store to get a headstart on your glassware collection. Then your wedding guests can choose a gift from the glass or crystal patterns you've listed as your preferences. And you'll avoid getting too many of the same glasses or patterns you don't like. Aside from the gifts you'll receive, you'll want to buy more glassware on your own. When you do, look for glass patterns that are sold "open stock" so you can buy any number of pieces to start, and still more whenever you want to order them. When you shop for glasses, hold the glass up to a white background (e.g., paper, cloth, a wall) to be sure it's clear and sparkling, smooth on the edges, and uniform in shape and thickness. Even colored glass should be radiant and clean-looking, not foggy. Especially crystal. All glasses should feel comfortable and evenly balanced when you hold them. While you're shopping ask to see a complete place setting of glassware so you can see the shape and design of all the pieces. The basic crystal place setting includes five—the goblet, sherbet, wine, iced tea, and salad plate. Of course you don't have to buy a complete place setting of glassware. You might need more iced tea glasses than salad plates, so you'll want to get those instead. When buying any glassware, look for items you can use in many different ways, such as the all-purpose, balloon wine glasses that can hold water, wine, or an ice-cream sundae; simple pitchers that can serve up icy lemonade or show off fresh daisies.

**TAKE PROPER CARE OF YOUR GLASSWARE** so it will last longer and always look its sparkling best. Store all your glasses and dishes in cupboards or cabinets to keep them free from dust and away from any steam

PATTERN NAME    Crystal _____ Everyday glassware_____

MANUFACTURER    Crystal _____ Everyday glassware_____

## GLASSWARE CHECKLIST

| | CRYSTAL | | | EVERYDAY GLASSWARE | | |
| --- | --- | --- | --- | --- | --- | --- |
| | Quantity on hand | Quantity desired | Price | Quantity on hand | Quantity desired | Price |
| Water goblets | | | | | | |
| All-purpose wine | | | | | | |
| Sherbet/champagne | | | | | | |
| Fruit juices | | | | | | |
| Iced beverages | | | | | | |
| Old fashioneds | | | | | | |
| Highballs | | | | | | |
| Sours | | | | | | |
| Cocktails | | | | | | |
| Pilsners | | | | | | |
| Cordials | | | | | | |
| Brandy snifters | | | | | | |
| Pitchers | | | | | | |
| Decanters | | | | | | |
| Dessert or salad bowl | | | | | | |
| Individual plates and bowls | | | | | | |
| Punch set | | | | | | |

or grease in the air. First, line your shelves with thick paper, plastic, or rubber covering to act as a cushion against chipping. Then stand glasses with the *rims upright*—not turned upside down. And don't stack them inside one another. When you handle glasses, hold those with stems by the stem, tumblers close to the base so they won't tip or drop. Most glassware is machine-washable, but check with the manufacturer if you're not sure—especially about glasses with gold or platinum decorations that may soften or scratch under high temperatures or strong detergents. When you wash glassware by hand, only do a few pieces at a time with warm, soapy water in a rubber or plastic dishpan. Use

a bottle brush or sponge to clean down inside glasses or jars. And drop in a bit of laundry bluing or ammonia to give glasses added luster. Rinse glassware in warm water, drain upside down on a dish rack or heavy dish towel, and once dry, polish to sparkle with a lint-free cloth. If your glass dinnerware or cookware has food stuck on it, soak it in cold, soapy water before washing. To prevent glassware from cracking, avoid sudden temperature changes: never put hot drinks into cold glasses or rinse a cold plate or pitcher in hot water. If you use glass cook-and-serve dinnerware, read the instructions carefully before you freeze food in it or cook with it over a flame to be sure you won't crack it.

# YOUR LINENS

Linens have come a long way since the well-stocked closet was piled with a snowdrift of white sheets, pillowcases, and towels. White—as well as black—is now only an accent to a complete palette of colors. Your linens can create any mood you want for your new home. So choose your favorite atmosphere, then make it happen with cool graphics or riotous florals.

Blended fibers cut down on your wash-day blues, making permanent press sheets that look just as crisp on your beds as freshly ironed ones. Be sure to follow the special laundering instructions on the new blends carefully. A 50-50 mix of cotton and polyester has the silky feel of percale. But don't overlook the merits of regular cotton percale and muslin. They're both extremely strong and long-wearing. Of the two, percale is more luxurious—and more expensive. Percale has more threads per square inch than muslin. The tighter the weave, the softer and finer the sheet. On a twin-size bed, you need a flat sheet measuring 66" x 96" if it's permanent press (cotton shrinks more). A full- (or double-) size requires a 81" x 96" flat sheet. A queen-sized bed needs a 90" x 102" flat sheet. A king-size bed takes a 108" x 102" flat sheet. Fitted sheet sizes match whatever bed size you choose. The National Association of Bedding Manufacturers designates bed sizes this way: full, queen, king, and dual-king (two twin beds together).

After you've picked your sheets, look for matching shower curtain, bedspread, even room accessories like waste baskets and tissue boxes. And if you want the same fabric for walls and draperies, check out sheeting by the yard now sold in many linen departments.

In towels, there are five textures to choose: sheared terry, plain terry, jacquard, huck and linen for hand, guest towels. Sheared terries have the look and feel of velvet with the familiar loops of plain terry on one side. But they are less absorbent than plain terries. Jacquard towels are sumptuous, with the design woven in. Get half your towels in a dark color, half light, to help make up a "full load" of each on laundry day.

## BASIC LINEN LIST

PER BED:
1 fitted mattress pad

6 sheets (fitted and flat)
2 winter-weight blankets—or
1 electric blanket with dual controls
pillows (as many as you like)
3 pillowcases for each pillow
1-2 bedspreads (to suit the seasons)

BATH:
8 bath towels
8 hand towels
8 washcloths
2 bath mats
shower curtain

FOR YOUR GUESTS:
4 sheets per bed
2 pillowcases for each pillow
1-2 blankets
2-4 sets of towels
6 fingertip towels

EXTRAS:
mattress covers
summer-weight blankets
comforter or quilt

In the bathroom, coordinate towels, rug, and shower curtains too. Harmony is achieved whether you have a perfect match or a pleasant contrast.

Don't neglect your table when choosing your linens. You should have at least one beautiful cloth, and several casual ones, for as lace or linen go with candlelight and Beef Wellington, red-checked gingham might be more suitable for fried chicken. Matching place mat and napkin sets are fun too and can even be set on a solid cloth for a dramatic dining effect. Pick tablecloths that are compatible with your china and glassware. The care you take now in choosing your linens will be reflected later in the beauty of your table.

As for the kitchen, choose potholders, dishcloths and dish towels that coordinate with the overall atmosphere so you won't have an unrelated jumble of colors and conflicting prints.

# LINEN CHECKLIST
## DINING AREA

Formal dinner cloth _____ size _____ color _____ rectangular ☐ round ☐ oblong ☐

Matching napkins (you should have as many
of these as you have china place settings)          on hand _____ needed _____

Card table or game set _____ pattern _____ price _____ on hand _____ needed _____

Informal cloth _____ size ____ pattern _____ price _____ on hand _____ needed _____

Everyday napkins _____ pattern _____ price _____ on hand _____ needed _____

Place mat set _____ pattern _____ price _____ on hand _____ needed _____

Heatproof table pads ____ size ____ pattern _____ price _____ on hand _____ needed _____

## KITCHEN

Dish towels _____ pattern _____ price _____ on hand _____ needed _____

Dishcloths _____ pattern _____ price _____ on hand _____ needed _____

Potholders _____ pattern _____ price _____ on hand _____ needed _____

Aprons _____ pattern _____ price _____ on hand _____ needed _____

## BEDROOM (for each bed)

Sheets flat _____ size _____ pattern _____ price _____ on hand _____ needed _____

      fitted _____ size _____ pattern _____ price _____ on hand _____ needed _____

Pillowcases _____ size _____ pattern _____ price _____ on hand _____ needed _____

Blankets winter _____ size _____ pattern _____ price _____ on hand _____ needed _____

      summer _____ size _____ pattern _____ price _____ on hand _____ needed _____

Electric blanket _____ size _____ pattern _____ price _____ on hand _____ needed _____

Blanket covers _____ size _____ pattern _____ price _____ on hand _____ needed _____

Comforter or quilt ____ size _____ pattern _____ price _____ on hand _____ needed _____

Mattress pads _____ size _____ pattern _____ price _____ on hand _____ needed _____

Bedspreads _____ size _____ pattern _____ price _____ on hand _____ needed _____

## BATH

Bath towels _____ pattern _____ price _____ on hand _____ needed_____

Hand towels _____ pattern _____ price _____ on hand _____ needed_____

Washcloths _____ pattern _____ price _____ on hand _____ needed_____

Bathroom rug _____ pattern _____ price _____ on hand _____ needed_____

Bath mats_____ pattern _____ price _____ on hand _____ needed_____

Shower curtain/liner _____ pattern _____ price _____ on hand _____ needed_____

Guest towels _____ pattern _____ price _____ on hand _____ needed_____

# BUYING A MATTRESS

What kind, what size, what price are choices you two will face when buying a mattress. Here's helpful information.

**Is a firm or a super-firm mattress best?** One company's "firm" may equal another's "extra-firm" so don't rely on names. Try them all and see what's comfortable for you. As long as your body is supported at all points, especially the hips, shoulders, and lower back, the degree of firmness is a matter of taste. You like a hard mattress—he doesn't? Order a special mattress that's hard on one side, softer on the other. Another solution: a dual-king bed (twin beds pushed together behind a single headboard). Fitted twin sheets go on the bottom, king-size on top. Or buy a foam T-shaped wedge to fill the space between the beds and make them up as one.

**What size should we get?** Is your husband tall? Are you? Your mattress should be six inches longer than the taller one. (See the mattress sizes sketched.) You'll be sleeping on that mattress together, so do shop for it together. Lie down. Can you roll over without bumping each other? Worried about the bed overpowering the room? Scale your other furniture purchases down for an uncluttered look.

**How much should we spend for a mattress?** With bedding, there are no bargains. If you want the best materials and workmanship, invest as much as you can afford.

**What's a waterbed like?** Like floating in the ocean. The wave motion soothes some people, makes others seasick. You'll both have to love it—if he turns over, you'll be set in motion. A waterbed needs professional installation, warm water (a heater is sealed into the frame), chemicals added every six months to freshen the water, and a building able to support its heavy

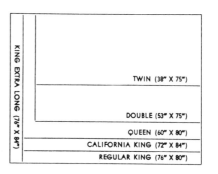

weight. Consult the Residence Building Inspector in your city if you're in doubt. King, dual-king, or queen, the length of most waterbeds is 84" so use flat sheets.

**What's the difference between innerspring and foam mattresses?** Solid foam bedding is lightweight (easy for you to turn), and may be used on a platform base with drawers underneath for storage. The new plastic foams come in different firmnesses and don't crumble or powder. Innerspring mattresses are more flexible than foam—and heavy! They've always been popular (you've probably slept on them *most*). Inside are heavy steel coils padded with upholstery fabrics so you don't feel them. Foam may be used as a cushioner in an innerspring. To prevent shifting and lumps, the padding is anchored by tufting or quilting. Signs of quality: reinforced edges to save wear and tear, strong handles backed with metal plates for easy turning, plastic or metal mesh ventilators to help air circulate inside the mattress. A good innerspring is guaranteed for 15 years. To get the most from your mattress, buy a foundation with it. A boxspring prolongs the life of the mattress by acting as a shock absorber. Bounce on the boxspring. It shouldn't squeak. Is there enough padding so you don't feel the springs? To hold mattress and boxspring off the floor, buy an adjustable metal frame with a center support for a king- or queen-size bed. Order casters—there are different ones for rugs or floors. A bed that rolls around is easier to make for the two of you.

**How do we care for our mattress?** Not many people know how important caring for a mattress is, and that it begins as soon as the mattress is delivered to your door. Avoid slashing the ticking with a sharp object when you open the wrapping. And protect your mattress with a cover that can be washed. A dust ruffle is not only decorative—it keeps the boxspring clean. If you don't like the look, use the vacuum to pick up surface dust. Alternate turning your mattress over side to side, then end to end every two weeks at first, later every few months. And so your boxspring wears evenly, reverse it once a year. Proper care will increase the life and enjoyment of your bedding.

# HOW TO BUY A SOFA BED

*A sofa bed should be handsome, sturdy, comfortable. Do read these tips before buying.*

**1. Analyze your needs.** A sofa bed's a good idea if: you live in a one-room apartment; you have one bedroom and want a place for guests to sleep; your bedroom is too tiny for a double bed. Ask yourselves: do you want to sleep on a sofa bed every night?

**2. Size things up.** Measure wall space, doorways (be sure movers can get the sofa bed into the room). Be realistic, and get the size that'll fit the space. Add the width of the sofa's arms to the mattress size—twin- 41"; full-53"; queen-58"; king-75". Most sofa beds open to 72-75".

**3. Shop around.** Visit a lot of stores, ask a lot of questions. Remember, discount marts may save you money, but offer little service, and better stores aren't necessarily more expensive. Find out about paying in installments.

**4. Plan to fall in love with the sofa bed you buy.** But don't be blind to its faults. Be sure seams are straight, patterns match, skirts are lined, cushions fit snugly.

**5. Test it out.** Push it. It should feel sturdy. Open it. The bed should glide out easily without jumping or balking. Feel it. Upholstery should be lump-free. Look at it. Hardware on the bed frame should have no protrusions that could scratch a leg, tear a sheet. Now lie on it. *Above all*, the mattress should feel comfortable.

**6. Latch onto a good value.** You can expect to pay between $300 and $1000 for a good sofa bed. Demand: a mattress that's protected against mildew, bacteria, odor (an innerspring or individually pocketed mattress will be more comfortable than foam); upholstery fabric that's stain-resistant; flawless construction, upholstery; a warranty (a promise of free service on defective materials or workmanship—up to a year).

# APARTMENT HUNTING

## How to find the right apartment for you

### By Doris Dickenson

Your first home—a cozy, comfortable apartment that reflects the warmth of your new life together. It's a beautiful dream, and it *can* come true if you two are informed apartment hunters who know what you want and how to get the best deal. But apartment living can also be a nightmare of unpleasant neighbors, tyrannical landlords, and restrictive leases if you're not careful about renting. So here's what to look for, what to watch out for.

**DETERMINE YOUR NEEDS.** Sit down together and decide what kind of apartment you both want. How many rooms do you need? Will one bedroom do for a year or so, or will you need two in order to start a family or have weekend guests? How much rent can you pay? (One-quarter of your gross income—before tax deductions—is the suggested guide.) Does that figure cover utilities (gas, water, electricity), garbage pickup, garage? (Add those costs on to the rent if they're extras in your area.) Do you want a furnished or unfurnished place? Where do you want to live? For how long? Does your apartment have to be within walking distance of your jobs? (Figure out if it would be less expensive to commute to work if rents are cheaper someplace else.) Last, list your needs according to importance—1-cost, 2-convenience to work, etc.

**SCOUT AROUND.** Read the newspaper rental ads to see what's available, at what price. Visit apartment buildings you like and ask if there are vacancies. Leave your name and current address with the landlord in case an opening comes up. Ask friends, fellow workers if they know of any good places. If you want professional help or don't have time to look yourself, register with a real estate broker. (Their fee? Usually a month's rent or percentage of a year's rent. But *don't pay anything* until they've found you an apartment.)

If you're moving to a new city, write the Chamber of Commerce there for maps, names and addresses of local newspapers, newcomers' organizations. Send for the Sunday Classified ads for an idea of apartment prices, sizes.

While you're out scouting, look for a copy of the local Landlord-Tenant laws stating your rights, the landlord's responsibilities. A consumers' group or renters' association may provide you with one. If not, look for a copy in the public or city/county law library. Find out what the law says a landlord must provide (heat, hot water, appliances?) before you look at apartments. That way you'll know what to expect.

**ASK QUESTIONS FIRST.** Before beginning the actual legwork of apartment hunting, save steps by phoning ahead. Find out if the apartment is right for you by asking questions like, "What's the rent? Are pets allowed? What floor is it on? When can we move in?" If the rent is much higher than you planned to pay, don't waste time even looking at the place. If it's far less than you expected to pay, find out why. Maybe the apartment's on the ground floor near a noisy street or next to an open-air roller derby. Ask before you look.

**LOOK CAREFULLY.** When you go to check out a possible apartment, pay attention to the neighborhood. Notice if it's pleasant, clean, quiet. (Visit at day *and* night.) See who your neighbors will be. Are there a lot of children around who may make noise you won't appreciate Sunday mornings? Or is there an abundance of elderly people who aren't likely to be new friends? Look for the nearest supermarket, dry cleaner, etc. If there are no laundry facilities in the building, you'll want a self-service laundry close by. Judge how far the apartment is from where you work. Is there a convenient bus stop, train station? Is there easy access to a freeway?

**CHECK OUT THE APARTMENT.** When you look at an apartment, try to have the landlord or superintendent with you so you can ask questions, get immediate answers. Take a tape measure along for sizing up rooms. What should you look for in an apartment? Clip this checklist of points to cover, questions to ask. Take it along when you apartment hunt.

# APARTMENT CHECKLIST

**By Joan Luddy**

**Space** Is the apartment big enough for you? Worth the rent asked?

**Condition** Is it clean, newly painted? If not, who paints, does other fix-ups? Can you move in without having to do a lot of work on the floors, etc.?

**View** Do you like what you see outside? Does a building next door mean no light, no sun for plants?

**Noise** Can you hear people in the next apartment, upstairs, traffic from the street below?

**Utilities** Is gas, electricity included in the rent? Are there appliances (stove, refrigerator) in the kitchen? Do they work?

**Heat/Air Conditioning** Are there heat vents in every room? Who controls them? When does the heat go on? If there are no air-conditioning units, can you install your own?

**Plumbing** Does the water run clear or rusty? Is the hot water hot? Do the toilets flush? Does the shower run?

**Wiring** Are there adequate outlets in each room? (The rule is about two per room.) Do the light switches work? Does the doorbell ring? Is there a fuse box in the apartment?

**Windows** Do they open? Are the panes in good condition? Are there screens, shades, blinds? Does the landlord provide window-cleaning?

**Closets** Is there adequate storage for clothes, linens, sports equipment? Is there basement storage?

**Pests** Are there roaches, ants, rodents in the apartment? Does the landlord exterminate?

**Service** Is there a full-time superintendent, maintenance staff? What facilities are there for garbage collection? Is there an incinerator room? Is there a laundry room with dryers? How many machines are there? Are they in good condition? How are mail deliveries handled? Is there a doorman, elevator attendant?

**MAKE AN AGREEMENT** Once you decide to rent an apartment, the landlord will probably ask for a security deposit. This deposit, usually amounting to one month's rent, should be considered as a "hold" on the apartment while the landlord checks your references. But make sure you understand its purpose, and do ask for a receipt that states what the deposit is for. In most states, your deposit is held as security against your breaking the lease or damaging the property. But it should be returned (plus interest in some states) when you move out, if you haven't broken any agreements. At the time you decide to rent the apartment, and before you sign a lease, make a list of anything in the apartment you want fixed—a leaky faucet, a broken window—and send a copy to the landlord by registered mail, return receipt. (This will also serve as proof of previous damages if the landlord tries to withhold your security deposit when you move out.) If the repairs haven't been made by the time you sign a lease, be sure the damages and work to be done are listed in the lease and initialed by the landlord.

**SIGN A LEASE** Not all apartment owners require their tenants to sign a lease. Some just make an oral agreement with their tenants to rent an apartment under the terms they've discussed. Others ask their tenants to sign a written agreement that gives them month-by-month tenancy. Either arrangement may be fine with you if you only plan to rent the place for a few months. But in both cases, the landlord can raise the rent whenever he feels like it, or ask you to leave. So your best bet is to sign a lease for one, two, even three years, to give you some protection against eviction and assurance that the rent is fixed for the length of the lease.

Before you sign a lease, *read it*. Take your time, even if people are waiting. Or ask to take a copy home and bring it back later. If you don't understand what it says, contact the local Housing Department, District Attorney's Office, or the Consumer Affairs Bureau for help. Things you should look for?

Name of the landlord, owner, not just manager
Apartment address and number
Amount of rent and date it's due
Amount of security deposit; conditions for return
Length of lease; what happens if you vacate before it expires
How much advance notice must be given by either party wanting to terminate the lease
Who pays utilities
Repairs the landlord must make; steps the tenant can take if such repairs aren't made (Can you withhold rent?)
Conditions under which the landlord may enter the apartment
Rules regarding pets
Conditions for making alterations—hanging pictures, wallpaper (Improvements may become the landlord's property.)
Conditions regulating subletting (A clause allowing you to rent the place to someone else is helpful if you must move before the lease runs out.)

If anything in the lease seems overly restrictive or unsuitable, discuss it with the landlord and suggest eliminating it from the contract. Don't be put off with, "Don't worry, we'll take care of it." If the landlord's sincere, he'll change the lease or add a written agreement that's signed and dated by him, initialed by you. Never sign a lease with blank spaces. Anything can be added later. Both the tenants and the landlord sign the lease. And once signed, be sure you receive a copy.

# FURNISHING YOUR HOME—YOUR WAY

*If you haven't a clue about the kind of furniture you want, decorating your new home may seem like an awesome task. It needn't be. With the right kind of planning, you and your husband can discover styles, colors, and moods that are really "you" and find furnishings you'll love for years.*

To get the best decorating results possible, you'll need to plan carefully. The key elements you'll need to balance: his taste and yours; the money you have to spend; the kind of space you have to work with in your first home. Follow the simple advice here, and you two can't miss.

## FIND OUT WHAT YOUR TASTES ARE

**Go ahead, mix your antiques with his modern. The trick of combining different styles in one room is to make it look as though you planned it that way.**

First, talk. You and your groom need to find out how your tastes are alike and how they're different, and to decide the ways you'll work out inevitable compromises. Window-shop, thumb through decorating magazines, visit model rooms—together. Get the feel of fabrics, flop into chairs, step onto rugs. Collect clippings of rooms you admire. Take home fabric swatches, wallpaper snips, color cards. What if your favorite possession is a collection of antique tin-types, his is a pair of Sister Corita's modern lithographs? How can you mix his Victorian sideboard with your flowered chintz-covered loveseat? A good way is to tie everything together with a strong uniform color scheme. If, for example, you choose warm yellow for the living room rug, curtains, walls, it will soothe the eye, allow a "hodge podge" collection of furniture to work together well. Be bold about devising your own furniture "mix"—if *you* like it, it will probably look great to everyone else.

## DRAW UP A FLOOR PLAN

**A floor plan helps you determine that the huge sectional you had an eye on is too big for your living room; a round table would be best for your dining nook.**

Work out a floor plan for each room you want to furnish. Sketch the room, indicating where windows, doors, radiators, and any other built-in features fall. Then measure the room with a folding ruler or metal tape and note each measurment in inches on the sketch. Also measure the width and height of doorways, stairs, and halls, so you'll know if large pieces of furniture will fit through them. Finally, draw each room to scale on graph paper. Draw and cut out furniture shapes on another piece of paper and arrange them on your floor plan. Rearrange those cut-outs until you can see what furniture pieces would be most practical and suitable to your daily habits, entertaining, tastes, hobbies.

## WORK OUT A BUDGET

**Plan to spend one-quarter to one-third of your annual income to furnish your home ($3750-$5000 of a $15,000 salary). Financial experts say one fourth should be cash, you may want to finance the rest.**

Figure out your needs, and test them agaìnt your budget. It's better, decorators say, to invest in a few good pieces than to skimp on quality in order to get everything all at once. Make a list of everything you want for each room, draw a line under items that really are essential *right now*. What can you buy new, what should you look for in second-hand stores, when will you allow yourselves to give in to whim? (If you're both dying for that big brass bed you saw in the antique store and don't mind waiting awhile for a dining table, why not?) Remember though, if you're going to stay within your budget, you need to use self-control most of the time. Also, you could start a savings account for furniture—set aside a certain amount each week toward a piece you crave, then buy it outright.

## GO SHOPPING

**The better stores are not always the most expensive. They often offer excellent service along with decorators who will go over ideas with you at no extra cost.**

When you've decided on a budget, on colors and styles you love, and on the mood you plan to bring home, you're ready to go shopping. Now set off with your room measurements, floor plan, and list of essentials to buy right away (see below). Where to shop? Visit several stores. Follow friends' advice on stores that have given good quality, financing, delivery. Stores you deal with should belong to the National Home Furnishings Association, or rate high with the Better Business Bureau. Test out all furniture before you buy it. Check wood pieces for sturdiness, secure legs. Place palms on table tops and shake. Sit in chairs, make sure they're wobble- free. Doors should swing freely, drawers should slide easily. Upholstery should be lump-free. Look for straight seams, matched patterns. Sofa, chair arms should be steady. Seat edges should be firm, but yielding. Run your hand under seats to be sure supportive webbing is closely woven. Most important, upholstered furniture should feel comfortable to both of you. Tags should give maintenance tips. Read labels on upholstered pieces, be sure fabric is resistant to dirt, that the stuffing is what you want. Expect to wait for furniture delivery, and be sure to ask the salesperson about the exact amount of time—you'll avoid frustration. Unless you buy "in stock" merchandise, you'll wait a minimum of four weeks (and possibly much longer) for a store to deliver your furniture. Ask if there are charges for delivery "up to and beyond the door." Ask about the store's damage policy—you should have time to check items thoroughly before the delivery people leave your home. Avoid paying before delivery. If you do pay, make sure the bill of sale is marked "paid in full." Pay by check, never cash. Read any contracts, and clear up ambiguities with an attorney or bank officer. And always demand copies of anything you sign. Keep them for your own peace of mind.

## USE YOUR IMAGINATION

**Indulge in rummage sales, "junkyard" finds, but be honest with yourselves. If you haven't the energy or interest in being "do-it-yourselfers," don't take it on.**

When you use your imagination, you'll add lots of your own touches to the decorating process. Besides buying in department and furniture stores, comb garage sales, auctions for the unexpected (a piano bench as a table, a wire egg basket as a desk organizer). Sew, refinish, hammer, and improvise. If you don't know how to paper a wall, there are books to show you how ("Crafty" friends can be a big help too.) You can build a bookcase of wood, or put one together from a kit. In-stock "K-D" (knock-down) kits give you the fun of do-it-yourselfing, they save on delivery time too.

### WHAT TO BUY FIRST

*Love that Franklin stove you saw in the antique store? It's not in your budget until you two have these basics.*

**FOR SLEEPING** You'll need a good mattress and boxspring (most couples choose queen-size). Two bedside tables. Linens (at least two sets). Blankets and a comforter for wintry nights. Pillows to sleep on, of course, and if you'll read in bed, lots of throws (with pretty ruffled shams, perhaps) to support you.

**FOR SITTING** A sofa should rate high on the list. Since the sofa gets more use than any other piece in your living room, it's a good idea to buy one of good quality. Chairs (preferably two) balance the sofa, end tables will hold lamps, drinks, pretty plants, books.

**FOR LIGHT** Lamps not only give light, they create a homey atmosphere too. You'll need several on his side of the bed and yours; by the living room sofa and chairs; on top of your desk.

**FOR PRIVACY** You can get by for just so long with blankets tacked across bedroom windows. In most rooms, you'll need curtains, wood shutters, or roll-up (matchstick?) shades.

**FOR EATING** A sturdy dining table (if in the living room, it can double as a desk). Chairs (at least two, preferably four) if space is tight, extra folding chairs can pop out of the closet to accommodate guests.

**FOR STORAGE** A chest of drawers (or two) in the bedroom with plenty of space for his shorts, T-shirts, socks; your lingerie, sweaters, hose. Bookshelves or a drawered cabinet in the living room for books, records, magazines, entertainment equipment, framed photographs you want to show off. Low sleek cabinets can double as end tables to support lamps, stash extras.

# DECORATING PLAN

## LIVING ROOM

Wall color _____ paint ☐     paper ☐

Floor covering color _____ carpet ☐    area rugs ☐  price _____

Drapery color _____ dimensions _____ fabric _____ price _____

Period or type of furniture _____ finish _____

Sofa_____style _____brand _____ color _____ price _____

Chair_____style _____brand _____ color _____ price _____

Chair_____style _____brand _____ color _____ price _____

Chair_____style _____brand _____ color _____ price _____

Tables _____ coffee _____ end _____ occasional _____

Television_____ brand _____ price _____

Stereo components_____ brand (s) _____ price (s) _____

Desk _____ price_____Desk chair _____ price _____

Lamps _____ floor _____ table _____ wall _____ ceiling _____

Storage units (chests, etc.)_____

Paintings, prints, wall hangings, other accessories _____

## DINING ROOM OR AREA

Wall color _____ paint ☐     paper ☐

Floor covering color _____ area rugs ☐ carpet ☐ flooring ☐    price _____

Drapery color _____ dimensions _____ fabric _____ price _____

Table size _____ style _____ finish _____ brand _____price _____

Chairs, number_____ style _____ finish _____ brand _____price _____

Sideboard or chest _____ style _____ finish _____ brand _____price _____

Serving cart_____ style _____ finish _____ brand _____price _____

Lamps _____ floor _____ table _____ wall _____ ceiling _____

Paintings and other accessories _____

## BEDROOM

Wall color _____    paint ☐     paper ☐

Floor covering color _____ area rugs ☐ carpet ☐    price _____

Drapery color _____ dimensions _____ fabric _____ price _____

Bed size _____ headboard style _____ brand _____ price _____

Mattress/box spring _____ brand _____ price _____

Dresser/chests _____ style _____ finish _____ brand _____ price _____

Mirror _____ style _____ finish _____ brand _____ price _____

Chair_____ style _____ finish _____ brand _____ price _____

Vanity table or desk _____ style _____ finish _____ brand _____ price _____

Night table_____ style _____ finish _____ brand _____ price _____

Lamps _____ floor _____ table _____ wall _____ ceiling _____

Paintings and other accessories _____

_____

_____

# YOUR APPLIANCES AND COOKWARE

## How to choose and buy them

**RANGES: Gas** and **electric** types both offer even heat for top-of-stove cooking; baking too. A plus for gas: burners cool faster. A plus for electricity: cleaner cooking. When shopping, consider the price of fuel and power in your area. **Built-ins** are space-savers, but **freestanding** models can move from place to place, cost less too. Features to consider: warming shelves, automatic timers, self-cleaning devices. **Microwave ovens,** generally in countertop styles, cook super-fast (a hamburger in 60 sec.) **Convection ovens** also for countertop, cook bit faster and more evenly, than con-ventional ovens.

**REFRIGERATORS AND FREEZERS:** There's a vari-ety of capacities and combinations to choose from. Two people need two to eight cubic feet for them-selves. They should also allow for two more cubic feet for entertaining and one cubic foot for every two addi-tional mouths to feed. In a freezer, it's two cubic feet per person. (A wise idea: buying with future family size in mind; appliances last a decade or more.) **Refrigera-tors,** mini to maxi, come with frozen food compart-ments, ranging from ice-tray size to several cubic feet. **Refrigerator-freezers** have two separate doors, side by side or top and bottom. Time limits on freezing various foods are listed in each model's instruction booklet. **Freezers,** as separate units, provide extra space, long-time storage. Options: automatic defroster, ice-maker, swing-out shelves, door storage.

**WASHERS AND DRIERS:** Separate or combination models range from doll-sized to huge-capacity ma-chines. **Automatic washers** perform the whole process at the touch of one button. Features to consider: durable press cycle, lint remover, presoak cycle. **Driers,** electric or gas, need time and temperature controls to keep permanent-press fabrics wrinkle-free. Some **combination washer-driers** won't wash one load while another dries; others will.

**DISHWASHERS: Countertops** and **full-size portables** hook up to the sink and move anywhere. **Built-in** types must be connected to the plumbing. When pricing, consider capacity, features like energy-saving cycles.

**DISPOSALS, INCINERATORS, AND TRASH COMPACTORS: Electric disposals** handle soft food wastes only. **Gas incinerators** burn all wet and dry wastes except metals, glass, ceramics. **Trash compactors** condense rubbish into small blocks. Before buying any one of these appliances, be sure they're permitted in your area.

**STOVE-TOP AND OVEN COOKWARE:** Ovenware need only retain heat, but a good pot or pan must do a more complicated job of transferring heat both evenly and quickly from the burner to the food. Copper conducts heat beautifully, but must be lined with another material (tin, stainless steel, silver) to be safe. (Unlined copper, however, is fine for cooking sugar, jam, beating egg whites.) Heavy aluminum is relatively inexpensive and conducts heat well, but unless properly cared for, can tarnish. Ceramic-like pyroceram goes from freezer  to oven to table.   In lots of great colors, enameled cast iron conducts heat fairly well, and is versatile (will cook in the oven, on stove-top too). Stainless steel is easy to clean, scratch-proof, and when heavily clad in copper or aluminum, conducts heat well. You needn't buy all your pots and pans in the same materials; expert cooks often enjoy using several different kinds for different dishes. You can tell a lot about the quality of pots and pans by looking at the way they're constructed. Check for dent-proof bottoms, and make sure pot balances flat on the cooking surface, has a heat-resistant, secure handle (preferably welded). Jiggle lids to be sure they fit securely, look for heat-resistant knobs.

There are many different kinds of ovenware that can work efficiently for you: glass, aluminum, enameled cast iron, ceramic, stainless unlined or lined with no-stick surfaces. Look for smooth, easy-to-clean surfaces, chip-resistant materials as well as beautiful designs, colors, handsome finishes.

**KNIVES:** A good knife will last decades. And you'll be less likely to cut yourself with a sharp knife than a dull one, since it will do the job on the first try. Insist on knives made of high-quality steel that will sharpen nicely and stay that way through many cuttings. Knives made from high-carbon stainless and combinations of stainless and other metals like molybdenum are tough, flexible, stainproof. The best ones are hand-forged, hand-sharpened, their handles of moisture-proof wood. Good knives are expensive, but since you'll have them a long, long time, they're worth the extra investment.

**INDISPENSABLE TOOLS:** Your kitchen is a workshop, and in a workshop you'll need tools not gadgets. Buy basics like mixing bowls, wooden spoons first and add your specialties as you discover the kind of dishes you enjoy cooking most. If you do lots of baking, you'll love a smooth marble surface for rolling dough, a little brush to butter-glaze pastry, and a good rolling pin and pastry blender to help turn out flaky crust.

**LABOR-SAVERS:** Every cook likes to use tools that take care of tedious jobs: a nifty food processor to puree, grate, chop; an electric mixer to froth egg whites, whip cream, mix batters; an electric fryer to crisp potatoes, chicken, donuts, tempura, vegetables.

# STOCKING UP YOUR KITCHEN

Garlic press, measuring cups, dish drainer . . . when you need everything, what should you get first thing? Here's a list to clip out, check off, and use as your buying guide.

## NECESSARY

- \_\_\_\_ 2 saucepans: 1-qt., 2½-qt.
- \_\_\_\_ 2 skillets: 8-in., 10-in.
- \_\_\_\_ Double boiler
- \_\_\_\_ Stockpot
- \_\_\_\_ Kettle
- \_\_\_\_ Dutch oven
- \_\_\_\_ Roasting pan with rack
- \_\_\_\_ 2-qt. round casserole
- \_\_\_\_ 2-qt. rectangular baking dish
- \_\_\_\_ 2 cake pans: 9-in. rounds
- \_\_\_\_ Cookie sheets
- \_\_\_\_ 2 loaf pans
- \_\_\_\_ Pie plate
- \_\_\_\_ Set of mixing bowls
- \_\_\_\_ Wooden spoons
- \_\_\_\_ Utensil set (ladle, masher, etc.)
- \_\_\_\_ Wire whisk
- \_\_\_\_ Rotary egg beater
- \_\_\_\_ Measuring cups and spoons
- \_\_\_\_ Salad bowl and servers
- \_\_\_\_ 3 knives: 3-in., 5-in., 8-in.
- \_\_\_\_ Bread knife with serrated edge
- \_\_\_\_ Knife sharpener
- \_\_\_\_ Wooden cutting board
- \_\_\_\_ Grater
- \_\_\_\_ Colander and strainer
- \_\_\_\_ Metal tongs
- \_\_\_\_ Corkscrew
- \_\_\_\_ Can and bottle opener
- \_\_\_\_ Vegetable peeler
- \_\_\_\_ Reamer (citrus juicer)
- \_\_\_\_ Salt and pepper mills
- \_\_\_\_ Kitchen shears
- \_\_\_\_ Funnels, large and small
- \_\_\_\_ Coffeemaker
- \_\_\_\_ 60-minute timer
- \_\_\_\_ Plastic storage containers
- \_\_\_\_ Ice trays
- \_\_\_\_ Vegetable and dish scrubbers
- \_\_\_\_ Dish towels
- \_\_\_\_ Potholders
- \_\_\_\_ Dish drainer
- \_\_\_\_ Drawer organizer for cutlery
- \_\_\_\_ Wastebasket

## NEXT

- \_\_\_\_ Vegetable steamer
- \_\_\_\_ Blender
- \_\_\_\_ Toaster or toaster oven
- \_\_\_\_ Electric mixer with dough hook
- \_\_\_\_ Kitchen scale

- \_\_\_\_ Marble pastry slab
- \_\_\_\_ Rolling pin
- \_\_\_\_ Pastry brush
- \_\_\_\_ Pastry blender
- \_\_\_\_ Flour sifter
- \_\_\_\_ Muffin tin
- \_\_\_\_ Spring form, removable bottom
- \_\_\_\_ Tube (angel food cake) pan
- \_\_\_\_ Soufflé dish
- \_\_\_\_ Quiche plate
- \_\_\_\_ Molds, different sizes
- \_\_\_\_ Custard cups or ramekins
- \_\_\_\_ Poached egg pan
- \_\_\_\_ Oven thermometer
- \_\_\_\_ Meat thermometer
- \_\_\_\_ Boning knife
- \_\_\_\_ Carving knife and fork
- \_\_\_\_ Knife rack or holster
- \_\_\_\_ Garlic press
- \_\_\_\_ Egg slicer
- \_\_\_\_ Salad spinner
- \_\_\_\_ Apple corer
- \_\_\_\_ Bulb baster
- \_\_\_\_ Barbecue skewers
- \_\_\_\_ Rubber bowl scrapers
- \_\_\_\_ Spice rack
- \_\_\_\_ Storage canisters or mason jars
- \_\_\_\_ Turntable for cupboard shelf
- \_\_\_\_ Serving trays
- \_\_\_\_ Paper towel rack
- \_\_\_\_ Apron

## NICE

- \_\_\_\_ Food processor
- \_\_\_\_ Microwave oven
- \_\_\_\_ Slow cooker
- \_\_\_\_ Coffee grinder
- \_\_\_\_ Juice extractor
- \_\_\_\_ Pressure cooker
- \_\_\_\_ Deep fryer
- \_\_\_\_ Waffle iron
- \_\_\_\_ Ice cream maker
- \_\_\_\_ Wok
- \_\_\_\_ Hot tray
- \_\_\_\_ Fondue pot
- \_\_\_\_ Clay cooker
- \_\_\_\_ Fish poacher
- \_\_\_\_ Melon ball scoop
- \_\_\_\_ Ice cream scoop
- \_\_\_\_ Biscuit and cookie cutters
- \_\_\_\_ Pastry bag and attachments
- \_\_\_\_ Trussing needle, lacing pins
- \_\_\_\_ Cookbook holder

# YOUR SUPERMARKET CHECKLIST

Your determined battle against today's high prices begins with a clear, disciplined shopping list. So clip out and make copies of our list, then check off your needs as they arise during the week.

## STAPLES
____Tea
____Coffee
____Granulated sugar/
 sugar substitute
____Confectioner's sugar
____Brown sugar
____All-purpose flour
____Baking soda
____Baking powder
____Yeast
____Cornstarch
____Vegetable shortening
____Vegetable oil
____Unsweetened
 chocolate/cocoa
____Spaghetti/noodles
____Rice
____Cereals

## CONDIMENTS
____Prepared mustard
____Mayonnaise
____Catsup/chili sauce
____Relishes/olives/
 pickles
____Olive oil
____Vinegar
____Worcestershire sauce
____Hot pepper sauce
____Peanut butter
____Jams/jellies
____Pancake syrups
____Vanilla extract
____Spices
____Herbs
____Salt/pepper
____Garlic

## SHORT-CUT FOODS
____Sauce mixes
____Bouillon cubes
____Pudding mixes
____Flavored/
 unflavored gelatins
____Spaghetti sauce
____Salad dressings
____Biscuit/piecrust mix
____Bread crumbs
____Pancake mix
____Canned/powdered
 milk

## CANNED AND FROZEN FOODS
____Soda
____Beer
____Fruit juices
____Vegetables
____Fruits
____Tomato sauce/paste
____Tuna/salmon
____Concentrated soups

## HOUSEHOLD NEEDS
____Paper napkins
____Plastic wrap
____Plastic bags
____Aluminum foil
____Waxed paper
____Toilet paper
____Facial tissues
____Matches
____Light bulbs
____Bars of soap
____Household cleaners/
 soaps/detergents

## DRUG ITEMS
____Toothpaste
____Adhesive bandages
____Aspirin
____Cotton
____Shampoo
____Razor blades
____Tampons/sanitary
 napkins
____Shaving cream
____Deodorant
____Mouthwash

## WEEKLY NEEDS
____Milk
____Cream: sweet/sour
____Eggs
____Butter/margarine
____Ice cream
____Cheese
____Dinner meats/
 fish/poultry
____Lunch meat/
 frankfurters
____Bacon/sausage
____Potatoes
____Onions
____Fresh fruits
____Salad vegetables
____Baked goods/bread/
 rolls
____Cocktail nibbles
____Crackers/cookies
____Alcoholic beverages:
 wine/liquor

# HIS-AND-HERS HOUSEWORK

How the two of you can divide and conquer those household chores

## VACUUMING  ☐ HIS  ☐ HERS

Once a week, give carpeting, scatter rugs, floors a thorough going-over. Use crevice nozzle along baseboards; upholstery brush on cushions; drapery tool on curtains and blinds. Do split up vacuuming—and all chores—fairly. How? First list everything that *has* to be done. Next choose what each of you prefers—if you're compulsive, make it "dailies" like dishes, if he's a procrastinator, "weeklies." See to it you're putting in equal time! Both *hate* what's left? Take turns.

## LAUNDRY  ☐ HIS  ☐ HERS

Sort clothes as you go—whites and lights in the washer tub (or one laundry bag), colored clothes in the hamper (or another bag). Check pockets for tissues, gum, etc. Once a week is easiest for launderette washings; at home, wash as hampers fill up. Never overload washer—soap and water must slosh around. Fold or hang clothes as they come from the dryer for least wrinkling, ironing. P.S.: Folding is one chore to share!

## DUSTING POLISHING
## PICK-UP  ☐ HIS  ☐ HERS

Skim sills, pictures, bookcases, furniture weekly. A damp, lint-free cloth (his old camp T-shirt?) or vacuum dust-brush does a super job. Furniture only needs waxing four times a year with wood wax or oil. Once a day, hang up clothes, put away books, knitting, shoes. Empty ashtrays, garbage cans. Throw out "junk" mail, newspapers (or stack to take to recycling center).

## WASHING DISHES  ☐ HIS  ☐ HERS

Sponge off dishes with soap and hot water, leaving the dirtiest pots for last. Be sure to clean in between fork tines, underside of dishes too. Rinse, drain, air dry. Have a dishwasher? Load after every meal, but run only when full. To save energy, turn the dishwasher off after "last rinse" and let dishes air-dry. Don't forget to wipe down stove, counters, and sink till sparkling.

## CLEANING THE
## BATHROOM ☐ HIS ☐ HERS

Clocking a minute or two of bathroom duty every day makes the weekly chores *much* easier. The "dailies": put combs, deodorant, makeup in cabinets or drawers; fold towels; cap toothpaste and check toilet paper. Rinse the tub or shower as you get out. Quick-sponge the sink. Then once a week, clean the toilet, bathtub, sink, and mirror. For the best results on tiles and the chrome trim on all fixtures—use some elbow grease!

## GARBAGE ☐ HIS ☐ HERS

Make garbage disposal part of your after-dinner routine. Once a week disinfect the container with an all-purpose cleaner or chlorine bleach diluted in *hot* water (hold your nose). Swish it around, then soak for 15 minutes. Rinse. Wipe down the outside too with cleaning solution. Dry container thoroughly inside and out.

# YOUR BUDGET

To get the most from your new family income, you'll need a spending plan you can stick to—one specially geared to *your* needs and goals. That takes careful, joint planning. So before you draw up your budget . . .

**Set clear-cut immediate and long-range goals.** What do you want your money to do for you during the first year of your marriage? In five or ten years' time? First year goals might be to buy a second car, to furnish your first home, to pay for a final year of school. Five- or ten-year goals might be to have the downpayment for a house, to have saved enough to start a family or to buy the sailboat you've always dreamed of. Keep in mind that no goals are too outlandish if you *both* agree on them. Record your goals on paper and estimate the amount of money you'll need to reach them.

**Size up your weekly income.** Write down what each of you makes after taxes, Social Security, and other deductions from your paychecks. If neither of your employers arranges for your health insurance, join a plan and count its premium as if it were deducted from your pay. Use *realistic* estimates if one of you works sporadically, or hasn't found employment yet.

**Calculate your fixed expenses.** These are ones you *know* you'll have monthly, quarterly, or annually: the cost of housing, utilities, insurance, planned savings, loan payments, medical check-ups, etc. (Note that planned savings is a fixed expense here.) Put aside as much money as you'll need to reach the goals you've set on time. The cost of housing? If you haven't found a place to live already, look for one that costs one-third to one-quarter of your monthly take-home pay. Then estimate the cost of utilities by going over any past receipts, or by asking other couples what they pay.

**Estimate your flexible expenses.** These are the ones that vary—in amount, significance, and payment date: food, transportation, clothing, entertainment, etc. The only way you'll be able to realistically estimate the amount of money *you'll* need to budget for each is by keeping running records for a month or so of what each of you spends weekly, item for item. At least for the time being, don't change your usual spending habits. You can economize later. After a month or so, go over each of your records to see how much money you spend as a couple on every category of the flexible expenses. For clothing expenses, figure last year's expenditure, plus or minus the cost of major articles you may or may not need this year.

**Draw up your weekly budget.** You can use the sample worksheet below to record your estimated income and expenses. It shows you how to convert fixed and flexible expenses to weekly totals. Add expenses, then compare against your income. If your expenses exceed your income, you can cut back on flexible expenses—the easiest to control. But if that's not enough, try to cut back on your fixed expenses; maybe move into a less-expensive apartment. If all else fails, start looking for a higher-paying job or extra work. But if, by chance, what you make is more than what you spend, decide how you'd like to use that extra money.

**Put your plan into action.** Keep track, at least in the beginning, of what you spend each week to see how' your budget *really* works. If you find that you are constantly "borrowing" from yourselves—maybe using household money to cover rent increases—it's a sign that your current budget is out of line with your needs. Don't feel guilty; change your budget. Once you've found the right spending pattern for *your* income, needs, and goals, records may not be necessary. Even if you're satisfied with your first budget, agree to sit down in six months to discuss your financial progress. Your budget should grow with you, adjusting to any changes in your plans, goals, or income.

# WEEKLY BUDGET

**INCOME**

|  | | **WEEKLY TOTALS** |
|---|---|---|
| Add: His weekly income | $_____ | |
| Her weekly income | $_____ | |
| Total | $_____ | $_____ |

**EXPENSES**
**Fixed: Monthly housing expenses**

| Rent/Mortgage payment | $_____ |
|---|---|
| Water | $_____ |
| Gas | $_____ |
| Electricity | $_____ |
| Telephone | $_____ |
| Total | $_____ |

Convert to weekly estimate:

$_____ x 3 = $_____ ÷ 13 $_____

**Periodic fixed expenses**
(Figure each annually)

| Loan payments | $_____ |
|---|---|
| Insurance premiums | $_____ |
| Medical check-ups | $_____ |
| Other (Tuition) | $_____ |
| Total | $_____ |

Convert to weekly estimate:

$_____ ÷ 52 = $_____

**Planned savings/Emergencies**          $_____

**Flexible: Weekly living expense**

| Food/Beverages | $_____ | |
|---|---|---|
| Transportation | $_____ | |
| Household (Upkeep, etc.) | $_____ | |
| Laundry/Dry Cleaning | $_____ | |
| Entertainment | $_____ | |
| Gifts/Donations | $_____ | |
| His Personal | $_____ | |
| Her Personal | $_____ | |
| Total | $_____ | $_____ |

**Periodic flexible expenses**
(Estimate annually)

| Her Clothing | $_____ |
|---|---|
| His Clothing | $_____ |
| Other (Vacations) | $_____ |
| Total | $_____ |

Convert to weekly estimate:

$_____ ÷ 52 = $_____

| Add total weekly expenses | $_____ |
|---|---|
| Compare to total weekly income | $_____ |